WHEELS AND DEALS

Wheels and Deals

People and Places in Irish Motoring

John O'Donovan

GILL AND MACMILLAN

First published 1983 by
Gill and Macmillan Ltd
Goldenbridge
Dublin 8
with associated companies in
London, New York, Delhi, Hong Kong,
Johannesburg, Lagos, Melbourne,
Singapore, Tokyo

7171 1292 6

Origination by Galaxy Reproductions Ltd
Printed and bound in the Republic of Ireland by E. & T. O'Brien Ltd, Dublin

Contents

The author and publishers are grateful to all who have helped them in photographic research for this book. Particular thanks are due to Mr W. J. Fitzsimmons of the Royal Irish Automobile Club for his kind assistance. Photographs on the following pages are reproduced by permission of the sources indicated:

3, 21, 132: National Library of Ireland. 22: Mansell Collection, London. 25: National Gallery of Ireland. 30: Kirwan Ltd, Dublin. 35, 73, 81, 94: BBC Hulton Picture Library, London. 37: Mr Denis Lucey, Portlaoise. 39, 41: Ulster Folk and Transport Museum. 42: Mr R. M. Humphreys, Dublin. 64, 65, 84, 87, 100, 121, 179: Science Museum, London. 88, 91, 103, 105, 145, 149, 171: Ford Motor Company. 108: Society of Motor Manufacturers and Traders, London. 118: Mr J. A. Byrne, Gorey. 142: Huet Motors Ltd, Dublin. 153, 191: Irish Shell Ltd. 159, 162, 164: The Smith Group, Dublin. 175, 177: Lucas Industries, Birmingham. 182, 196: Mrs Maureen Lemass, Dublin. 184, 188: Motor Distributors Ltd, Dublin.

This publication was undertaken by John O'Donovan at the request of the Society of the Irish Motor Industry which was anxious to make available a readable history of the development of the Irish motor industry. In this regard the Society wishes to acknowledge the financial assistance which it received towards the cost of preparing this book from three member companies: Irish Shell Ltd, Lucas Service Ireland Ltd, and the Smith Group.

Introduction

About five years ago Robert Prole, secretary of the Society of the Irish Motor Industry, invited me to lunch with himself and Matt McQuaid, formerly notable in the motor trade and now retired. Their objective was to find out if I as a professional author thought a book could be made out of the collected reminiscences of veteran motor traders, it being felt a pity that this unique stock of first-hand information should perish with them. I replied that books could be made out of far less promising material, and often had been, and gave them the names of a few writers who might be interested in compiling such a book for them. It transpired that a lady had assured them that *I* was the only possible man for the job. As the lady had never met me and was therefore uninfluenced by my innate charm, she had based her recommendation upon esteem for my writings.

Naturally I assured my hosts that this lady's judgment was perfectly sound, that so perceptive was she, her advice should be sought on other matters too. But I declined the proffered commission because I was already fully engaged in other directions. Besides, the proposed book was not in my line, and anyway I knew nothing about the motor trade apart from what I had picked up as a junior costing clerk in Huet Motors of Mount Street Bridge for a year or so before the outbreak of war in 1939 brought motor trading to a standstill for its duration.

I noted at the time that my refusal of the offer did not discompose Bob Prole in the least, and I went away and thought no more of the matter.

A year passed. Then out of the blue another luncheon invitation came from SIMI. This time, Bob Prole being engaged elsewhere, my host was Leo Keogh, chief executive of SIMI. He brought Terry Balfe of Irish Shell with him and I was told, as something which should interest me, that enough guarantees of financial backing had been secured to make it possible for me to start the book. I protested that I had not given any undertaking to do so, reminding them that I had in fact declined the commission with thanks. The protest had as little perceptible effect on Leo Keogh as on Bob Prole. He simply went on talking as if my role as author-in-chief

1

of SIMI had been ordained by heaven, assuring me that every assistance would be given, all records laid open to me, and even though the preliminary research and the writing of the book might take as long as a month or even six weeks no pressure would be imposed upon me to make haste.

If I now declare that I am teetotal this is not an irrelevant assertion of virtue: it is that you may rule intoxication out of possible explanations of how it came about that by the end of the luncheon my still protesting self was being thanked by Leo Keogh for so graciously and unfussily agreeing to do the book.

What then is the explanation? The answer is I do not know.

The reminiscences of the veteran traders were duly tape recorded but were found to constitute merely a few threads in what was turning into an elaborate tapestry. Besides, the inevitable development had occurred over the years with anecdotes and stories. Good yarns had become better in repeated tellings, details of one event were mixed up with those of another, hearsay had assumed the mantle of personal observation. In other words, the reminiscences would have to be verified before being offered as history. Nevertheless, all was grist that came to my mill.

An odd feature was that the reminiscences invariably dealt with minor characters and walk-ons. Even reminiscences of reminiscences seldom if ever touched those in the lead roles. I waited in vain for any mention of John Boyd Dunlop, Harvey du Cros, the Booth brothers, Frederick Woods, R. J. Mecredy and so on. The trouble about the minor characters is that they were minor and, being minor, had done or said little to interest succeeding generations. The story of how X or Y slipped on a patch of grease and ruined his grey suit, the kind of yarn that sets the table on a roar in the later stages of an annual dinner, would fall as flat as the victim if offered to the general reader as a historical memoir. Even if I had been given oodles of material about the major characters of the Irish motoring drama I had to bear in mind how relative a description major can be. On the world stage the heroes and unheroes of our little drama would not be discernible to the naked eye.

And what, you may ask, about documentation?

Well, I have long been amused by the common academic assumption that if a thing is written down, especially in an old unpublished record, then it's true. I for my part never leave out of account that it was written by a fellow human being, at best fallible, perhaps inaccurate, and quite possibly a malicious libeller. Having worked in newspapers for many years I know too much about how things come to be printed, from ordinary reports of the day's occurrences to art criticism, not to take their every word without a grain of salt. Official records of proceedings I view with even dourer suspicion, the minutes of meetings I have attended differing too often from my own recollections not to have taught me to be wary of taking such documents at their face value. The experienced committee man develops an instinct for sensing what's between the lines. Not that all slanting of information, evasion or suppression are deliberate. It can be an unconscious process. Moreover, allowance must be made for some people's sheer inability to express clearly and unambiguously what they intend to convey.

Do not conclude from this that I make a point of not believing anything or anybody, and that I place no trust in documentation. In practice, like the rest of mankind, I believe a great deal of what I read or am told, provided it is credible, or as with the saint, because it is incredible. We have no alternative. We cannot be everywhere and verify everything for ourselves, so that the fiercest sceptics can be deceived in much that they accept as true. It is common knowledge that a birth certificate often states that which the mother knows to be untrue, but death certificates are as a rule more dependable, even though reminiscence may contradict them. Thus, fortified by the evidence of a death certificate, I willingly accept that God allotted Ireland's first motorist twenty-eight years more of active and colourful life than Mr John Moore allows him in his recently published *Motor Makers in Ireland*. Reminiscence

Dame Street, Dublin, at the turn of the century.

3

asserts that Harvey du Cros was strangled in the Phoenix Park in 1915 by an infuriated Dublin cabman. I prefer the evidence of a death certificate which contradicts this at every point.

So if there is a science of communication there is an art of interpreting communication, and this art I practise in so far as I am able. You will therefore find in the pages which follow that the traditional praises of certain firms, institutions and personages are not re-sung. Moreover, I have permitted myself more latitude in comment than I fancy Leo Keogh and Bob Prole and their management committee expected to find in the book they had called into existence, although comment remains, I trust, within humanitarian limits. But even when they happened to disagree with my opinions they honourably respected my freedom to report as I found. I am happy to render them this tribute.

In compiling this chronicle of certain aspects of Irish motoring life I have drawn on every source open to me that time, funding and energy permitted me to avail myself of. Everything was checked so far as this was possible from independent (or at least alternative) sources. If there was direct conflict of testimony and no independent evidence I did as judges do, or are supposed to do: evaluated

4

credibility and decided accordingly. Many of those who were kind enough to submit themselves to my close questioning must have found their patience taxed by probings they might well have vetoed as too intrusive. But they showed no resentment and did not object to second and even third visits or to requests that they importune friends on my behalf for information or for the loan of publications which are now collector's items. I was more than once flattered by the trust placed in me to treat with discretion matters which the worldly wise usually keep strictly to themselves. One merry soul made the skeletons in his cupboard dance so amusingly — *and without enjoining me to secrecy* — that I was briefly tempted to tell all. But you are entitled to damn the consequences to yourself, not those to others, so I leave it to some future grubber amongst my notebooks to amuse his or her contemporaries with the merry soul's uncensored narratives, he and I being then returned to dust and beyond caring.

So many people have helped me in so many ways that I shall not append a formal list of acknowledgements lest I inadvertently leave someone out and cause offence in the last place I would wish to. I shall not even express my gratitude to Leo Keogh and Bob Prole for their untiring assistance because they have specially asked me not to, and I must respect their wishes. But to all, hearty thanks.

1

Ireland's First Motorist

1

Ireland's first motorist had a habit, when the humour seized him, of pulling out a revolver and firing in the direction of some passing neighbour. At first sight this might appear striking proof of how the automobile, from its earliest days, brought out more of the devil than the angel in its drivers. But it's only fair to add that by the time Ireland's first motorist had developed this habit he had become convinced, like his almost exact contemporary the shady financier Horatio Bottomley, that champagne should be the staple of one's daily diet, a bottle of it constituting a complete meal in itself, satisfying and stimulating. Fortunately for the neighbours' peace of mind it soon transpired that despite the champagne he was an excellent shot and was not aiming for a hit. He practised regularly, his target being a row of empty bottles forty paces distant. The crash of breaking glass was a reassuring tribute to his marksmanship even if, with the noise of the shooting, it was a little wearing on the neighbours' nerves. Besides, Ireland's first motorist was a medical doctor and it was some comfort to know that in the event of his accidentally failing to miss a neighbour, first aid would be immediately available.

By the way, lest the reader leap to the conclusion that only in Ireland or the United States of America would such behaviour be tolerated, let it be recorded that it took place in England, in the peaceful Berkshire village of Cookham Dean. For in 1922 Ireland's first motorist, having for some time observed with his experienced eye that the average marksmanship of Irish gunmen presented serious risks to the innocent bystander, decided to emigrate to safer surroundings.

The date of the first Irish motor trip has not yet been established beyond question, and probably never will be. We are told that the first *steam* car in Ireland was imported into Belfast and delivered on 6 March 1896, to a Mr John Brown, F.R.S. England was ahead of Ireland with the petrol engine, for it was on 16 May 1891 that the first engine of this kind was imported by Frederick Richard Simms, a consulting engineer, later the founder of the Society of

6

Motor Manufacturers and Traders and of the Automobile Club of Great Britain and Ireland (the RAC). Britain's restrictive legislation concerning self-propelled vehicles on the public highway inhibited Simms from importing a fully assembled car. (He did import a petrol-engined boat, which he tried out on the Thames between Charing Cross and Westminster.) The petrol-driven car didn't really get going on British roads until 1895.

Sir William Davis-Goff and his chauffeur in a car marked WI 1, the first registered car in Co. Waterford.

The Countess of Fingall claims in her memoirs that 'the very first motor-car in Ireland' belonged to Sir Horace Plunkett, high priest of the agricultural co-operative movement in Ireland and first head of the Department of Agriculture and Technical Instruction.* It was a De Dion Bouton and Lady Fingall publishes a photograph of Sir Horace at the wheel, the car standing outside Merrion Square. (Lord Dunsany tells me the car was afterwards kept at the family seat, Dunsany Castle, Co. Meath.) But the claim that Sir Horace was our first motorist is quite unfounded.

The descendants of Sir William Davis Goff (1838–1917), a Waterford businessman, claim Sir William as the first motorist. The Goff family photograph albums have many pictures of Sir William and his chauffeur in a car numbered WI-1, which makes it unquestionably the first car officially registered in Co. Waterford. But the car is clearly younger than the 4½ h.p. Benz of *c.* 1896 on which rests the claim of Dr John Fallon Sidney Colohan to be Ireland's first motorist. The claim can be admitted only *faute de*

*Elizabeth Countess of Fingall, *Seventy Years Young,* London 1937, p.227.

mieux. It was repeatedly put forward in print from at least as early as 1901, without contradiction so far as I can find. For instance the *Irish Field* of 13 April 1901 published a photograph of the doctor and his party in a Daimler, the caption declaring, 'Dr Colohan owns the distinction of having been the first Irishman to take up motoring. He is now acknowledged to be the leading expert in this country.' A write-up in the official programme of the Gordon Bennett Race of 1903 declares him:

> about the first British subject to begin motoring, having driven in France and Germany long before the law allowed motors in England. Was the pioneer of motoring in Ireland, and is recognised even on the Continent as one of the leading motor experts. Several of his inventions are in use on well-known French and English cars.

But although the *Irish Times* of 5 January 1907, in stating that he was 'among the first to drive a motor in Ireland', may appear unwilling to award him the primacy, the context does not suggest that such was the reporter's intention. He would seem to have been merely speaking loosely. The Gordon Bennett programme mentions that Dr Colohan, having retired from medical practice, 'devotes all his time to motoring and engineering. Is an expert with the sporting gun, and a clever photographer, having secured a gold medal for photography.' This account and many others which deal with Colohan and the coachbuilding and engineering firm in which he had become controlling partner, Hutton & Sons of Summerhill, Dublin, bear signs of having been written by himself. Some of the assertions of his excellence may be taken therefore with a grain of salt. It also has to be borne in mind that self-puffery was commercially vital in those early days to 'inventors' (the word simply has to be put in quotes) who were ambitious for a Dunlop-like success. So in seeking the limelight Colohan was not merely indulging an exhibitionistic streak but was being a businessman. When he saw the opportunities for big commercial success as engineer and inventor passing beyond his reach, his publicity-hunting stopped.

2

John Fallon Colohan (the Sidney came later) was born in Dublin in 1862, the son of James Colohan, a bank manager and a connection of the Galway Colohans, a medical family with an extensive practice in that county. Being a Roman Catholic, the bank manager did not send his son to Trinity College, Dublin. Instead Colohan was sent to the Edinburgh Medical School where he qualified as physician and surgeon at the age of thirty and the following year was in practice in London and in Long Ditton, Surrey. One of Colohan's

Dr J. F. Colohan.

characteristics was an almost neurotic restlessness. He was a man of many addresses and many posts, and often gives the impression of being, like Boyle Roche's bird, in two places at the same time. For instance, in 1896 he was Medical Officer for Health in Athenry, but had resigned this post by the following year and while apparently maintaining the Athenry address had another at 44 Albermarle Street in London. He had also become a medical referee for the Edinburgh Assurance Co. He is recorded as attending the university in Frankfurt-on-Main in 1897.

By 1898 he had added Woodville*, a detached house in the village of Blackrock, Co. Dublin, to his addresses, was attached to St Vincent's and Dr Steevens's Hospitals in Dublin as well as to St Thomas's and Brompton Hospitals in London and had briefly

*Demolished in 1981 to make way for a shopping centre.

been a police surgeon and sanitary officer. Presently he became physician to the convalescent home at Linden, Blackrock, Co. Dublin, and continued to hold his other appointments (according to the medical directories) long after he was stated to have retired from practice. From this it would appear that Dr Colohan was enjoying a high standard of living. He also, by his own account, enjoyed a low standard of health. In 1891, when he was in Germany, he studied the motor and visited factories where experiments were being carried out. Some years later he was able to have some motoring in Paris and in the South of France (always a favourite place with him), and was much inclined to buy a car. What stopped him was a fear that the UK parliament would not enact the promised Light Locomotives Bill, but as soon as this became law he placed his first order. It is on the importation into Ireland of this vehicle that his claim to be our first motorist rests. His enthusiasm for the new sport (as it was regarded) and his love of tinkering about with machinery made him a pioneer of motoring, in fact a missionary for the cause. He was not above doing a bit of buying and selling for profit, on his own account. By supplying paragraphs to the newspapers and motoring journals he would publicise whatever car he happened to have for some unique or superlative attribute and then sell it. For example, towards the end of 1901 he claimed to own the largest and most powerful car in the country, a four-cylinder 24 h.p. Daimler which he had himself boosted to near 30 h.p. ('sufficient proof of the owner's expert knowledge').

> The gear is a very much improved type which enables any adjustment to be much more easily effected than formerly, and considerably reduces the size of the gear box, which in such a large car with broad gear wheels would otherwise take up a great deal of room. Two side levers are provided, each connected with two different gears, the first and second speed being made to slide on the shaft by one lever, while the other works the third and fourth. A third lever is also fitted with three fixed positions, 'forward', 'out of gear', and 'reverse'. The counter shaft and differential gear are in the usual position, and the gigantic sprocket wheels on the former give one an idea of the great speed this car is capable of. Heavy chains connect counter shaft and road wheels.
>
> The car has roller bearings throughout, which in spite of its size, make it a wonderfully easy mover, and saves [sic] a great deal of energy which is usually wasted in friction. Tube and electric ignition of an improved design are both fitted, also the owner's patent self-starter, which has now been largely adopted. Gravity feed supplies the carburetter, while pressure feed is adopted for the burners, as they are less likely to be affected

by draught. Both forced and sight feed lubricators are used connected to every bearing in the car. A throttle is fitted in conjunction with the 'cut-out' governor, resulting in great economy, almost complete absence of noise and vibration, and greater efficiency. A water circulating index is fitted within view of the driver and the column of the wheel steering of the latest type forms a convenient position for the ratchet fittings connected with accelerator, electric ignition, etc. Artillery wheels, shod with 5 in. Clipper-Michelin pneumatic tyres, make driving a luxury; while for touring, an interchangeable set are provided with 3 in. solid rubbers.

An early group of motoring enthusiasts. Lord Louth is on the left and Dr Colohan is second from the right.

The *Motor News* coyly admits that the less said about the car's speed the better (the legal limit at the time being 12 mph). Nevertheless it claims that before the addition of the extra horse power the car did over 50 mph over a measured mile. With the boosted engine power 'it will require no stretch of the imagination to credit that another 15 miles an hour is within its capabilities.'

In spite of the *Motor News's* tribute to Colohan's 'patent self-starter which has now been largely adopted', history has not so far enrolled him amongst the notable motor engineering inventors of his time. The Irish Patent Office can turn up no record of any invention registered there by him, although it could be argued that the absence of the official record proves nothing more than that

Colohan did not bother to register his discoveries. However in this connection a word may be said about the general patenting situation in those early days. It is hardly an exaggeration that every second person in Western Europe was taking out patents for this, that, and the other, because every invention connected with the motor car, except when obviously absurd, had a market value. This arose from the fact that a proposed British Motor Syndicate, organised by three financiers, was buying up patents wholesale in the hope of getting a legal stranglehold on the newborn motor industry that would enable them to hold every manufacturer and probably every driver up to ransom. St John C. Nixon in his book about the British Society of Motor Manufacturers and Traders dismisses most of these patents as 'over-valued had they been bought at a sixpenny bazaar', and cites one patent which was offered to the syndicate. It was from a clockmaker who had designed a vehicle powered by a giant clock spring. The disadvantage was that you had to stop every few yards to wind up the spring. Even the syndicate declined this offer.* So while there is no good ground for placing Dr Colohan amongst such charlatan inventors there is none either for classing him amongst the Daimlers and the Benzes. His claim to fame, such as it is, must rest on his being our first motorist and on his being one of the new sport's most enthusiastic supporters. Of the genuineness of his enthusiasm there need be no doubt. The motor car, with its potential for instant and speedy mobility, would have appealed to his restless nature, and it had the great advantage over the railway train of being much more personal and flexible. So we find Dr Colohan not only pursuing commercial advantage with the motor car but helping to organise all kinds of driving events for sheer love of the thing. It comes as no surprise to see him listed as a founder member of the Royal Automobile Club of Ireland.

The coachbuilding firm in which he became so important a partner, John Hutton & Sons, was established in Dublin in the 1770s. The Huttons became Ireland's leading coachbuilders and the seal was set on their reputation with an order for a state coach for Queen Victoria in 1851. In due course they received royal warrants and, when Colohan began his connection with them, were coachmakers to the Queen and to her sons the Prince of Wales and the Duke of Connaught. They were almost equally proud of having been mentioned in novels by Lady Morgan and Charles Lever. Their workshops and yards were at Summerhill: a large premises conveniently situated on the fringe of fashionable Mountjoy Square, now CIE's Summerhill depot. (But the coachbuilders' name lives on in Hutton's Lane.) Huttons employed between sixty and seventy skilled tradesmen and when they opened a showroom at 2 Dawson

*St John C. Nixon, *The Story of the S.M.M.T. 1902–1952*, pp.18–19.

12

A general view of Huttons' garage and workshops, taken about 1910.

Street established an association between the street and the motor trade resembling Harley Street's with the medical profession. Colohan's whiz-kid descent upon Huttons in 1898 yanked them out of the eighteenth century and into the twentieth. Up to then they had been happily providing Ireland's gentlefolk with Queen's pattern phaetons, four-wheel dog carts, Stanhope wagonettes, polo and village carts 'and many other examples of the coach-builder's art in various patterns and of the highest excellence of material and finished workmanship'. Colohan now had them carrying a stock of oil and steam cars, also motor-cycles, and all were ready for immediate delivery. He flooded the country's newspaper offices with handouts telling how 'Dr Colohan, a celebrated motorist and expert engineer', had introduced to Huttons 'a number of valuable patents, which gives the firm a big pull and advantage in the market'. He also plugged Huttons' readiness to arrange hire-purchase facilities, a point of some delicacy at that time which the various provincial papers handled in amusingly different ways and the Dublin papers snobbishly declined to mention at all. The *Fermanagh Times* of 15 August 1901 stated with Northern bluntness that 'they have furthermore arranged to supply all makes of cars and cycles on the easy payment system', whereas the *Ballina Herald* of the same date tiptoed much more gently through the tulips:

As there may be a large number of persons wishing to buy motors, who are prevented from doing so by the large initial outlay, they have arranged to supply all makes of cars and cycles on the easy payment system.

As Huttons had by now doubled their staff to 160, and moreover had the redoubtable Dr Colohan at hand, they could reasonably claim to be able to cope with any repairs, so that out-of-order cars no longer needed to be sent to England for attention. Some of their coachwork must have been very ingenious if the claims made for it were genuine. For example, a Mr O'Grady ordered a 10 h.p. Daimler from them with a 'composite body which by simple change can carry two, four, or eight passengers' and had a hood 'which can at will protect passengers in the front or back of the car'. The *Motor News* of 8 August 1902 adds:

> This car when complete will not only be 'up to date' but 'before its time', as Messrs Hutton have the happy knack of forestalling the desires of even the most ardent motorists.

Huttons had always aimed 'up-market', a tradition which must have been quite congenial to Colohan, a dyed-in-the-wool Dublin snob. He himself ran a Daimler, the preferred car of Edward VII, and the model was pushed hard by Huttons, the principal Irish agents. They organised behind the scenes a number of miniature motor shows in the provinces, really advertisements for the Daimler. But pushing this model was tough in the metaphorical as well as in the literal

14

sense, partly because the sporting element loomed large in early motoring and Daimler did not cultivate a sporty image, but chiefly because the Daimler was an expensive car and there simply weren't enough people in Ireland who were at once motor enthusiasts and rich enough to run one. The bread and butter of Huttons's motor department came from the relatively cheap models and of course from repairs. This situation seems to have continued even after the Daimler got a terrific boost in prestige when King Edward brought a string of Daimlers over for his 1903 Irish visit.

Colohan was also dealing on his own account. In the autumn of 1902 he sold his souped-up 24 h.p. Daimler to R. G. O'Callaghan of Brackenstown, Swords, Co. Dublin, for a reported £1400. The *Irish Times* was induced to commit itself to the declaration that Mr O'Callaghan had thus secured 'what is unquestionably the fastest, most powerful, and the most elaborately furnished car at present in Ireland.' But Colohan was not the man to allow himself to be upstaged by his former car.

Dr Colohan is having a 12 h.p. touring car built, also a high-powered one, with which he expects to cause a sensation in motor circles.

Assuming that only one car is being referred to in this somewhat ambiguous sentence, it may have been the 60 h.p. Mercedes racing

One of Dr Colohan's early cars, a 14 h.p. Daimler.

car he sold at a profit of £400 the following February, having allegedly abandoned his intention of racing it on the continent. It all sounds as if Colohan, in the matter of motoring, was becoming one of yesterday's men.

3

It is only to be expected that as time passed and motoring lost its novelty some of the edge would have gone off Colohan's interest in the engineering side of Huttons. The rapid development of motor technology was making irrelevant his skill as an amateur mechanic, and it was an uphill job trying to get Huttons' heart away from horse transport. One feels that if it had been within their power Huttons (and all the other Irish coachbuilders) would have done away with the noisy, smelly, troublesome internal combustion engine and returned to the noisy, smelly horse transport, the troubles of which they were long used to and therefore not so much aware of. The Hutton heart leaped up when, in 1902, they received orders for their well-known one-horse jaunting cars from the Nizam of Hyderabad, from an unnamed Boston millionaire, and from HRH Prince Henry of Prussia. When they sent over a handout about Prince Henry's vehicle to the English *Sketch* it backfired. The *Sketch* of 11 June 1902 sneered at the jaunting car's colour scheme (olive-green picked out with red, with green cushions to match), saying that:

> If the Prince goes jaunting about Berlin in this conveyance, he will look so like a pickled cabbage that the colours must have been chosen out of compliment to the national Sauerkraut.

Huttons for their part were probably glad they had their jaunting cars to fall back on when a recession hit the Irish motor trade in 1908. Colohan's health was also giving him concern around this time. Perhaps one should say it was giving him more than usual concern, for he seems to have always been something of a hypochondriac. Besides, he had found a new interest. He had acquired the Grand Hotel, Malahide, Co. Dublin, and was having a great time tinkering with every bit of machinery in the place.

His personal life had changed too. His wife, as keen a motorist as himself, had died and he had remarried, the new Mrs Colohan agreeing (or deciding) to live in the Grand Hotel. A brief formal announcement in March 1908 let the world know that the doctor and Hutton & Sons had dissolved their partnership, an equally brief paragraph in the *Motor News* said the doctor had retired from the firm through ill health. The hotel seems to have held his interest for another decade, but by 1922 he was again a widower and, judging by remarks to his confidential manservant and friend

Richard McAllister, disenchanted with women. Disenchanted with Ireland also, for he pulled up his few remaining roots and moved to elegant retirement in the Thames Valley; his final years being spent in Dean Cottage, Cookham Dean, a village near Marlow-on-Thames. He had managed to persuade the seventeen-year-old Richard McAllister, an employee at the Grand Hotel, to come with him as a kind of personal attendant. The doctor proved a kindly and grateful employer, treating Richard more as son than servant. Later, Richard's sister Margaret joined them at Cookham Dean as housekeeper.

The Cookham Dean years let us get a closer look at the man than do the Dublin years. Some of the older inhabitants still remember Ireland's first motorist as 'the mad doctor' or simply as 'the Irishman'. Percy Garrett, local pub landlord, told me about Colohan's passion for shooting. Colohan would often ask Mr Garrett, then a boy, to say which person in some approaching group should be shot at. Without waiting for a victim to be nominated he would fire in the direction of the oncomers. His trigger-happiness was confirmed by other villagers. Ernie Tuck, who used to deliver bags of coal to the doctor, recalled that one day he picked a plum from a tree growing beside the path in the doctor's garden. Immediately the doctor appeared at his bedroom window, gun in hand. 'Do you want me to blow your head off?' Without waiting for a reply he fired.

I asked why the police did not intervene but was assured that the local constabulary quite understood that Dr Colohan meant no harm and that he was a good enough shot not to have any

Dr Colohan and his first wife are on the left in this photograph of an early motoring party.

The Motor Tour of 1901 was the first major Irish motoring event. Dr Colohan's photograph shows some of the cars before the start outside the Shelbourne Hotel, Dublin.

accidents. Or perhaps they were waiting for him to make a mistake and provide them with an interesting prosecution. As already mentioned, he kept in practice by shooting at rows of empty bottles in a field beside the cottage. A villager showed me the shattered glass, still lying where it had fallen sixty years before. Cookham Dean evidently respects its historical relics.

Miss Ricketts, who as a girl worked as a clerk in a wine merchant's in Marlow, recalls taking Dr Colohan's large and frequent orders for champagne, which had become the staple of his diet. Mr A. H. Peddle, the spritely octogenarian now (1980) living in Marlow, who witnessed the codicil to Colohan's will in May 1932, remembers the doctor telling him that his first intake of champagne for the day was a half bottle served with full honours on a silver tray by Richard McAllister at eleven o'clock in the morning. Colohan's death certificate reveals that he suffered from heart trouble, cirrhosis and chronic nephritis. In his will he praised Richard McAllister for rendering

> constant service and devotion to me during the past thirteen years during which time he has nursed me through three serious illnesses, sitting by my bedside practically night and day thus risking his own life and having been to me as a son, never taking a day off for his own amusement.

The villagers remember him as being about five feet eight inches in height and well covered without being obese. He was brisk and lively, humorous and talkative, and generous to the local children

18

in the matter of pennies for sweets. His passion for novelties was not confined to motor cars. He was Cookham Dean's first wireless owner and fitted his set with an extra loudspeaker so that on Sunday evenings, from his open bedroom window, he could relay to the neighbours the church bells and the service broadcast by the BBC. Although he had been bred a Roman Catholic he was not, according to the McAllisters (who were Anglican) a particularly devout one, and apparently was not a Mass-goer. Yet in his will he left £50 to the local curate for Masses for his soul ('three to each one pound'), with a further £25 to the Bethlehem Institute near Lucerne for Masses for himself, his two wives, and his second wife's first husband. At the foot of his not very elaborate tombstone in St Peter's churchyard at Marlow is the request

Please pray for his soul.

He made a number of £10 bequests to various Dublin charities, and two in Tralee, and a bequest in clause 5 of his will suggests that he may have had cause for a troubled conscience.*

The faithful Richard McAllister and his sister inherited the bulk of his £15,191 estate and left Cookham Dean soon after the doctor's death. Richard eventually returned to Malahide and married. He did not enter the motor trade himself, but a brother did, and it was Richard's sons who succeeded to the business. McAllister's Garage occupies a prominent corner site just outside Malahide itself. The site, La Mancha, has more than a little local interest: it was the scene of a sordid murder in the late 1920s when an elderly man and his two sisters were murdered by one of their workmen.

Richard's widow and his sons told me that Richard held the doctor in the highest regard, never having anything but good to say of him. I am indebted to them for permission to reproduce some photographs taken by the doctor of the Gordon Bennett Race, which Richard had piously preserved.

*See Appendix 1.

2

Roads, Red Flags, Horses

1

In the eyes of the law mechanically propelled vehicles didn't exist until 1832. In that year, following the report of a select committee of the House of Commons the Stage Carriage Act was passed, prescribing maximum measurements of stage carriages, regulating their conduct on the highway, the carriage of passengers, and ordering the identity of the owner to be stated on every vehicle. As the British House of Commons legislated for Ireland from 1801 until the establishment of the Irish Free State in 1922, this act applied here. It was much invoked by the constabulary in the hey-day of the Gaelic League, when carriers were held to have breached it by painting their names on their carts in Irish instead of in English.

The next legislation was the Highway Act of 1835. It was concerned with the regulation of traffic on the highways, prescribing penalties for damage done to the highways by vehicles, for obstruction, and it permitted anyone who saw a person driving furiously to the danger of the public to arrest the driver without a warrant. The Locomotive Act 1861 was a comparatively liberal enactment, since it named 10 mph as the maximum permitted speed on the public highway, with 5 mph through any city, town or village. Four years later the Commons saw fit to cut these limits to 4 mph and 2 mph respectively, and laid down the notorious regulation that a man carrying a red flag should walk before each and every mechanically propelled vehicle.

Needless to say the taxman had to be propitiated as well. Since 1869 all vehicles had been subject to a tax. From 1878 a tax of £10 was imposed on 'locomotives'. But the policeman was less easily propitiated. He seemed to regard the motor car as a kind of personal affront, one requiring to be avenged by the most rigorous application of the law. Not that the policeman was indiscriminate in his retribution: he was reluctant to molest the influential or the well connected. For instance, in June 1895 when

20

the Hon. Evelyn Ellis, having imported a 3½ h.p. Panhard from France, introduced Queen Victoria's neighbours at Windsor to the horseless carriage, later driving from Windsor to Malvern at an average speed of 10 mph, he experienced little trouble with the police. 'They were generally satisfied by my producing my ordinary carriage licence', he said. But things had changed by the following Feburary when a Roxburghshire man drove to Berwick-on-Tweed, arriving at three in the morning. By his own account he was having a quiet snack outside the Town Hall when he was suddenly surrounded by thirteen constables. They charged him with using a horseless carriage without having a man walking in front to warn pedestrians and others that the mechanical monster was nigh.

As a result of this kind of vexatious prosecution parliament passed the Locomotives on Highways Bill of 1896 which exempted lighter vehicles propelled by mechanical power from almost all the earlier enactments. But a speed limit of 14 mph was imposed and the central authority empowered to prescribe a lower limit.

Only in 1903 did the law refer to the motor car as a motor car. In that year the Motor Car Act acknowledged the light locomotive

Patrick Street, Cork in the early days of the motor car. Note the solitary car in the foreground.

College Green, Dublin in the early twentieth century.

to be a motor car, raising the speed limit to 20 mph (although allowing local authorities to prescribe lower limits for their areas), and making regulations for driving licences, registration of vehicles, provision of index marks and the size of number plates. The following year a government order propounded the legal definition of a motor car (the width, tyres, brakes, and so forth), and provided against excessive noise. All vehicles have been subject to a tax since 1869, an annual tax of up to £10 being imposed from 1878 on 'locomotives'. A century later road tax on private cars was abolished in the Irish Republic but was reinstated after a couple of years, thus confirming the motorist's belief that as well as being the innocent victim of other road users' bad temper and malevolence, he has been chosen as the special victim of all powers that be. For their part the powers that be must feel that road users have always been unreasonably hard to please. Criticism of eighteenth-century mud and potholes was no doubt justified. Yet when in the nineteenth century Dublin Corporation tried to rid the capital of its traditional ankle-deep mud by paving the main street with cobbles, road users still complained. On 12 October 1861 the *Irish Times* published a letter in which the writer said he was glad to see public attention called to 'the dangers and inconveniences of the new pavement'. He went on:

22

A wag said that so great is the veneration of the horse for the inventors of it, that he rarely even crosses it without going on his knees. There is, unhappily, much truth in the remark. It may be argued by those who advocate the continuance and extension of the pavement that it is only bad drivers who have let their horses fall. I know the reverse to be the fact, however. An eminent Veterinary Surgeon was driving his private car up Grafton Street lately, and his valuable mare fell and broke her knees. I could cite other instances *ad infinitum*.

There are users of the road who will declare that *exceptis excipiendis* things were not much different in the 1980s.

One of the surprising Ireland v. England comparisons is, as will be duly related, that for many years Irish roads were actually better than English. Another is that Irish policemen were more reasonable, more understanding, less officious than their British counterparts. The English pioneer driver Charles Jarrott tells how when he was having a practice run on an Irish country road for the 1903 Gordon Bennett Race, a policeman appeared suddenly from behind a cart and halted him. The speed limit at the time was 14 mph and the policeman accused Jarrott of doing 15. This did not annoy Jarrott as he knew he had been doing at least 30. The policeman asked for his name and address, but on finding that Jarrott was one of the drivers in the forthcoming race apologised for stopping him and bade him go free and at all costs 'beat the Germans'.

Charles Jarrott said he doubted if there was, from the motorist's point of view, 'a more sporting body in the world than the Royal Irish Constabulary'.

Sir Henry Robinson, vice-president of the Local Government Board in the early 1900s, claims in his *Memories: Wise and Otherwise* that he was the first Irish car owner to be caught in a speed trap. He had just bought a 10 h.p. Argyll from William Roger McTaggart of South King Street in Dublin, and McTaggart was delivering it to Robinson's home in Foxrock when he was caught speeding on the Donnybrook Road. His reply to the police sergeant's request for the usual particulars was: 'My name is McTaggart and I am a cycle and motor agent and I let out bicycles on the hire system. I have a good many clients among the police, and it is pretty well known that if they are in arrears with their instalments McTaggart & Company don't press them very hard.'

The sergeant hesitated.

'Did you happen to notice my subscription to the Dublin Metropolitan Police Benevolent Fund?', McTaggart continued. 'No? Well, at any rate I suppose you saw the cup I presented to the DMP sports?' The sergeant capitulated.

I'll tell you what we'll do, Mr McTaggart. We'll leave the matter entirely in your hands.'

'Very well, Sergeant, I think that will be fair to both sides.'
And off McTaggart drove.

2

The clouds of choking dust which even the slowest moving vehicles raised on non-macadamised surfaces in dry weather appear to have been accepted by the motoring people as unalterable, inescapable facts of nature, like the wetness of rain or the chill of the east wind. A competitor in the 1,000-miles car trial organised in England in April 1900 described how the dust got into every exposed part of the car, to say nothing of smothering the face and hair of the crew. When rain fell it merely substituted mud for dust as it had always done.* Little improvement was effected in road surfaces from the early eighteenth to the late nineteenth century. Even in England the situation was horrific. Arthur Young in his *Six Months' Tour in the North of England*, published in 1770, warns travellers to avoid the Wigan turnpike road 'as they would the devil, for a thousand to one they break their necks or their limbs by overturnings or breakings down.' He measured one rut and found it an incredible four feet deep 'and floating with mud only from a wet summer'. He reports that the only repairs consisted of loose stones thrown into the rut at random, 'which serve no other purpose than jolting a carriage in the most intolerable manner'. And he adds that he passed no fewer than three broken-down carts along 'those eighteen miles of execrable memory'.

If this was the state of important English roads, one may well wonder what Irish roads were like. The surprising thing is that they were reputed to be better than the English, and we have the word of English travellers for this. Possible explanations are that labour for road building was always cheaper and more plentiful in Ireland than across the water, and traffic being less dense and vehicles lighter, the same havoc was not wrought on road surfaces. Again, road maintenance in England was nobody's business in particular and suffered accordingly. Irish roads were the responsibility of the grand juries, who were prepared to do something about them. Moreover, in Ireland there had been the application of improved methods of surfacing suggested by that odd genius Richard Lovell Edgeworth, father of the novelist Maria, methods which are claimed to have anticipated McAdam's.

According to John Joly (1857–1933) one-time professor of geology and mineralogy at Trinity College, Dublin, Edgeworth 'stands as one of the most far-seeing and scientific road engineers of all time.' He maintains that Edgeworth anticipated McAdam, in

*Quoted in D. Noble and G.M. Junner, *Vital to the Life of the Nation*, London 1946, p.23.

24

Richard Lovell Edgeworth, whose ideas for road surfacing anticipated those of McAdam.

priority of publication at least, and that in any event his principles of road building, which differed from McAdam's, were in fact those adopted by later engineers in the mistaken belief that they *were* McAdam's. It is interesting to note what early nineteenth-century engineers regarded as a satisfactory main road. Even the great Thomas Telford was content to have only stones of *more* than 2½ inches diameter removed from its surface. Edgeworth for his part demanded that the largest stones allowed to remain on the surface be less than 1½ inches in diameter.

An amusing story is told of the methods of measuring these stones. In England, before the invention of a ring through which the stones had to pass before they could be used, the criterion was: could the stone fit into your mouth? When outsize stones began appearing on road surfaces, an investigation revealed that these had been passed as suitable by an Irish labourer. He had conscientiously fitted every stone into his mouth — but he had no teeth.*

Until the end of the eighteenth century in England and until at least the mid nineteenth century in Ireland, the city streets were as bad as the country roads as regards the surface, with the added disadvantage that they were filled with household refuse and used as open sewers and animal cemeteries. A heavy shower, which on today's hard surfaces acts as a cleanser, in the old days merely added to the horror. Jonathan Swift in his *Description of a City Shower* (in London) paints a ghastly picture:

> Filths of all hues and odours seem to tell
> What street they sail'd from, by their sight and smell,
> They, as each torrent drives with rapid force,
> From Smithfield or St Pulchre's shape their course,
> And in huge confluence join'd at Snowhill ridge,
> Fall from the conduit prone to Holborn Bridge.
> Sweepings from butchers' stalls, dung, guts and blood,
> Drown'd puppies, stinking sprats, all drench'd in mud,
> Dead cats and turnip-tops come tumbling down the flood.

3

The nineteenth century saw Irish roads losing whatever superiority over the English they may have enjoyed. Today the only comparison that can be drawn in their favour is that they are not so crowded. One can jolt along over the potholes and the chips of unrivalled looseness at one's leisure, largely unharassed by other drivers apart from the occasional elderly farmer in an elderly car, both of them autumnally tinted with rust, and proceeding in the middle of the road at a pace which is a reminder that Ireland is the only country left in Europe where time still isn't money.

Writing in 1906 in his *Ten Years of Motors and Motor Racing*, Charles Jarrott reported that 'the roads in Ireland were not made for speed. I would even assert they were not made for motors', although he admitted that a car could be driven over them. But he preferred driving over the worst Irish roads to negotiating some of the many bad stretches of *pavé* in France. 'If scorching is desired, then Ireland is unsuitable, but for variety of scenery and climate, and the making of a grand tour on a small scale, it should not be missed.'

Jarrott was speaking from experience. He had taken part in August 1901 in the tour organised by the recently formed Irish Automobile Club.

*Communicated by Mr Maclean of the Irish Patents Office.

26

The adaptation of Irish roads to the needs of the motor was a long and slow process because the roads in their then condition were deemed to be adequate to the needs of the horse; and, Ireland being chiefly an agricultural country, the horse's rôle in Irish transport seemed permanent. Motoring was deemed to be no more than an expensive sport for the few, a sport which even enthusiasts would grow out of as children grow out of their fondness for spinning tops. Besides, the motor had to contend with mankind's inborn resistance to change, innovative change in particular.

Charles Jarrott, one of the pioneers of motor sport in Britain and Ireland.

It is hardly an exaggeration to say that people everywhere tended to raise an outcry on the appearance of anything that moved other than on feet or hooves. The furious resentment of the pre-Revolution French citizenry against the speeding carriages of the nobility is an old story, and there is no reason not to assume that similar feelings stirred the peoples of other countries. At the coming of the railways those perennially comic characters the medical specialists declared that the human body simply could not withstand the strain of travelling at 20 mph, that the rush of air would build up so much internal pressure that travellers would literally explode. People accepted this as good and sufficient reason for trying to stop the railways, just as their descendants in the 1920s wanted the tomato

27

added to the list of scheduled poisons following another medical pronouncement that eating tomatoes gives you cancer. (I forbear to cite more recent examples.) True, the anti-railway campaign gained a certain plausibility when, at the opening of the Liverpool and Manchester line in 1830, a well-known politician who ventured on a stroll along the tracks was cut down from behind by a train, although the death of a replaceable politician was not to prove in the long run an effective barrier to the combination of progress and high finance. A later generation denounced the bicycle as a fearsome traffic hazard and the handlebar bell was dismissed as no proper safeguard for those who were hard of hearing or slow of foot (or both) and thus liable to be mown down by the dread penny-farthing as poor Mr Huskisson was by the Manchester train.

The motor car was seen as the greatest menace of all. It threatened not merely life and limb but the viability of the many crafts and industries based on the horse. The horse breeder, the farrier, the harness maker, the carriage builder, the vet, the oats grower saw their existence threatened by any real effort to encourage or facilitate the use of the motor car. Above all there was the deep attachment to the horse felt by men from time immemorial, an attachment nowhere more fervent than in the bosom of British generals, a group of men who still had not recovered from the emotional disturbance of seeing the musket ousted by the machine gun. No war could be waged, no military ceremony be conducted, no member of the royal family born, married, or buried without the active participation of many Houyhnhnms. Since history began the horse had been the honoured chief symbol of gentility and dignity. The most ardent enthusiast for mechanised transport had to admit that, as we Irish would say, the horse was your only man for dignified ceremonial. Even the squat and obese Edward VII ('Tum-Tum' to his lady friends), in spite of the additional disadvantage of a musical comedy uniform, became the embodiment of majesty when on a horse. Lords lieutenant invariably made their state entry into Dublin on horseback until the events of 1916 suggested it would be prudent not to make themselves so convenient a target for snipers. The horse-drawn carriage in its landau form was used by the elderly for jaunts into the country until the 1930s. I can recall the crushing boredom of being provided as a child with the treat of being jaunted from Ranelagh to Killiney and back, one broiling summer's day, in the company of the ladies of the family, the expedition being under the command of my maiden great-aunt. The experience left me with no sentimental illusions about the leisured comfort of jogging in a landau. It was seven interminable hours of heat, thirst, tedium, flies, and the dank odour of ancient cloth upholstery.

The dawn of the twentieth century found the public apparently

still invincibly horse-minded. By calling the first motor car 'horse-less carriages' they showed that to them the car's most notable attribute was that it was not drawn by a horse. Indeed the popular nineteenth-century ghost stories about 'headless coaches' — four headless horses and a headless coachman — are plausibly attributed to country folk coming on somebody experimenting with a steam carriage and being unable to conceive of a vehicle travelling without equine assistance. The first car rallies were called 'meets' even by motorists themselves and to this day you can convey a clearer notion of engine power to the general public by expressing it in terms of horsepower rather than in cubic centimetres.

The age of the horse had been a long one, and cruelly arduous for the horse. The Victorians, in the name of efficiency, had found it more economical to work omnibus horses to death in four years than to work them humanely for fourteen. It was a common sight in cities to see these horses dropping between the shafts and expiring in a few minutes with a mixture of blood and froth issuing

This photograph, taken in the early part of the century at the Canal Bridge near Monasterevan, Co. Kildare, is a good illustration of an unsurfaced Irish country road. Note that the car is on the 'wrong' side of the road.

*The line of motor
hearses and mourning
coaches for the
funerals of the victims
of the North Strand
bombing, 1941, going
up Seville Place, Dublin.
Even at this late date,
motor hearses were
still a relative rarity
in many parts of
Ireland.*

from their mouths. If the jarvey didn't drive his bony nag so hard it was probably only because he hadn't the working capital to provide himself with a quick succession of horses. The jarvey therefore developed a trick of appearing to lash the horse into a gallop to satisfy an impatient passenger, while in fact he was only striking the shafts. Many stories are told of touchingly affectionate relationships between drivers and horses, and one Dublin jarvey, a Fenian, became almost a fan of the detective (Mallon) who had arrested him because the detective 'had been good to th' oul nag' while the jarvey was in jail.

It can be added that while certain Edwardian eccentrics left weird and wonderful directions for their funerals, from being entombed seated in an armchair in a vault excavated under their hall door, to having their coffins suspended in mid-air by ropes from the roof of their barns, apparently none was so eccentric as to demand that his remains be borne to the grave in a horseless hearse. Indeed the role of the horse in Irish funerals was preserved long after it was dismissed from the refuse collection departments of our corporations and county councils, those staunch upholders of ancient methods and attitudes. The twentieth century was well advanced into middle age before the horse-drawn hearse finally yielded to the motorised vehicle. The changeover was not without pain to the feelings of the mourners, who seemed to mourn the passing of the black horses and their plumes more than the passing of the deceased. I recall the local scandal in Rathmines and the frisson of horror that caused the residents of Mount Pleasant Avenue to catch their breath when an adapted Chrysler Imperial with a white steering wheel arrived instead of a traditional horse hearse to bear away a defunct maiden lady. But the ultimate in funeral horror was reached in 1939 when a plum-coloured Ford V8 saloon swept out of the back entrance to Sir Patrick Dun's Hospital in Dublin, with a coffin roped to the roof, and hurried off down Mount Street towards the city centre. From the second-floor window behind which I worked as a costing clerk in Huet Motors, I had a grandstand view of the scene, and Yeats' line about the indomitable Irishry sprang to mind when I saw a passing garda commandeer a messenger boy's bicycle and pedal off in pursuit of the V8.

The horse cab enjoyed a revival during the petrol-less years of World War I but the passengers didn't. A couple of refurbished cabs still clatter through Dublin's streets, but the occupants are invariably tourists willing to undergo a brief personal experience of Ye Olde Times.

Curiously, horse transport died almost as hard in England as in Ireland. Dogged Irish conservatism may have kept sedan chairs in use into the 1870s even in Dublin (although availed of only by

This photograph, taken
by Dr Colohan during
the Gordon Bennett
Race of 1903, shows
the dust rising in
spectacular fashion
behind one of the
competitors.

elderly ladies and invalids), but Kathleen Ni Houlihan was far more tolerant of the transport revolution than was John Bull. His first observable reaction to the horseless carriage was ridicule, but as the number of cars increased so did John Bull's dislike of them. He felt that motorists were a small minority of cranks who were trying to deprive the majority of their jealously guarded ancient freedom of the highway — driving the public off the road in every sense. A typical outburst came as late as 1903 from an MP, Cathcart Wason (Orkney and Shetland), who publicly gave thanks that 'there is not one of these slaughtering stinking engines of iniquity in the whole of my constituency'. Mr Wason continued: 'A strong feeling is growing up of irritation in the country districts at the fact that owing to inaction, apathy and carelessness of the Department, these cars are monopolising the whole of the public roads.'

Mr Wason and his supporters were of course perfectly right. The motor vehicle has for years totally monopolised the roads, extinguishing for ever, so far as one can see, the public's right to walk unmolested along the highway. One now strolls along a country road merely on sufferance, and should the road be narrow you may have to hop smartly on to the grass verge lest your coat be literally torn from your back by the juggernaut. Not that pedestrianism was altogether carefree in the early days of motoring, judging by the Countess of Fingall's recollections:

Our hats, including Father Finlay's clerical one, are tied on with enormous veils. We are all just about to start on one of our expeditions. We shall rattle over the bad roads, terrifying the donkeys and cows who graze on the strip of grass by the roadside and who never before have seen such a contraption as ours. Hens and chickens and ducks will fly before us and we shall have a sensation of moving at desperate speed through space. We are going (at twelve miles an hour!) to wake up the Irish countryside.*

The Irish countryside however did not always take kindly to being woken up. We are told that when motorists went to pass a horse and cart on a country road, the carter often jumped down, tore off his coat, threw it over the horse's head, yelled that the motorists were killing the people and demanded damages. Sir Henry Robinson has another story in his memoirs of how an old man fell on his back in jumping off his cart, and lay with his legs working like a beetle as he shouted, 'Ye're after killing a man, I'm the man that's killed.' The victim then rose and requested Robinson to report the fatality at the next police barracks. Robinson recalls yet another incident on the Belmullet road when, turning a corner, he encountered a herd of cows. He knocked down a young heifer and she retaliated by driving a hind leg through one of the wheels. The car had to be jacked up and the wheel removed before the heifer could free herself and run off. Her proprietor now advanced, wailing that the fleeing animal was dead, that she had been the sole support of himself and his wife and family, that she had cost him £8 at the fair in Ballina and was due to have a calf in September. The usual crowd had collected and supported in chorus every wild statement. Before Robinson could point out that cattle are not supposed to be on the road unless being driven to a fair or a farm, an old woman who had just come down from the mountain pushed her way to the front of the crowd and declared, 'I was driving them to the fair.'

In spite of such occurrences, from early in the motor age Ireland was regarded as the motorist's paradise. Its sparse population, less than a twelfth of Britain's, meant there were fewer road users. Ireland had fewer rich people, and since motoring was a rich man's hobby, there were very few mechanically propelled vehicles about. Ireland was not a heavily industrialised country, so that such little heavy commercial traffic as existed was largely confined to the railways and the canals. Thus conditions made it possible for the motorist to achieve the ideal of having the road virtually all to himself. True, there were few of the long straight stretches that made for fast and easy driving, but then easy driving was not a prime objective of the pioneer motorist. He was more of an

*Elizabeth Countess of Fingall, *Seventy Years Young*, London 1937, p.227.

adventure-loving sportsman, relishing the challenge of winding, hilly, bumpy roads with sharp corners.

Needless to say women contributed from the beginning of motoring to the merriment of the male. In March 1902 the *Motor News* alleged that a lady had patented a new body for cars which was something between a bathing machine and a phaeton. The lower, bathing machine part accommodated the 'mechanician', the phaeton seats on top of this providing for two persons, one of whom would drive. The upper seats were to be reached by a small iron staircase. The *Motor News* suggested that some cellarage be added to the basement and a roof garden to the top.

The loyalty of ladies to the drivers of cars they were travelling in was demonstrated in a claim for damages heard in Dublin in December 1904 before Lord Chief Justice O'Brien ('Pether the Packer') and a jury. Mr William Le Waters of Kildare had left Punchestown Racecourse on the evening of the previous 27 April, and was travelling in his pony and trap at five or six miles an hour along the road towards Naas. Suddenly there came down a passageway known as the King's Gap, a motor car driven by Mr George Whitfield of Cloughjordan, Co. Tipperary, with Mrs Ethel Smith as his passenger. Mr Whitfield was allegedly driving so fast that when he got to the public road he was unable to turn 'in the proper way, and the consequence was that he went slap into the plaintiff's trap, upsetting and smashing it.' Plaintiff and passenger were thrown onto the road. But according to Mrs Ethel Smith it was the pony and trap which had come 'flying down and hit the motor'. The Lord Chief Justice asked Mrs Smith if she was *certain* the pony was going quickly. 'I am certain it was flying,' she replied. 'It seemed to come like a flash of lightning.'

Sir Charles Barrington, who had arrived on the scene shortly after the accident and who was also giving evidence, testified that motor cars could be stopped very suddenly. 'His own little car could be stopped so suddenly that it would throw its occupants out.' The jury found for Mr Le Waters, awarding him £15 damages. (He had claimed £500.) Incidentally, the solicitor-general, appearing for Mr Le Waters, declared in his opening statement that he

> quite recognised that the motor industry gave much employment, and that it might be useful to members of the public, but owners of motor cars ought to be taught that the roads of the country do not belong to them. With the motorists it was sort of *faugh an ballagh* — clear the road for them.

Mr Tim Healy, KC, for the defence, denounced his opponent's case as an attempt to use the very just feeling that existed — and which he himself shared — against motor cars 'to prejudice one who had driven carefully and who was within his rights.'

34

4

*The Irish Automobile
Club reliability trial,
1907, leaving Newry,
Co. Down. The car
in the foreground is a
15 h.p. Clement Talbot.*

Most of the photographs of the early cars and their occupants are misleading. They generally show people in immaculate morning dress, the gentlemen in shining toppers, the ladies with wide-brimmed and heavily ornamented hats, just the kind of headgear to be blown off in an open car doing more than five or six miles an hour. The reality was that the dust and dirt of the roads obliged drivers and passengers to protect themselves with tent-like head-to-toe dust coats ('utility garments' they were called), caps, veils and goggles. But the motoring organisations made a point of urging drivers and passengers to put on their poshest clothes before being photographed in order to improve the image of motoring, thus associating it with impeccably attired ladies and gentlemen rather than with mechanics in grubby utility garments. Rare indeed is the photograph showing the motorist after a long journey: filthy with dust from the potholed stony mudtracks which served even as main roads, bedraggled from wind and perhaps rain. If that was the worst to be suffered, he was lucky. The unlucky driver who suffered one or more major breakdowns which he would have had to try to put right himself on the side of the road (or the middle of the ditch) would have looked like a World War I foot soldier who had rolled his way out of No Man's Land back to the home trench. Recollections of the hazards of motoring die hard in Ireland. Mr Andy Ahearne, who in 1970 retired after fifty years service in W. B. Crawford Motors, recalls how a Mr Yapp bought an Austin 7 in the late 1920s and arrived at the showrooms to take delivery, attired in a long leather coat, crash helmet and goggles.

3

The Do-it-yourself Men

1

It goes without saying that the first cars in Ireland arrived more or less completely assembled. Since there was no mass production every car was an individual and unique vehicle, the body being built usually to the personal specification of the purchaser. Samuel Butler has pointed out that no matter how revolutionary a new thing is people will still find ways of bringing it into conformity with the old. Because of this determination to give the new vehicle a comfortably familiar look, the bodies of the early cars were made to look as much as possible like those of the horse-drawn carriages. No doubt coachbuilders did little to lure customers into daring experiments. Coachbuilders, no more than other people, would not deliberately try to make life difficult for themselves.

There was of course a complete range of accessories available to coachbuilders and to prospective motor car owners: horns, lamps, and so forth. Some of the horns were almost fantasy instruments, with an elaborate dragon's or dolphin's head for a mouthpiece, situated near the front of the car, and a long serpentine body winding back to the rubber bulb, the power source, near the driver's hand. The lamps were, again, recognisably the blood relations of the old carriage lamps, and, like most Edwardian objects, seemed to aim as much at heaviness and largeness as at utility and efficiency.

Most purchasers turned to England for cars. They patronised even English coachbuilders, although Ireland had plenty of highly skilled craftsmen in that line. Some Irish motorists, however, decided on do-it-yourself. It was quite fashionable for the nineteenth-century country gentleman, living on his rents and dividends, to be an amateur carpenter, scientist, or engineer. Many a country gentleman who didn't choose to fill his life with hunting, drinking, gambling and philandering, spent what may well have been his happiest hours in his workshop or laboratory. Inevitably some of these men had a go at making their own motor cars. They didn't necessarily start from scratch. The engine would be acquired and they would carry out their own modifications, make their own additions and so forth. Jim Ryan in his *History and Traditions of*

The unique Silver Stream, now restored to its former glory.

Knock and Timoney (Roscrea 1980) tells of a clergyman named Morris who lived in the Tipperary townland of Cappalahan and about 1912, having built himself a wireless receiver, started to build his own car. The local forge made parts from his own carefully prepared patterns, but the outbreak of war prevented him from obtaining necessary components so he had to abandon the project. The unfinished vehicle was auctioned a few years later, but concerning what happened to it eventually history and Jim Ryan are silent. More successful was the car built by a retired railway engineer named Somerville-Large between 1906 and 1909. The car, called the Silver Stream, is now the choicest item in Denis Lucey's collection of vintage cars at Portlaoise and has taken part in several rallies. It was one of the vintage models put on display at the 1980 Irish Motor Show at the RDS in Ballsbridge.

Philip Townshend Somerville-Large, who had worked with the

Indian State Railways, was born and bred in Cork (1848) and studied at the university there. But after his early retirement through ill health from the railways in 1897 (he was only forty-nine) he chose to settle in Carnalway, a village on the banks of the Liffey near Kilcullen in Co. Kildare. By 1906 he was running a 16/24 h.p. four cylinder De Dietrich but came to believe he could build a better car himself.

He imported through a London firm a French engine, a Gnome six-cylinder 6DMB side valve with a bore and stroke of 85mm x 90mm, and a chassis from another French firm, Malicet et Blin. Most of the other hardware originated in France too, and the cape cart hood came from Birmingham. The body was also made in England. An estimate exists dated 5 March 1909 from Alford & Alder, Carriage and Motor Body Works, of 53 Newington Butts, to build a body to specification for the sum of £90. They offered to use aluminium in place of steel for an extra £3 10s 0d (£3.50). But the estimate Somerville-Large accepted was that of Salmons & Sons of Newport Pagnell, Bucks. This was for £60. It would seem that the only Irish-made parts were the head and rear lamps (the side lamps were by Frankonia).

With these materials Somerville-Large constructed a luxurious five-seater open tourer. The Silver Stream was finished in August 1909 and ran well enough to encourage Somerville-Large to set up a company in Kilcullen to produce the model in quantity. Nothing further came of the project, so there was only one Silver Stream. It remained on the road until Somerville-Large died in 1929, when it was laid up. Eventually it was bought by Denis Lucey and lovingly restored. It represented Ireland at the 'Fanfare into Europe' celebrations in Brussels to mark Ireland's accession to the EEC.

2

Another essay in car making in Ireland was that of the Burke Engineering Co. of Clonmel, Co. Tipperary. The Burkes were a local family who had made their money as grocers and spirit merchants in Bagwell Street (an appropriate name for a business thoroughfare), with one of the sons opening in the 1880s a few doors away as a solicitor and a fire agent. By the early 1900s William Burke was moneyed enough and leisured enough to be a keen motorist and to have patented an ignition plug inspector. In February 1905 he set up, with A. C. Williamson, the engineering company bearing his name and went into car making with the intention of producing vehicles solely with Irish labour and materials.

The factory was in buildings which used to be the headquarters of the famous Bianconi car service, a name still fragrant with the odour of sanctity in the annals of Irish transport. But although

The Fergus, designed and produced in Belfast in 1915. The First World War and rising production costs killed it off commercially.

the company was favoured with an early order for three cars (total cost about £2,000) and fortified with assurances of further patronage, it stopped making cars in 1907. Although in accordance with its expressed policy chassis and gearbox were made in Clonmel, the Burke company's cars were powered by French engines in which the final drive was by twin side chains.

The Alesbury brothers of Edenderry, Co. Offaly, built a light car around an 8/10 h.p. two-cylinder Stevens engine and advertised it as having a body 'constructed entirely of Irish wood'. Little more was heard of the 'Alesbury' after about 1908.

An interesting car was produced in Belfast in 1915 at the motor works of J. B. (Joe) Ferguson, eldest brother of Harry of tractor fame. Designed by J. A. McKee, the car, named the Fergus, was ahead of its time in some ways. It had automatic lubrication and the four-cylinder 2.6 litre engine had rubber mountings, the earliest recorded instance of this device. Because of wartime restrictions the car could not be manufactured in quantity in Ireland, so a factory was set up in Newark, New Jersey. America's entry into the war in 1917 put another stop to the manufacture of the Fergus, and the project did not get under way until 1921. But the model was too costly to produce and was abandoned the following year.

But by 1921 Joe Ferguson had another car on the stocks, the O.D. (Owner-Driver), which lived up to its name. Ferguson had aimed at a vehicle which above all would be easy to maintain.

Among other advantages he produced a clutch that could be relined in twenty minutes without having to remove the gearbox. Moreover the O.D. had an air compressor which could inflate the tyres (a feature of the Fergus also), and power an air jack. But here again was a vehicle which appeared too costly for ordinary commercial production, although like the Rolls Royce it might have proved economic in the long run. The prototype, which had been built during 1918–19 in Belfast, could reach 75 mph and remained in service for 250,000 miles. Its bodywork was destroyed during the World War II blitz but the chassis survived and is now in the Belfast Transport Museum together with Joe Ferguson's own Fergus. Joe had driven this in America until 1950, for he had emigrated and prospered in New York as an importer of European cars. When he died in New York in 1969 the Fergus was found in the basement of his premises and was offered by Joe's son to the Belfast museum.

Also in this museum is a Chambers car, representing the most successful of the Irish car manufacturing ventures. Robert Chambers, who was in business in Belfast as a maker of machines for wiring corks on to soda water bottles, began making cars in 1904. His brother J. A. Chambers had worked with Vauxhalls and, as has been pointed out, the early Chambers models owed not a little to Vauxhall design. The first car had a flat twin engine of 7 h.p., three-speed epicyclic transmission located in the rear axle, with chain or worm final drive. Until they ceased production around 1925 Chambers were to stick to worm final drive. The firm is estimated to have produced between 200 and 300 cars in all, mostly 2 and 2.4 litre models, although in the early days they had also turned out some light vans and ambulances. Chambers remained in business until 1929, when they fell victim to the Depression.

3

Somewhat surprisingly there was little stirring in the car-making line in Dublin in the early 1900s. A Shamrock model was produced by the Shamrock Motor and Cycle Works of Mark's Lane (off Pearse Street), who had made their name with bicycles retailing at ten or twelve guineas (£10.50/£12.60) and who not only made gears of every description (offering 'Spur, Bevel, Worms, in Steel, Bronze, or Fibre') but undertook 'to replace in the shortest time all parts of Engine Gears or Chassis of any make of car . . . Crank Shafts re-turned – New Bronze or White Metal Bearings fitted . . . Cylinders re-bored true'. So far no Shamrock has been found to have survived, nor even any details of its construction. Many years later, in 1959, a company called Shamrock Motors Ltd was formed

in Tralee, Co. Kerry to build another Shamrock car, but the enterprise does not appear to have prospered, although some Shamrock cars were actually produced in Castleblayney, Co. Monaghan.

During the 1920s and 1930s J. A. Jones ran a garage and motor works at the Baggot Street Bridge end of Haddington Road (a site long associated with cars: in the 1950s it was W. G. Wilkinson's service station and is now occupied by Murray Rent-a-Car). In 1925 Jones assembled his Thomond saloon, 'the first car built in the Irish Free State'. It was powered by what is believed to have been an engine supplied by Meadows, a 1750 cc four-cylinder overhead valve job with a four-speed gearbox. Like other Irish cars the Thomond seems to have drawn ideas for its design from many sources. Michael Worthington-Williams describes it as 'an attractive car with a V radiator not unlike the contemporary Imperia, and boasted three-quarter elliptic springing at the rear, and four stud wire wheels reminiscent of the Riley Monaco'. There were also some sports-type Thomonds which are said to have distinguished themselves on Ireland's worst hills, including Glengesh in Co. Donegal, and they won first-class awards in twenty-four trials including the Dublin-Glengarriff. These successes inspired R. M. ('Dick') Humphreys, a successful motor-cycle trialist of the late 1920s, to invite Jones to build him a Thomond to Mr Humphreys' own specification. Mr Humphreys got a load of motor accessory booklets at the 1928 London Motor Show and spent some happy months designing a dream car. Early the following year he ordered the main components from England:

Three early 10 h.p. Chambers cars, photographed in Ormeau Park, Belfast, before the Irish Trials of 1907. Jack Chambers, on the left, won first place in Class C; the other drivers are Charlie Chambers and Dr J. Hurst.

41

The Humphreys Thomond, with Mr R. M. Humphreys seated on the running board.

an X-braced channel-steel frame of heavy gauge metal, a two-carburettor Meadows 1500 cc (12/50 h.p.) four-cylinder engine, four-speed gearbox, conventional propeller shaft and rear axle, C.A.V. electrical equipment, wire-operated four-wheel brakes and bolt-on wire wheels with 5.00 x 19 in. tyres. Fletcher & Phillipsons of Dublin made the radiator.

The Humphreys Thomond was a two-door coupe and the costs were:

	£
engine	48
electrical equipment	28
front and rear axles	26
radiator	12
steering equipment	10
miscellaneous parts	14
import duty	22
wheels, tubes, tyres	24
body (inc. screen, dashboard and accessories)	45
labour charge on chassis and body	70
bonus to J. A. Jones	50
Total	£349

42

The bodybuilder for all the Thomond cars was B. A. Parsons, then head assistant in the Jones garage and later the proprietor of a garage at Mespil Road, a few yards away from the original Jones premises. The early Thomonds were of wood and fabric, the later included four-door saloons made of metal and these, according to Mr Humphreys, 'boasted a truly professional finish and were indistinguishable from the average coach-built body of that period.' Mr Humphreys often drove to Connemara (where his fiancée lived), leaving Dublin soon after five o'clock in the morning and particularly enjoying the twenty-mile stretch between Kilbeggan and Athlone which he usually covered in twenty minutes and once managed in under eighteen. Petrol consumption averaged 26—30 mpg, tyres lasted 25,000 miles, he never had to touch the engine (excepting the plugs), and during 74,000 miles experienced only one serious breakdown. This was when the propeller shaft fractured because of insufficient margin of movement on the shaft where it entered the gearbox collar. Rudimentary methods of testing for this movement when building proved unreliable. Mr Humphreys says the Thomond gave him four of the happiest years of motoring in his life, and he thinks it a pity the public didn't give greater support to this courageous Jones-Parsons venture.

The futuristic De Lorean sportscar, built at a special plant in Dunmurry, Co. Antrim. The De Lorean company collapsed spectacularly in 1982.

43

The 1950s saw the brief emergence in Belfast of two new Irish cars, the McCandless and the Crossle. With the exception of the ill-fated De Lorean venture of the early 1980s, these and the Tralee-born Shamrock represented the last gasp, for the present at any rate, of the commercially produced native Irish motor car. It will be noted, however, that *produced* is not a totally accurate word in the circumstances. Since so many important components had to be imported it could be argued that early cars like Somerville-Large's Silver Stream were not so much *made* in Ireland as assembled here. The Irish contribution was in overall design, in modification, adaptation and ingenuity, and had these been backed and exploited by the business world, as Dunlop's tyre was by Harvey du Cros, Ireland's motoring history might well have been different.

4

The Motorist fights back

1

The 1903 Motor Car Act raised the speed limit to 20 mph but gave *local* authorities the irritating power of cutting this for their own areas. The act also dealt with dangerous driving, the licensing of drivers and registration of cars, and presently an Order in Council provided for index marks and the shape and size of number plates. In other words, the motorist had both gained and lost, for the liverish policeman now had a wider array of offences to deploy against the driver. Speed traps were set up along every road which afforded the motorist a chance to see what his car could do, and as he bowled along in a cloud of dust, visibility further hampered by goggles, the dark shape behind the hedge which he had assumed to be a cow could prove to be a constable.

Even allowing for justifiable prosecutions, motorists were probably right in believing that in most cases prosecution was being intensified into persecution. They resolved to fight back. Individually or in small groups they operated private warning systems along certain stretches of road, especially the London-Brighton road. Warnings had to be to all appearances entirely innocent. A pedestrian scratching his left ear could be really informing the motorist that there was a speed trap around the corner. A disadvantage was that any warning code was necessarily known only to a few, but soon this was to be overcome.

In March 1905 a letter from a Wolverhampton man named Walter Gibbons appeared in *The Autocar*, proposing an anti-trap club. Cyclists wearing special badges, their wages to be paid from the club's annual subscriptions, would patrol the roads to spot where the traps were and give warning. By good luck (from the motorists' point of view) Charles Jarrott and a friend were already operating a private warning system on stretches of the Brighton road. By the following month, encouraged by *The Autocar* letter, they had recruited members for a body they proposed to call The Automobile Mutual Association. By June the AMA executive had

shortened the title to Automobile Association and were notifying motorists through the motoring magazines that they were open to receive new members. The association had its critics: *The Motor* denounced any warning system as 'a proceeding of questionable dignity'. But the sufferings of motorists guaranteed the AA's speedy success.

Ladies were enthusiastic early motorists. This photograph shows Miss Phyllis Dare (no relation to the legendary Dan) at the wheel of her Darracq, in 1907.

2

As a motoring organisation the Automobile Association had been anticipated by the Automobile Club, a body whose speedy acquisition of the prefix Royal hinted at a higher degree of exclusiveness than the AA's. A fraternal group, the Irish Automobile Club, was founded in Dublin in January 1900, its first committee being headed by Randal Pilgrim Ralph Plunkett, 14th Baron Louth, of Louth Hall, Ardee (3,760 acres). The baron was fortified by the support of a covey of colonels and captains, a few esquires, a brewer (Smithwick) and a distiller (Jameson). It is true that the committee also included two non-bluebloods, R. J. Mecredy, a journalist and publisher of a cyclists' magazine which later blossomed into the *Motor News*, and Dr Colohan. Mecredy had his use as that harmless necessary drudge, the Hon. Sec., but his profession and the need to earn his bread through commercial pursuits prevented him from being accorded full genteel status. Dr Colohan, however, was more fortunate. Not only could he wear a tall hat with total conviction (see page 17) but he had acquired a kind of honorary blue-bloodship by marrying a lady connected with the illustrious Sidney family of Penshurst Place in Kent, a circumstance which inspired him to include Sidney in his litany of names.

It was not long before Lord Louth yielded primacy in the club to his cousin Sir Horace Plunkett who belonged to the richer branch of the family (the Lords Dunsany of Dunsany Castle, Co. Meath: 5,549 acres). Sir Horace's blood was so unquestionably blue that he had no need to wear a tall hat while in the driving seat. With Sir Horace as its president, the club became an organisation of gentlemen run by gentlemen for gentlemen, the rest being left out in the cold. But then cars were still only for the rich. Prices for run-of-the-mill models ranged from £200 to £800, and a 60 h.p. Mercedes set you back some £2,500. When you relate these prices to the weekly earnings of tradesmen at the time — about twelve shillings (60p) a week for unskilled labour and seventeen shillings and sixpence (87½p) for skilled, perhaps Irish motoring in those days could be more aptly described as only for the rich-rich.

The Irish Automobile Club had its premises at the St Stephen's Green end of Dawson Street, so that with Hutton & Sons at the other end the thoroughfare received additional confirmation as the Harley Street of the trade. The Mansion House was opposite but, more significantly, there was a shoeing forge and livery stables next door. Inevitably the club was ennobled with a Royal, and for the sake of convenience we shall henceforward refer to it as the RIAC.

In the spring of 1902 the RIAC opened Dublin's first car park, albeit a private one. The club took over a stores at the rear of Hutton's showrooms, with the entrance from Dawson Lane, announcing that members' cars could be parked there free during the day but with a charge of a shilling for cars left overnight. A 'washer' was there to wash cars 'at an almost nominal figure', and a skilled mechanic to do adjustments or other minor repairs. As the *Motor News* justly remarked, 'This garage should prove a very great convenience to the members, and will no doubt be enlarged later on if the club develops.' The writer added that membership was increasing steadily and that amongst a batch of nine recently elected members was the Marquess of Anglesey. Later the RIAC was to take on the motor traders over price fixing (more politely, price maintenance), but in these very early years the club's most important function was the control of motoring competitions and other such events within its own territory. (The club's authority in this area derives from its membership of the Federation Internationale de l'Automobile.) The most famous competition held

47

Sir Valentine Raymond Grace, one of the entrants in The Motor Tour of 1901.

under its aegis was of course the Gordon Bennett Race of 1903, but its first big event had taken place in August 1901. This was called simply The Motor Tour and was hailed by the papers as 'the first motor club meet which has ever taken place in this country'.

3

It is usually stated that about a dozen cars set off from the Shelbourne Hotel on The Motor Tour, but the newspapers print a list of eighteen and include amongst the drivers a Mr Dunlop, presumably the tyre man himself because 'Dunlop junior' is named amongst the passengers. There was also Mr Harvey du Cros junior (16 h.p. Panhard), Charles Jarrott (7 h.p. Panhard), the Rev. and Hon. Benjamin Plunkett, one of the Guinness clan and a future Bishop of Meath (De Dion), and inevitably Dr Colohan ('in his well-known 7 h.p. Daimler'). Last but not least there was Mr (later Sir) Valentine Grace who thirty years later was much given to appearing in amateur drama contests to recite Mark Antony's speech in a sheet (double-bed size, to accommodate his Falstaffian figure), but on that August morning in 1901 content to appear before the public merely at the controls of a small motor tricycle. With R. J. Mecredy as their pilot (9 h.p. Daimler), the tourists headed via Terenure for Naas, and on to Castledermot, Carlow and Waterford, where they were received by a local magnate, Alderman (later Sir) William Davis Goff, that year's president of the Club.

The only disappointment was that J. H. Edge had fallen ill and so was unable to bring over from England the fearsome 60 h.p. (*recte* 40 h.p.) Napier which he had driven in the recent Paris-Innsbruck race. The only fatality was an unfortunate dog which had been killed 'before County Dublin was left'. The roads were declared to be for the most part in first-class order. One reporter became ecstatic:

Through Dublin and Kildare the cars sped along over what were described as the surfaces of billiard tables.

It was not a race. The drivers made a point of keeping to their agreed place in the procession ('the machines could scarcely have been more nicely conducted') and

It was remarkable to note how little the motors frightened horses. The 'friend of man' for the most part, indeed, evidenced a lofty contempt for them, and went on his way regardless altogether of their triumphant progress. Even the village blacksmith did not hesitate to come smiling to the door of the smithy as if the motor was his best friend.

From Waterford, accompanied by Alderman Goff, the travellers made for Cork, stopped at Lismore to inspect the Duke of Devonshire's Irish seat. From Cork they went across to Parknasilla and Killarney, returning via Galway, Kilkenny, the Vale of Avoca and Glendalough.

While at Killarney Jarrott, another English driver Roger Fuller, and Harvey du Cros junior decided to take their cars through the four-mile ravine known as the Gap of Dunloe. They had heard that many years before a two-horse car had actually got through the Gap and into the Black Valley, the only time anything on wheels had been known to do so. Their Irish colleagues assured them they hadn't a hope but the trio decided to find out for themselves. Setting off for the Gap they discovered that the road ceased at its foot and the lake began, the road resuming on the other side. The locals told them the lake was impassable, which was rather unusual, the Irish practice being to assure wayfarers that getting up something like the North face of the Eiger is only a matter of a ten-minute trot, the speaker having frequently done it himself. But the trio, having waded into the lake to test the depth, concluded that they could get across by making a dash. The long steep climb up to the Gap was worrisome, for the track was too narrow to turn around in and if the car in front conked out they all would have had to crawl down backwards, with a cliff wall on one side and a precipice on the other. There was one nasty moment when Du

ALL THE WAY
UP SNOWDON!

On Thursday, May 26th, 1904,
Mr. Harvey Du Cros, Junr.,
succeeded in driving an Ariel
motor car

TO THE SUMMIT OF SNOWDON,

using the identical set of

DUNLOP MOTOR TYRES

used by Mr. S. F. Edge in the

GORDON-BENNETT RACE IN IRELAND, 1903.

These Tyres can now be seen at

14 REGENT STREET, S.W.

DUNLOP PNEUMATIC TYRE CO., LTD., ASTON, B'HAM.

Where Dunlop Motor Tyres can be obtained in Paris:
14 RUE PICCINI, AVENUE MALAKOFF, PORTE MAILLOT.

Harvey du Cros junior did not confine his daredevil driving to The Motor Tour, *as this tounge-in-cheek advertisement from* The Motor News *of June 1904 illustrates.*

Cros's radiator was found to have boiled dry and they hadn't a bucket to fetch water. They had to climb the cliff and bring back supplies in a waterproof rug from a mountain stream.

Incredibly, they managed to drive their cars to the top of the Gap, and lived to tell the tale. Their only bad experience was that one Billy Murphy scrawled his name with a sharp stone on the rear panel of Du Cros's expensive Rotschild carriage body. But the

50

prevailing opinion was that the event had been a splendid success, and from many quarters a note was sounded that has a very familiar ring — that it had all proved a good advertisement for Irish tourism.

4

The greatest Irish motoring event of those days was the 1903 Gordon Bennett Race. It brought this country into the international racing scene years ahead of Britain because of a loophole in the law.

James Gordon Bennett was the millionaire owner of the *New York Herald*. His father, James Gordon I (1795–1872), was a Scot who after training for the Catholic priesthood had emigrated to America at the age of twenty-four. He worked as a teacher, a proof-reader, a journalist and a lecturer, and would never have been heard of if he had not, at the age of forty, started the *New York Herald*, price one cent. He did not spare the dollars in the pursuit of news, and indulged in what the Old World would have considered dis-graceful intrusions into privacy (for the Old World was a recently reformed character in this matter and therefore very intolerant of its own old vices in others). The second James Gordon Bennett (1841–1918), while bettering his father's instruction, added the pursuit of prestige to that of news and scandal. In an intensely snobbish era it was not enough to have millions to be accepted socially by the people who mattered. We shall presently learn about the lengths to which Arthur du Cros was prepared to go, both in toadying and in cash expenditure, to get into England's inner circle. The short cut available to women, of marrying into the peerage, was obviously not equally effective for men, and the purchase of a British title (the only title that mattered), was quite difficult until Lloyd George, in search of ways to fill the Liberal Party coffers, democratically threw open the doors of the House of Lords to downtrodden millionaires. As a citizen of the Republic which staunchly upholds the principle of the equality of man in every-thing except money, James Gordon Bennett was debarred from even a humble knighthood. The only thing in that line open to him was membership of the mystic Order of the New Maecenas, and membership was to be achieved only by large purchases of prestige. Here again the only prestige that mattered was British prestige or, at a pinch, French, with German coming a very poor third. When not even Germany would touch you with a bargepole, you had to turn, like Tammany's Boss Croker, to the last social refuge of a scoundrel, Ireland.

Meanwhile James Gordon Bennett purchased prestige by send-ing Stanley to find Livingstone and supplied funds for his Congo journey. But the chief result of this investment was to turn Stanley and Livingstone into household names while leaving James Gordon

The Gordon Bennett trophy for road racing, the competition for which took place in Ireland in 1903.

Bennett relatively unknown outside the readership of his *New York Herald*. It wasn't until he was well into middle age that he realised that the quickest way to make his own name known worldwide was to attach it to international sporting trophies. So the Gordon Bennett prize for yachting was founded and, in 1900, the Gordon Bennett Trophy for automobile racing was put up for grabs.

5

In appearance the trophy was massive and preposterous. It was an essay in silver statuary on a mottled marble plinth. It showed what would now be called a vintage car, two-seater and chain driven, with flames issuing inexplicably but alarmingly from the wheels, a respectably draped lady with wings from her shoulders and feathers from her feet, standing erect on the seat in the recommended Victorian pose of 'bosom out, bum in', with a youth, naked except for a bit of strategic seaweed, sitting on the bonnet regardless of the heat from the engine, clutching in his extended left hand what is either a giant ice cream cone or a midget flaming

52

torch, and steering the car from the wrong side of the steering wheel with the fingertips of his other hand.

The rules and conditions were simple enough. The cars had to be made of materials and components manufactured in the country of origin, the nationality of the winning car determining the venue for the following year, although the winner could, if he wished, nominate France where the first race had been held. The nationality of the driver was immaterial, and the race itself was a kind of point-to-point affair.

The 1902 race, the third, was run between Paris and Innsbruck (325 miles). It was won by S. F. Edge of London in a British-made 40 h.p. Napier, and although his average speed was, at 34 mph, nearly six miles below the average of the previous year, Edge was the only driver to finish the course. The 1903 race was therefore due to be held in Britain, but between the restrictions on driving imposed by statute and by local by-law, and public opposition to the horseless carriage which had been raised to hysteria by the fanatics, the idea of a British Gordon Bennett Race had to be abandoned. At first it was assumed that France would have to be made the venue yet again, as provided by the rules. But the lawyers found that although Ireland was in the UK the legislation, through a technicality, did not apply there. This left Ireland and the Isle of Man as two possibilities, and in the ensuing auction the Irish bid was the successful one.

The phenomenal energy and enthusiasm always generated in Ireland in support of any venture uncontaminated by honest toil, were immediately released, as usual. From the farmer to the philosopher, the jerrybuilder to the geriatric, the whole Irish nation appeared to lose interest in everything except promoting a race between horseless carriages, these having the added fascination of being driven by foreigners. It is said that support was sought from 120 MPs, 30 county councils, 450 hotels, 13 parish priests and the bishop in whose diocese the race would be run, Dr Foley of Kildare & Leighlin.

Officially, organisation was in the hands of the RIAC, which chose a course consisting of a triple circuit of a figure-of-eight run from Ballyshannon Crossroads, Co. Kildare to Kilcullen, down to Carlow and back to Kilcullen via Athy, then across the Curragh to the town of Kildare, and back to Ballyshannon via Monasterevan, Stradbally and Athy, with an extra loop of the western circuit, 368 miles and 765 yards in all. The race was fixed for 2 July. By June the local authorities had galvanised themselves into repairing the roads on the course, straightening bends and rounding off sharp turns.* As the highway near Maryborough

*Hutton & Sons suggested the launching of a fund for improving the course roads, and offered £20.

S. F. Edge, the winner of the 1902 Gordon Bennett race from Paris to Innsbruck.

(Portlaoise) was considered unsuitable for racing, the county council obliged with an entirely new road. Hedges were cut down for two hundred yards before corners, danger flags were put up, and a large force of police (variously rumoured to number between two thousand and seven thousand) was detailed to guard the course. The race-roads were to be closed from 6.00 a.m. on the big day, side roads were blocked off, all animals were to be kept in the fields, and human spectators were to spectate only from behind the hedges, and on the understanding that they were strictly to obey the police and club officials.

All residents along the road had been personally served with warning notices in case they failed to read the scores of public notices along the course, and at 6.30 on the morning of the race, two pilot cars set out in opposite directions to cover the entire course and give warning that the race was on. In short, if a tithe of the energy, care, foresight and dedication lavished on the horse-less carriage race had been expended on running the country, Ireland would have been Utopia.

In the weeks before the race a number of the entrants were putting in practice runs, and it was only to be expected that they would be joined by exhibitionist drivers out to create the impression that they too were taking part in the event. Complaints were heard about 'motor scorching' in the locality and about the number of hens being run over. A semi-official compensation rate of half-a-crown (12½p) per hen was fixed, the owner being allowed to keep the carcase. This only caused the number of hens on the road to shoot up dramatically, especially when a horseless carriage was heard chugging along in the distance. But there wasn't a corresponding rise in the number of compensation payments as the hens quickly learned something of the art of self-preservation.

The London and North-Western Railway for its part put on extra boats to meet each of the four trains running daily from Euston to Holyhead for the race,* so there must have been a large cross-Channel attendance. The French, however, had chartered a steamer to bring their cars over. It anchored in Dublin Bay and became a floating garage, servicing the twelve Panhards and eight Mors that had arrived for the event. Finally, the Bishop of Kildare sent a circular to his priests, requesting them to warn parishioners about the danger of getting drunk on the day of the race. They were to be exhorted to abstain from alcohol, at least until after the race.

6

The race itself turned out to be without serious accident except for one rather nasty but non-fatal crash. The weather was reasonably good and although there were a few showers they were not unwelcome as it was deemed they would support the German-made emulsion which had been sprayed over the roads to keep the dust down. The two pilot cars, one a Star, the other a Wolseley, both went around the western circuit, leaving the eastern without official warning that the race had begun. But this didn't matter: no one suffered harm as a result. There were twelve competitors, three apiece from Britain (deemed to include Ireland), France, Germany and the USA. Charles Jarrott (Britain) ran into trouble near the Rock of Dumamase outside Stradbally, on what Jarrott described in his memoirs as 'a perfectly straight stretch of road'.† Something went amiss with the steering gear of his Napier and he went into the ditch at about 60 mph. He was thrown out of the car, which passed over him, dislocating his shoulder and breaking a collar bone, and finally overturning on the unfortunate mechanic, who was unhurt except for the red hot exhaust pipe pressing on his chest. Medical attention was rendered by Dr Kennedy, who had been

*Cars up to 50 cwt. were carried at 6d (2½p) a mile at owner's risk, the railway company bearing the risk for an extra 25 per cent. An additional ten shillings (50p) was charged if the car was loaded on to a covered truck.

†Charles Jarrott, *Ten Years of Motors and Motor-Racing 1896—1906*.

summoned to the scene by bicycle. But Kennedy was soon shoved aside by a more eminent practitioner, Lambert Hepenstal Ormsby, president of the Royal College of Surgeons in Ireland and very soon to be a knight, a man of such formidable presence that although after marrying a girl named Anastasia he had invented a device for anaesthesia, no one dared crack jokes about it in his hearing.

The accident effectively put Jarrott out of the race. A couple of other competitors had started with their handbrakes on, stalling their engines. Another got carburettor trouble and had to push his car over the starting line, losing forty minutes. In all, seven cars turned over or ran into the ditch, and it seemed as if the race were turning into a duel between the 1902 winner, Selwyn Francis Edge of Britain, driving an 80 h.p. Napier, and Camille Jenatzy, a Belgian driving for Germany in a 60 h.p. Mercedes. But Edge, as well as going into a ditch, developed fan belt, radiator, and tyre trouble. (He is said to have got through seven tyres.) He did manage to finish the course but came in last with a gross time of 12 hrs 50 minutes (net time on the road, 9 hrs 18 minutes, 48 seconds) and was disqualified into the bargain for obtaining 'outside assistance'. Jenatzy was first, with respective times of 10.18.01 and 6.39.00, and an average speed of 49.2 mph. He went on to indulge in an

56

appalling display of crude, vulgar exultation. On hearing about Edge's accident he had jumped out of his car and danced around, screeching, 'Edge bust up!' On being declared winner Jenatzy went nearly berserk, shouting, waving his hands aloft and standing up in his car to revel in the applause. A spectator said 'he looked like a man possessed.'*

The reader may well be wondering why Dr Colohan did not take part in the race. As a matter of fact an *Irish Times* reporter put this question to him in an interview published just before the event. 'I am glad you mentioned that,' replied the doctor, 'for I am rather tired of the question myself.' Reminding the reporter that there were only twelve cars in the race, he said, 'The cars and drivers are selected by the automobile clubs in each country, and, naturally, the men who have been most prominent in the continental races have been picked out.' But he had been around the course 'about four times' and each time liked it better. 'There are some splendid long stretches and the surfaces most of the way are not at all bad . . . I think passing will be the greatest difficulty unless the grass sides are levelled up a bit.'

Dr Colohan did, however, perform a useful service in connection with the race. He used his photographic skills to take a number of action pictures, some of which we reproduce.

*Jenatzy was later killed through fool-acting. In 1913, while on a wild boar hunt in Belgium, he went out one night and began imitating a boar's growl. A fellow hunter mistook him in the dark for a boar and shot him.

The car that won the 1903 Gordon Bennett race. Jenatzy's 60 h.p. Mercedes was specially built for the race at the Daimler works in Cannstadt, Germany.

Camille Jenatzy's winning car driving up Ballybannon Hill, Co. Kildare. It is being driven at this point by Jenatzy's co-driver, Werner.

It was generally agreed that the Gordon Bennett Race would do wonders for motoring in Ireland and for the tourist industry. R. J. Mecredy proposed that another international race be held on the same course the following year, the cars running on alcohol instead of petrol. Each competing country would manufacture its own alcohol, British cars being entitled to use Irish alcohol but not Scotch. Since alcohol could be distilled from potatoes and beet, not alone would Ireland's farmers profit from the enterprise but through self-interest would become ardent supporters of the cause of motoring. A new Irish industry would have been founded, and a national trophy, declared Mecredy, soaring, could be awarded by the Irish government or by the Irish people. His proposals were generally applauded by his fellow journalists, most of whom had been running on alcohol themselves for years.

5

Travelling on Air

1

Next to the internal combustion engine itself the most important early contribution to the development of the motor car was the pneumatic tyre, and this was developed and first manufactured in Ireland. As far as the general public is concerned, the inventor of the pneumatic tyre was a Belfast vet, John Boyd Dunlop. His claim takes the rank of an article of faith in Belfast and has gained the tribute of a plaque on the premises where the epoch marking tyre is said to have first come into being. To this day Dunlop's name is associated with a famous manufacturing company. The truth is, John Boyd Dunlop collected much credit and cash that strictly speaking were not due to him at all.

Although often referred to as a Belfast man, John Boyd Dunlop was in fact a Scotsman through and through. He was born in the village of Dreghorn in Ayrshire on 5 February 1840, the son of a farmer. When he was young somebody told him he had been a two months premature baby. This convinced him he was basically a delicate man, too delicate to work on the family farm, so he trained for a veterinary career. Believing that any kind of stress or undue exertion would be fatal to him, he got into the habit of speaking and moving very slowly, and this, coupled with a white beard of Father Christmas amplitude, gave him while still in early middle age the aspect of an Old Testament prophet. Nevertheless, within twenty years of coming to Belfast he is reputed to have built up the largest veterinary practice in the country, although he was still considering retirement at fifty-two in the hope of being able to cling on to existence for another year or two. He seems never to have had a day's serious illness until at eighty-one he changed his health tune, declaring, 'I am happy to say I am still hale and hearty and feel as young as when I was fifty.' Shortly afterwards he died quite unexpectedly.

His son Johnny appears to have picked up the paternal concern with maintaining a desperate hold on life. At ten years of age Johnny was complaining of the bumpy ride he suffered while travelling over Belfast cobbles on a solid tyred tricycle. Since the

CHAUFFEURS' OUTFITS
READY FOR SERVICE.

———

Chauffeurs' Smart Dark Blue, Green or Grey Liveries, with livery buttons, **55/-** and **65/-** each.

Chauffeurs' Caps to match liveries, **7/6** and **8/6** each.

Chauffeurs' Oxford Grey Frieze Overcoats, warmly lined, livery buttons, **48/-** each.

Chauffeurs' Overcoats in Dark Blue or Green, **65/-** each.

Chauffeurs' Driving Gloves, **9/6** and **12/6** each.

Chauffeurs' Leggings, **8/6, 10/6, 12/6, 16/6, 18/6.**

———

Illustrations and Price List on application.

PIM BROS., LTD.,
South Gt. George's St., DUBLIN.

This 1914 advertisement is a reminder of the extent to which motoring remained a rich man's hobby until the 1920s.

father suffered similarly while jolting along country roads in a dog cart, his mind was concentrated wonderfully on the problem of preventing vibration. So he conceived the notion of an air-filled tube tyre, and thus it came about that the pneumatic tyre was to be first commercially developed in Ireland.

Three families were concerned in the project: Dunlop, du Cros and Booth, the last two being settled in Dublin for many years.

60

The first Booth we need concern ourselves with was James, of Kilbeggan, Co. Westmeath, born in 1802, who was sent up to Dublin as a teenager to be apprenticed to an uncle. He travelled on the roof of the Kilbeggan coach, his feet tucked into a wisp of straw, his capital consisting of one shilling (5p), a parting gift from his father. Presently he and his uncle opened a store in Dublin's somewhat misleadingly named Golden Lane, a narrow thoroughfare linking the curtilage of Dublin Castle with the precincts of St Patrick's Cathedral. They traded as R. & J. Booth, describing their business as an 'artists' warehouse and timber yard', although the directories also list them as machinists. James married a Miss Wilson of Longford, breeding four sons and seven daughters.*

The Booths, strict Methodists, were members of the nearby Whitefriar Street congregation, transferring to the more imposing Centenary Church on St Stephen's Green when that was opened in 1843.

In due course James's sons, Robert and Richard Wilson Booth, took over the business, concentrating on the engineering side. They moved to new premises in Stephen Street, about a hundred yards away from where they had been in Golden Lane, and continued to prosper. Richard appears to have been the dominant brother, assuming leadership in the family enterprises almost as of divine right. Both brothers were enthusiastic members of their congregation, but along with their love of the Good Book went a love of music, an inheritance, they believed, from their Wilson mother. Family worship, morning and evening, was the rule, with a hymn added on Saturday evenings and Sunday mornings. They regarded the efficacy of prayer as beyond question and accordingly treated God as an expert consultant, propounding problems of business and social and family life for His consideration with a view to obtaining sound advice.†

Now the great test of your sincerity in supporting any cause is the extent to which you spend your own money for it. The Booths pass this test with flying colours in the matter of their congregation's orphanage. James Booth had built himself a handsome house in Harrington Street (No. 37) next door to Walker's Methodist Female Orphan School.** After James's death in 1896 (he was ninety-two),

*One daughter married into the Henshaws, for many years one of Dublin's leading hardware and ironmongery firms; another married into Fannins, the medical suppliers of Grafton Street.

†See *Methodist Centenary Church, Dublin Commemorative Record*, 1943, p.108.

**The school, founded in 1804 by Solomon Walker, was for girls of between seven and thirteen, *both* of whose parents were Protestant thought not necessarily Methodist. Since the 1930s it has been the headquarters of the Catholic Girl Guides.

his son Richard acquired the house and presented it to the school. Richard, who was secretary to the school, also bought a house in Skerries for it, so that the orphans could have holidays at the seaside.

In addition Richard had been choirmaster at the Centenary Church since 1863, his first act being to reinstate women sopranos and altos, they having been excluded from the choir for many years. He successfully urged that an organ be acquired, took lessons, and became the church's first organist. Richard began the Christmas morning service at 7.00 a.m. until, in 1908, by general agreement, it was postponed until 11.00 or 11.30 a.m.

Robert Booth for his part dedicated some of his time to the Methodist Widows' Alms-House and Aged Female Charity in nearby Grantham Street. ('Candidates must be over sixty years of age, and members of the Methodist Church for at least four years immediately preceding their admission.') Robert acted as honorary treasurer to this ancient charity (it had been founded in 1866), but he also provided the Centenary Church organ with an electric blower, a thing that makes one suspect that it may have been he who had to work the laborious bellows for his dashing brother.

But Richard's energy and enterprise paled beside those of William Harvey du Cros, in many ways the most important member of the pneumatic tyre trio and easily the most colourful.

The du Croses were amongst the many Huguenot refugees who settled in Ireland at the end of the seventeenth and beginning of the eighteenth centuries. William Harvey du Cros (usually known as Harvey) was born in Dublin in 1846 and was entered at the Blue Coat School* at the age of nine and a half. He left the school in December 1860 and, at the age of fifteen, having fled from an unhappy home, launched himself into Dublin's business world. He worked for seven years in the counting house of Brooks Thomas, the builders' providers of Sackville Place, apparently for starvation wages. He was fond of telling his sons how in youth he was always hungry. From Brooks Thomas he moved to Gatchell's the iron-mongers of Dawson Street (later Maguire & Gatchells), where he kept the books for £90 a year. For the period and for Dublin, it was an excellent salary (Gatchell was a Quaker). Just around the corner in Molesworth Street was the genteel land agent's office where the young George Bernard Shaw was soon to start work for less than one-sixth of that sum.

At twenty-two, Harvey du Cros married Annie Roy of Durrow, Laois, who was five years his senior. She seems to have introduced into the du Cros line the sense of humour which Harvey himself notably lacked. To her dapper little five-foot-five husband Annie

*Officially the King's Hospital, founded in 1670 for the education of the sons of Dublin's poorer freemen.

presented in fairly rapid succession half-a-dozen sons of whom Arthur Philip, born in 1871, became the most prominent. Like Schumann, Harvey du Cros seems to have needed the addition of a wife to spur him into forging ahead. Soon after marrying, he applied for the post of assistant secretary to the Irish Commercial Travellers' Association. The application, which his son Arthur suspected was drafted with Annie's help, was successful. Before long Harvey was full secretary. He operated from a room in 32 Lower Abbey Street, next door to the editorial office of *The Flag of Ireland* and other patriotic magazines run by the pornographic photographer and future Parnell forger, Richard Pigott. Presently du Cros added two more strings to his bow: a commission agency and the Commercial Travellers' Building Society. He was soon in the paper business as well. Such then was the founder of the first of the 'Dunlop' companies.

3

Tyres of one kind or another had been in use for thousands of years, partly to secure resilience but chiefly to protect the wood with which the wheel was made and to bind the component parts together. That highly resourceful race, the ancient Egyptians, used leather tyres for their chariot wheels. Later generations used bands of iron until the invention in 1839 of vulcanisation* suggested that bands of solid rubber could be substituted. It then became merely a matter of time before someone invented a pneumatic tyre. This was in fact what happened in 1846, seven years later.

As already mentioned, the discomfort experienced in the 1880s by Dunlop and his young son in having to travel over Irish boreens in solid-tyred vehicles set him thinking about ways to overcome the vibration problem. He was to brood over various solutions for the remainder of his life.

Dunlop's first experiment was to make a tube with thin ($\frac{1}{32}$ inch) rubber sheeting, and affix this to a solid wooden wheel with strips of linen from one of his wife's old dresses. Using a teat from a baby's bottle as a valve, he inflated the tube with a football pump and set the wheel rolling down his back yard. He found that instead of soon toppling over like the solid-rubber tyred front wheel of his son's tricycle, it travelled the length of the yard and rebounded off the wall.

He developed the idea by fitting to two wooden hoops of three foot diameter inflated rubber tubes encased in canvas jackets. These were wrapped in an outer jacket of sheet rubber, reinforced with two additional strips of rubber on the threads. All adhesions

*Vulcanisation was a process in which the heating of mixtures of raw rubber and sulphur rendered the substance more elastic and less plastic.

were effected with rubber solution, which was also used to secure the tyre to the rim. The hoops were affixed to the rear wheels of the tricycle with copper wire. The job was completed on 28 February 1888, and on that evening Johnny made a trial run in the moonlight. After making further improvements and demonstrating the tyre to favourably impressed Belfast businessmen, Dunlop ('Veterinary Surgeon, 50 Gloucester Street, Belfast'), applied for a patent for his invention —

64

A hollow tyre or tube made of india-rubber and cloth, or other suitable material, said tube or tyre to contain air under pressure or otherwise and to be attached to the wheel or wheels in such a method as may be found most suitable.

Unfortunately he was not aware that forty-two years earlier, on 10 June 1846, another Scotsman had anticipated him by being granted a patent for an invention consisting of

The application of elastic bearings round the tires of the wheels of carriages, rendering their motion easier, and diminishing the noise they make when in motion. I prefer employing for the purpose a hollow belt composed of some air and water-tight material, such as caoutchouc or gutta percha, and inflating it with air, whereby the wheels in every part of their revolution present a cushion of air to the ground or rail or track on which they run.

The man who had thus completely anticipated Dunlop was Robert William Thomson, a civil engineer, then in practice in London. His pneumatic tyre, although not named as such, was written up in *The Mechanics' Magazine*. Descriptions of carriage rides with the 'elastic tyre-wheels', or 'Thomson's Patent Aerial Wheels', appeared in its pages and by 1849 the magazine was reporting that

A replica of Dunlop's first pneumatic tyre of 1888.

The tyres are perfectly elastic as well as soft. They do not sink into loose gravel or soft ground as common wheels do. Nor, on paved streets, do they retard the carriage by receiving constant concussions from every paving stone or other obstacle they pass over — they yield to every inequality, permit the carriage to pass over it without rising up, and the elastic tyre expanding as it passes from the obstruction, returns the force borrowed for a moment to compress the tyre.

As will be noted presently, these claims were to be repeated on behalf of the Dunlop tyre in due course. But the magazine's 'confident expectation that these wheels will speedily come into general use' was not realised. Mankind in general has a built-in resistance to revolutionary discoveries and, unlike Dunlop, Thomson had not been lucky enough to encounter a commercial adventurer like Harvey du Cros who would force the public to accept the benefits of his invention. As things turned out, Thomson remained virtually the sole user of pneumatic tyres for nearly thirty years. On his death at fifty-one on 8 March 1873, his tyre returned to the obscurity from which it had never really emerged.

4

So in the autumn of 1888, not knowing that the rug would soon be pulled from under him, John Boyd Dunlop induced a small Belfast firm, Edlin and Co., to start manufacturing bicycles suitable for his patent tyres. Whatever the agreement was between the two parties it was informal and oral, a thing Edlin must have regretted later on. But even though Dunlop had improved the valve mechanism and the tyre materials, the problem remained of how to get cyclists to accept the pneumatic tyre. Dunlop's first effort in this direction took the form of a *coup de théâtre* at a college sports in Belfast on 18 March 1889.

One of the contestants in the mile race, William Hume, agreed 'for a consideration'* to use Dunlop's tyres on his machine. Spectators were amused at the man with the rag-and-rubber tyres which looked so clumsy in comparison with the neat looking solid rubber ones. When the race started, Hume deliberately kept well to the rear. Somebody cracked a veterinary joke, 'no wonder he's slow, his mare's in foal'. But on the third lap Hume started moving up quickly and when two hundred yards from home pelted past the leaders to win by sixty yards.

To this victory can be traced the foundation of the Dunlop Rubber Company. For amongst the defeated cyclists were some of Harvey du Cros's sons and du Cros, who was amongst the

*M. McDonnell Bodkin, *Recollections of an Irish Judge*, 1914, p.262.

R.J. Mecready, the founder editor of The Motor News. *He was involved in nearly all motoring activities early in the century, and was an original director of Dunlops.*

spectators, perceived the commercial possibilities of the new tyres. Later events give us good reason to suspect that neither Dunlop nor du Cros greatly cared for one another from the very beginning. It appears that at first either Dunlop would not do business directly with du Cros or vice versa, so du Cros remained in the background while moves were made by others in the following sequence. Dunlop approached William Bowden, a cycle agent of Bachelor's Walk in Dublin, offering to part with some of his patent rights in return for Bowden's help in setting up a company to manufacture Dunlop tyres. Bowden in his turn approached (with Dunlop's consent) J. Malcolm Gillies, manager of the *Freeman's Journal*, offering a part of his own share in return for Gillies's assistance in getting their joint enterprise puffed in the *Journal*. Both invited their mutual friend Harvey du Cros to join the project. Harvey agreed to do so without any stipulation at this stage as to his share of the profits, but on the Napoleonic conditions that he should have complete control, appoint the directors, write the prospectus and make the issue to the public.

As can be seen, John Boyd Dunlop was already relegated to a back seat. He was however appointed a director of the new company with du Cros, the others being Frederick William Woods, a partner in a tea and coffee importing business; Richard J. Mecredy, who came from a family of solicitors but whose chief interests were cycle racing and editing *The Irish Cyclist*; Richard W. Booth and his brother Robert, now running a well-established 'mechanical, engineering, lathe and tool manufactory' in 63 and 64 Stephen Street. Booth Brothers were also agents for various leading makes of British bicycles. The company, which had been floated on 18 November 1889, was called the Pneumatic Tyre & Booths' Cycle Agency Ltd. The capital was £25,000 in £1 shares (known as Booth's Babies), of which some £15,010 was offered to the investing public but not fully subscribed. Mathias Bodkin tells how he applied for a hundred shares but was allowed by the company to withdraw the application on being assured by a stockbroker that it was a wildcat concern, and by a champion cyclist that the pneumatic tyre was worthless.*

Dunlop was given £500 and three thousand shares for surrendering his patent rights, and presented half to Bowden and Gillies for their not very strenuous part in the promotion. Edlin & Co. of Belfast, instead of finding themselves with a snug place on the ground floor of the new enterprise, were taken over for £490, afterwards reduced to £400 and payable in shares, and were given jobs in the new concern. Edlin, preferring independence, soon cut the connection but the 'Co.' in the person of Finlay Sinclair stayed on, became works manager, was treated well, and could unctuously remark that 'hard work is a pleasure when we have appreciative masters'. Richard and Robert Booth received £4,000 in cash and four thousand shares for contributing the premises and goodwill of their agency.

The company, having declared in its prospectus that the pneumatic tyre was 'indispensable for ladies and persons with delicate nerves' (is it too fanciful to see Annie du Cros's drafting hand in this section?) held its first formal board meeting at 65 Stephen Street on 30 November 1889. On the motion of R. W. Booth, seconded by F. Woods, it was resolved that Harvey du Cros be elected chairman. Dunlop was not at this meeting, although 'also present' were Robert Booth and J. Malcolm Gillies. The latter, having walked on for this interesting scene, then walked off into the wings, followed by the other minor characters, leaving the centre of the stage to Harvey du Cros.

Du Cros handed over his paper business to his son Arthur in order to devote himself wholetime to promoting the pneumatic tyre. His claim that the tyre minimised vibration at its source — 'that fruitful cause of nervous exhaustion which is frequently more

---

*M. McDonnell Bodkin, *Recollections of an Irish Judge*, 1914, p.258.

68

trouble to the rider than the actual labour of propelling the machine', as well as 'accelerating the speed', certainly interested the British cycle manufacturers. Their corporate request that a 'licence for supplying and fixing pneumatic tyres should be granted to manufacturers' was sympathetically considered by du Cros and his colleagues. The first decision was to grant licences to not more than ten makers at a royalty of 9d (approx 4p) for each wheel, but a fortnight later there was a new decision 'to throw the pneumatic tyre open to the trade'.

5

For six happy months du Cros believed his company held the pneumatic tyre monopoly throughout the British dominions and that in the words of a later tycoon, the directors had been given a licence to print their own money. The company set up its headquarters in Oriel House, a large building on the corner of Westland Row and Harcourt Place, where in six showrooms it exhibited 'splendid specimens of the leading makes of bicycles, tricycles, and safeties fitted with the new tyre'.* Then came the discovery of the

*Stratton's *Dublin, Cork and South of Ireland*, 1892, p.80.

Harvey du Cros at the wheel of his 16 h.p. Ariel.

earlier Thomson patent, which had long expired, compelling Dunlop to make the forlorn admission that his 1888 patent, the company's bulwark, was invalid. The position now was that anyone was legally entitled to manufacture pneumatic tyres. Du Cros seemed to have nothing to offer. His factory was an attic, its plant consisted of half a dozen sewing machines, some wooden racks, a few pairs of scissors. Everybody except Harvey du Cros accepted that the Pneumatic Tyre and Booths' Cycle Agency lay under sentence of death. But his motto in the various sports he had practised was 'Never accept defeat'. A foolhardy motto judged by commonsense, nonetheless it paid off in this emergency. With, as virtually his only ammunition, certain minor patents taken out by John Boyd Dunlop for methods of fixing tyres to wheels, and other patents dealing with valves, du Cros took on the cycle manufacturers and the world's rubber industry. To add to his troubles, Dublin Corporation prosecuted the company for creating a public nuisance with the disagreeable smell caused by smearing the tubing with a solution of rubber in naphtha during manufacture. The Corporation lost its case but threatened to appeal. This was the last straw. Harvey du Cros had already realised that a factory in Dublin was inconveniently distant from the main market outlet in the British midlands. Moreover, business contacts had already been made with a Coventry firm run by an expatriate Irish family named Byrne. These considerations made du Cros and his colleagues decide to move to England.

They set up a factory in Coventry, in Dale Street, and were soon claiming to employ between 200 and 500 hands according to the requirements of the season. The Coventry factory was placed under the command of du Cros's son, Arthur Philip. Arthur, having wound up the paper business his father had earlier entrusted him with, was taken into the company in 1892. Barely twenty-two, he was a chip off the old block. This future millionaire, baronet, and occupant of two of England's stately homes, had been educated at the Kildare Place School and had started in the lowest grade of the civil service. With his appointment to the company, the du Cros family really began to go places. Arthur struck up an acquaintance with Ernest Terah Hooley, a Nottingham stockbroker turned financier who more than once was to see the inside of a jail. Hooley organised the sale of the company for £3 million and refloated it at £5 million on the strength of its having established, after much litigation, possession of valuable patents for detachable pneumatic tyres. The patents were based on inventions by a Londoner named Charles Kingston Welch (who was even more diminutive than Harvey du Cros), and by the American Erskine Bartlett. These inventions embodied the principle of a wired, beaded-edge tyre secured to the wheel 'by means of a hooked rim under which the edges of the cover were held and kept in place by air compression'.*

A condition of the £5 million re-flotation was that the original shareholders should have the prior right of taking shares in the new enterprise. First subscriber to the new company, which was called the Dunlop Pneumatic Tyre Co., was Harvey du Cros, who took 66,666 preference 66,667 ordinary and 66,667 deferred. Similar amounts were taken by Arthur du Cros and by Charles Wisdom Hely of the former big stationers in Dame Street.

Dunlop himself had little or nothing to do with the company that bore his name. For some time his unease in the presence of the spry little du Cros had become obvious. The collapse of his patent had made him a smaller boy than ever at board meetings, and his narrow view of the possibilities of the tyre, especially his pessimistic insistence that it would never do for heavy vehicles, must have made him particularly tiresome to the venturesome du Croses.

Dunlop had a hang-up on the problem of vibration. Ignoring the existence of the motor car, he was devoting himself to the perfection of a system of springing for big cycles that would absorb shocks and ensure the rider's comfort, and he felt the company was not giving him wholehearted support. There was also the touchy matter of finding a job in the company for his son Johnny. Harvey du Cros sent him soothing letters but Dunlop continued to sulk. He sulked more than ever after Welch joined the company and the detachable tyre was named the 'Dunlop-Welch'. Dunlop made statements about Welch that provoked a dignified letter of resignation from Welch on 31 October 1894. Dunlop immediately climbed down and tendered an apology. Welch withdrew his resignation, but on 16 March 1895, Dunlop sent a snooty note to the company secretary, announcing that he would cease to be a director as from 1 May. He could not resist a further allusion to his frail condition. 'I may mention that I expect my time will be fairly well occupied during the summer *considering the state of my health.*' Harvey du Cros replied in the stately style that comes naturally to men of small stature. Accepting the resignation he added a sentence with a sting in its tail: 'The Directors desire me to say that for their part they are sorry to receive a letter from you couched in this form; but, on their behalf, I am desired to express a hope that your health will improve and that you will enjoy many happy years and even greater success than that which came to you through your connection with the Pneumatic Tyre Company.'

*Sir Arthur du Cros, *Wheels of Fortune*, London 1938, p.145.

The story of the development of the Dunlop Rubber Company (as it became in 1901) belongs more to England than to Ireland. A Dunlops branch was always maintained in Ireland and Harvey du Cros never lost contact with his native city although he gave up his homes there at the turn of the century and made Cornbury Park, a historic Jacobean mansion in Finstock, Oxfordshire, his 'seat'. Dunlops continued to owe much to his shrewd guidance. He steered it carefully through the rubber plantation scandals exposed by his fellow-countryman Roger Casement, enabling it to emerge without any visible stain on its character. Casement's report (1904) on the horrifying circumstances in which latex was being collected from the rubber trees in the Belgian Congo would have created a greater stir than it did had it not been played down by the Foreign Office.* For one thing, the grasping Leopold II, King of the Belgians, the most repulsive of the villains of the piece, was closely related to the British royal family. For another, the Foreign Office did not wish to have any mud flung at the rapidly developing and prospering British rubber industry. Then word got through that Casement was at it again, this time in the Peruvian plantations. Moreover, speculators had forced up the price of Brazilian rubber in 1910 to the then astronomical figure of 12s 9d. (63¾p) a pound. Harvey acted. Dunlops laid plans for growing their own rubber in Malaya. They also built factories for spinning their own cotton. Eventually they were to diversify into general rubber goods, footwear, weatherproof clothing, sports goods and 'Dunlopillo' cushioning.

Harvey du Cros had himself diversified into other branches of the motor industry. He was not only pursuing wealth but security. The hardships of his early youth developed in him a reluctance to keep all his eggs in one basket. He even had two houses in Dublin, both quite near each other. The bigger was South Hill, set in some twelve acres of pleasure grounds, hardly a mile from the sea (and from Dr Colohan's house in Blackrock); the other, Inniscorrig, which was actually on the sea's edge at Dalkey. Some of his spare energy was devoted to setting up, with the help of his brother Ernest, an extraordinary firm in St Stephen's Green called Dobsons. Dobsons claimed to be builders' providers, electrical engineers, opticians and house painters, dealers in glass, wallpaper merchants, suppliers of mouldings, wood and marble mantlepieces, sanitary goods, and makers of photographic instruments. It was a range of diversification unusual even for Dublin. But when Dunlops really

*Among Casement's horrifying revelations was that the white overseers on the plantations encouraged the black workers to fulfil unreasonably high quotas by hacking the hands off defaulters.

took off, Dobsons became too insignificant even for Harvey and was abandoned. He was now into car agency.

He had acquired the English rights to a French car, the Panhard-Levassor. His choice of a French model was inspired not so much by sentimental regard for the land of his forefathers as by France's reputation as the leading manufacturers at that time. The reputation owed less to their engineering skill than to their intelligent exploitation of car racing. The first official car race had been held in June 1895, a race from Paris to Bordeaux and back. This had been won by Levassor in a 4 h.p. Panhard; he covered the 732 miles at an average speed of 14.91 mph in 48 hours 48 minutes. The following year's race, Paris to Marseilles and back, was also won in a Panhard. Harvey's choice of Panhard was therefore shrewd. He hired the 21-year-old former law student, Charles Jarrott, to handle the rights for him in England. Harvey du Cros was the eternal middleman.

Harvey chose Jarrott to teach him to drive. He refused to be a docile pupil, declining to keep the car in low gear, insisting on perpetual top and on hanging on to the steering tiller with both hands. Luckily for Jarrott the lesson was a short one, for the car swayed and rocked about alarmingly. 'If temerity and boldness may be counted,' murmurs Jarrott tactfully, 'Mr du Cros would have been a proficient driver forthwith.'

In spite of his growing wealth and increasing commercial import-

The Panhard-Levassor was one of the most popular and prestigious early French cars. Harvey du Cros was the English agent for the marque. This photograph shows a 1907 model.

ance, not even Cornbury Park and weekend house parties made Harvey du Cros and his family quite acceptable as 'county'. But he laid the foundations upon which his son Arthur was able to build. At any rate Harvey was made à J.P. for Sussex and in the 1906 general election became MP for Hastings in the Conservative interest. Following an Irish tradition he passed the seat to Arthur who held it as a Conservative from 1908 to 1918. Harvey became a Chevalier of the Legion of Honour, truly a fate few can escape, and with a Christian forgiveness rare in a Dublin Huguenot accepted a knighthood of the Order of Isabella la Catolica. He had also married again, his first wife having died with the century.

Although the Dunlop Rubber Company made its most spectacular strides under the managing-directorship of Arthur, these were made possible because, as in the case of the family's social rise, Harvey had prepared the way. It is virtually certain that were it not for his commercial skill the name of the surly, small-minded, ungracious Dunlop would not have been heard of any more following the discovery that he was not the true inventor of the pneumatic tyre. Arthur also benefitted more than a tycoon would dare to admit from his father's caution and far-sightedness. Success came early and easily to Arthur because Harvey had provided the opportunities for him. His rewards, being on the English scale of finance where pounds are more rapidly made than pence in Ireland, turned him with relatively small effort on his part into a millionaire. Harvey's thornier way gave him the habit of picking his steps with care and masking his autocratic temperament to some degree with polished courtesy. In its obituary notice, the *Irish Times* praised Harvey's 'marked ability in dealing with points raised by shareholders, especially with regard to suggested new enterprises in furtherance of the company's development'. Where Harvey shone and was seen to shine was when as chairman he presided at company meetings. He had a gift for presenting facts and figures lucidly and briefly, and for reducing complexity to simplicity. He could remain cool, tactful and conciliatory under stress and seldom put a foot wrong. Never would he have got into the kind of scrape that Arthur got himself into over the King Edward love letters affair. Harvey du Cros remained chairman of the Dunlop Rubber Company until his death, but the reins slipped from his hands in 1914. In that year, at the age of 68, he suffered a completely disabling stroke and never recovered. His illness was hushed up as much as possible and he was brought back to his old Dalkey home, Inniscorrig, where he lingered for four years. On Saturday, 21 December 1918 he suddenly took a turn for the worse and in a couple of hours his exhausted heart ceased to beat. Six days later he joined his first wife Annie in the imposing mausoleum he had built for her at Finstock. Their sons were reunited with them there in due course.

Obviously most of Harvey's fortune disappeared into a family trust, for the record shows that he left a mere £42,144 in England and £5,641 in Ireland. In his will he requests 'my dear Sons . . . to preserve a unity towards each other and I beg that they may love each other to the end'. Having thanked 'my dear wife for her unfailing attention to me during our lives', he further prayed 'that she and my daughter Pat will always look up to my sons as true and worthy friends'.

Nor can Arthur du Cros's £47,000 estate have accurately reflected *his* true financial position when he died in 1955 any more than the £15,080 left by Richard Booth who died on 11 April 1930. (Richard's son Edwin's £262,000 was nearer the mark.) As for John Boyd Dunlop, he died aged 81 on 23 October 1921 at his home, Leighton, Ailesbury Road, Ballsbridge, Dublin, leaving the sum of £119,378 5s. 9d., of which £101,293 17s. 8d. was prudently salted away in New South Wales, far from the hazards of European wars and Irish civil strife.

Dunlop himself always lived more modestly than the others. For some years he lived in a smallish house in Mount Merrion Avenue ('on my father's estate', said Arthur du Cros, which was stretching the truth quite a bit), and tended to describe himself as Vet. Surg. rather than Esq. But presently he moved from Harvey du Cros's 'estate' and settled in Ailesbury Road, then the city's most select inner suburb, and, a victim to middle-class morality at last, replaced Vet. Surg. with Esq. He invested some of his savings in Todd Burns, the big drapers in Mary Street, eventually becoming chairman of the board. He often travelled to board meetings on a bicycle, on which he looked incongruous and uncomfortable, and which Dubliners maliciously noted he couldn't ride properly. He was often heard to rumble into his beard that the Booth brothers had become rich without doing anything. The name of du Cros he could hardly bring himself to mention.

As already related, John Boyd Dunlop died shortly after announcing that at long last he was beginning to feel rather well. He is buried with his wife and young Johnny in Deans Grange Cemetery under a tombstone inscribed 'Behold the upright for the end of that man is peace.'

8

Until his father's death Arthur du Cros had been vice-chairman and managing director of the Dunlop Company: he then became the chairman he had been in effect since his father's disablement in 1914. The years 1914–18, the period of the war, were no real test of his ability as Dunlop emperor. The requirements of war kept the Dunlop factories working at peak capacity: Arthur had little to

do apart from placing his buckets under a continuous shower of gold and emptying them into his bank account. He had become more English than the English themselves, a thing which generally amuses that race more than it flatters them. He was now rich enough to hobnob with peers but not yet rich enough to have the right kind of peer hobnob with him in return. For years he had ached for a title and had acquired a stately home so as not to be caught napping should a coronet arrive expectedly. Unfortunately for him the Conservative Party, of which he was a pillar, had been out of office for many years and so was not in a position to add his name to the annual honours lists. Arthur had, therefore, to be on the watch for other paths to nobility and when Ernest Terah Hooley dangled before him what appeared to be an opportunity to rescue the British royal family from an embarrasing situation, he snatched it greedily. Such a rescue could reasonably be assumed to be worth a peerage.

There was a lady in the case but this only made the susceptible

Arthur all the more eager to rush in where old Harvey would have feared to tread.*

Since Arthur's career belongs more to Dunlop in England than in Ireland, to follow it in any detail doesn't fall within the scope of this book. It must suffice to say that as an expert on motor transport he tried hard to induce the British military authorities to substitute mechanised horsepower for actual horses. Not even when he assisted the Automobile Association to transport a battalion of Guards by motor from London to Hastings in 1909 could he favourably impress the generals and field-marshals. Undaunted, in the same year he formed the parliamentary aerial defence committee whose aim was to ensure that funds would be made available to develop an air-arm for the army. He and Harvey actually presented the British Army with its first airship, and on the outbreak of the 1914 war he set up, at a cost of £25,000, three motor ambulance convoys which he maintained, again at his own expense, until the war ended. Obviously this was the period in which he must have been amongst the richest men in England. Like his father he maintained a seaside home, Craigweil House, Bognor, which he made a treasure house of art and which he placed at the disposal of George V in 1929 when the monarch was convalescing after serious illness. But by then he was no longer in the millionaire class, so that the expense of the royal visit must have been a serious drain on his resources. One suspects that he was still hankering after a coronet.

He hadn't been able to maintain the prosperity of the Dunlop Rubber Company during the post-war recession and his personal fortunes suffered with the company's. Nineteen twenty-two was a year of catastrophes. In a palace revolution Arthur was kicked upstairs as 'president' while Sir Eric Geddes and Sir George Beharrel came in as chairman and managing director respectively. These two men had won tremendous reputations as wartime administrators, Geddes having been a First Lord of the Admiralty and later Minister of Transport. As chairman of the Chancellor of the Exchequer's committee to advise on all aspects of national expenditure he became notorious for his Thatcher-like wielding of 'the Geddes axe'. He solved the Dunlop Company's 1920s problems by expansion. Believing that the company had become too dependent upon the motor and cycle industries, Geddes and Beharrel acquired the Charles Mackintosh group of companies and diversified into the manufacture of a wide range of rubber products, including footwear, sports goods, and of course 'mackintoshes'. Two highly profitable developments were latex foam cushioning, marketed

*Nor would Harvey have allowed himself to be diddled by royalty, the judiciary, and of course the lady, as easily as Arthur was. Arthur lost about £64,000 by the affair.

as 'Dunlopillo', and, in the 1930s, a rapid growth in Dunlop's output of aeroplane tyres, wheels, and braking equipment.

It had not taken Geddes and Beharrel long to completely extinguish Sir Arthur du Cros's flickering flame in Dunlop's. He was to experience domestic troubles too. Soon after his deposition from the Dunlop chairmanship he and his wife were divorced after twenty-eight years of marriage. The last straw in his tense relationship with Dunlop's was when he discovered that his father's portrait had been slung out of its one-time place of honour in the board-room. Arthur, in a transport of filial indignation, had to rescue Harvey's likeness from further indignity, but we can be sure that his reproaches to Geddes and Beharrel bounced off those toughies like a beach ball off Dunlopillo.

Arthur married again in 1929, his second wife being Florence May, daughter of James Walton King of Walton, Buckinghamshire. She died in 1951 and a few months later at the age of eighty he married Marie Louise Joan Beaumont (but born Buhmann, the daughter of a German railway official).

Latterly Arthur lived on a more modest scale than in his heyday. His home was Nancy Downs House, Oxhey, Watford, Hertfordshire, and his last years were clouded with heart trouble, arteriosclerosis, with, finally, prostatic obstruction. He died aged 84 on 28 October 1955 at his home, leaving £47,019.13s.10d., a sum which, as already mentioned, would not have accurately reflected his true financial position. He mentions in his will that during his lifetime he had made 'adequate provision' for his family and descendants. This appears to have been the truth.

9

After the removal of the tyre factory to England, the Dublin branch of Dunlops became chiefly a sales point for tyres and the company's various other rubber goods. The manager was Arthur H. Huet (later of Clanwilliam Motors, Mount Street Bridge), originally a worker in the Bessbrook Spinning Company in Armagh, who became another of the du Cros proteges. His efficiency earned him a transfer to the Birmingham headquarters where, whatever his official title was, he was generally referred to as the commercial manager. But his fortunes at Birmingham were eclipsed with the eclipse of the du Cros hegemony. During the reorganisation of the firm under Geddes and Beharrel he was packed back to Ireland as managing director of the Dublin branch. This now moved to imposing new headquarters in Lower Abbey Street (now the offices of the Voluntary Health Insurance Board but still retaining the name Dunlop House). The 1920s and early 1930s were no boom time for Dunlops either in Ireland or in England, so that Arthur Huet probably had to keep running hard in order to stay in the same place. During this period he was an eminence in the Irish Motor Agents' Association, at the meetings of which his extremely clear mind and general formidability must have made him a disconcerting presence. Respectful attempts were made to get him to accept the chairmanship but he waved these aside. Troublesome honorary positions were not to his taste. It was left to a later managing director of the Irish Dunlop Company, John Sheridan, to serve as a president of the Society of the Irish Motor Industry (1972–3).

In 1935, after Huet's retirement, Dunlops accepted an invitation from the government to start making tyres here once more. This time the factory was to be set up in Cork where Fords had already been going strong for a generation. That year the factory was opened at Marina, taking on 300 workers. After the paralysis of the war period the company expanded and prospered. At its peak in the 1970s it employed 1,600 workers at factories in Cork, Waterford and Templemore, exporting not far off 20,000 tyres a week, including 250 truck tyres. As well as marketing tyres and tubes it was offering footwear, sports goods, inflatable dinghies, and Dunlopillo divans, mattresses, pillows and continental quilts, and carpet underlay. In short, the company was carrying on the tradition of its founding father Harvey du Cros, although his portrait had been slung out of the boardroom at headquarters half a century before and his connection with Dunlops totally forgotten. Any ancestral piety felt by the firm was concentrated on John Boyd Dunlop, who was at one time threatening legal action against them to have his image removed from their trade mark, and who in any event was not the inventor of their most famous product.

6

The Two Henry Fs

1

They were Henry Ford and Henry Ferguson, the one of Co. Cork descent, the other of Co. Down birth; and but for a generation gap they might have made a formidable partnership and one very beneficial to Irish agriculture.

Fords of Cork has been the major car firm in Ireland for nearly three-quarters of this century. The belief has gained ground that Henry Ford opened a factory in Cork chiefly for sentimental reasons although it was also acknowledged that Cork's site and labour advantages made a factory there a profitable proposition. The truth appears to be that there was little sentiment in the venture. Henry Ford's attitude to Cork is summed up in his attitude to the little cottage in Ballinascarthy that used to be the Ford family home. Henry wished to buy it, dismantle it, and re-erect it near his American mansion. But he regarded the price asked as too high, so he dropped the project and later on acquired just the hearthstones for Fair Lane, his home at Dearborn, Michigan. The name Fair Lane itself represented a little family sentiment. It was the Cork thoroughfare, now renamed Wolfe Tone Street, where his maternal grandfather had been born. Later a large area of Dearborn was named Fair Lane and the name was given to one of the most successful of Ford's American cars.

To the naive Irish observer Cork in the second decade of this century must have appeared an eccentric place to start a motor engineering factory. There was already a well-established Ford factory in England which presumably could look after the English market and be developed to supply the growing continental demand. Ireland herself was too sparsely populated (4,390,219 by the 1911 census) and the average household income too low to provide an economic home market. The natural conclusion would be that a large-scale factory in Cork was a Quixotic gesture by a sentimental American-Irish millionaire to the city of his fore-fathers. But the real motive was probably that a Ford factory in Cork would be another base within the British empire and, as such, a way of evading the high tariffs that protected British

FIRST · CAR

industry throughout the empire against foreign competition. Cork was nicely positioned between America and the European mainland. Ford's commitment to it is best seen when one realises that this was the first all new manufacturing plant he had built outside the USA with its own foundry. The Irish labour force was cheaper and more plentiful than the British, and more docile. Big Jim Larkin's Dublin dock strike fiasco in 1913 seemed an indication that docility would be maintained for some years to come. An ideal site was available on the South Bank of the River Lee, virtually in the heart of Cork city. Henry Ford seems to have spotted the site's potentialities during his brief and unpublicised visit to Ireland in August 1912. The fact that the land was public property doesn't appear to have bothered him. He was either told or he divined that the Irish citizen could be more readily persuaded than the English to part with his heritage without kicking up a fuss.

I doubt if Henry Ford had many mistaken notions about Ireland

Henry Ford in 1896, at the controls of the first Ford motor car.

that weren't speedily corrected by his 1912 visit. The Fords were originally English Protestant settlers who had acquired land in Munster in the days of Good Queen Bess (she had confiscated some 600,000 acres). In the 1830s three Ford brothers left Cork and went to America 'with the desire and determination to establish homes in which the fullest sense of freedom and independence could be had.' (Hardly the words of people who were enjoying complete residence-satisfaction in Ireland.) In the worst days of the 1847 Famine Henry's grandfather followed the others to America with the rest of the family. Among this second batch of emigrants was 21-year-old William who in due course bought a farm at Dearborn and fathered Henry.

2

Henry, born in 1863, was brought up to be a farmer but loathed the work. He found no joy in personally working the soil: to him it was the dreariest drudgery, and he had no romantic Irish notions about the horse. A fall off one at the age of nine didn't promote any *tendresse* in Henry Ford for an animal he regarded as bothersome to attend to and expensive to feed. 'What a waste it is for a human being to spend hours and days behind a slowly-moving team of horses', he said, 'when a tractor could do six times as much work.' He spoke as one who had 'followed many a weary mile behind a plough and I know all the drudgery of it'. As a consequence 'to lift farm drudgery off flesh and blood and lay it on steel has been my most constant ambition'. So the basic difference between Henry Ford and the other automotive designers of that era was that whereas they aimed at a passenger vehicle which perhaps might be later adapted for more general traction, Ford aimed at a farm tractor which might later be adapted as a motor car. His first successful car was built in 1896 when he was thirty-three years of age. At forty he founded, after a few false starts, the Ford Motor Company.

We can pause here to take a closer look at Henry Ford the man through the eyes of a shrewd observer, the financier and banker Edward Beddington-Behrens. Beddington-Behrens met him during a visit to America in the early 1920s and acknowledged that Ford was the most extraordinary person he had encountered in the States. Ford received Beddington-Behrens and his companions, Albert Thomas (a Frenchman) and Edward Phelan (Irish), both of the International Labour Organisation, at the Detroit factory. His office was surprisingly modest for a man reputed to be amongst the world's richest. It was like other rooms in a ground-floor row of concrete buildings, the upper half of the room being of glass so that he could see and be seen. Ford himself was tall, thin, white-haired and austerely handsome, looking over seventy while still

82

under sixty, and somewhat given to monologue. He seemed to find it hard to sign his name, writing it 'with the painful application of a pupil writing in a copy-book'.

> He attempted to talk about general political questions but his ideas had no logical sequence. So much so, that it was difficult to carry on any sustained conversation with him. He did not know which currency was the lowest: the dollar, the pound sterling, the Austrian crown, or the mark. He thought Czechoslovakia had an outlet on the Adriatic.*

According to Beddington-Behrens he was intensely anti-Jewish ('The Jews were the source of all evil in the world'), he held Frenchmen in contempt, likewise 'aliens' in general, and seemed hostile to any man not engaged in producing machinery. The visitors found, however, that when he remained in his element and talked about machinery he was 'a different man', although Beddington-Behrens's final verdict was that Henry Ford was 'a complete megalomaniac'. He further noticed that Ford had several *aides* who organised his propaganda, and he surmised that these exploited their chief because 'apart from his wonderful engineering activities, he displayed a naiveté and ignorance of world affairs which would have been surprising even in an average schoolboy'.†

But in spite of (perhaps because of) these limitations, Henry Ford ran a highly efficient factory in which little energy and material went to waste. He showed his visitors his technical school for the children of his workers, where the curriculum followed by the 500 pupils included the making of spare parts. The spare parts more than covered the cost of the school.

3

The Ford Model N was the first low-priced four-cylinder car to be built by the company and the first Ford to be seen in Ireland. It was exhibited in the 1907 Irish Motor Show in the Royal Dublin Society's grounds at Ballsbridge. Three versions of the Model N were on display: a standard runabout, one with a polished chassis, and a special-bodied crimson two-seater.

The Model N, like its creator, was spare and lanky in appearance. Its wheelbase seemed disproportionately wide, critics declaring 'it won't fit the ruts on byroads'. It was further condemned as 'too light for Irish roads' and 'too American', but amongst those who had a good word for it was the influential R. J. Mecredy, by now

*Edward Beddington-Behrens, *Look Back — Look Forward,* London: Macmillan 1963, pp.46—7.

†Beddington-Behrens, p.47.

Ford's first great success as a motor manufacturer, the Model N, first seen in Ireland in 1907.

the founder and editor of the *Irish Motor News*. Another admirer of the car at the show was one R. W. Archer.

In 1903 the 26-year-old Richard W. Archer and his eldest sister had gone on a tour of the West of Ireland in a 6 h.p. Wolseley. He found it 'a great little car' although it had certain drawbacks. The carburettor was directly over the exhaust outlet and if it flooded, everything under the coal scuttle bonnet went on fire. Archer accepted this hazard as one of the inescapable facts of motoring life and carried an old sack as a fire extinguisher. On the return journey from Galway the engine started knocking so the car was parked in Clara and the passengers got home as best they could. A few days later Archer and a friend, Arthur Hopkins, an enthusiast for cycles and motor cycles, went to Clara and partly dismantled the engine. They found the crankshaft broken across at the centre of the connecting rod and held together only by bearing on adjacent parts. In this condition the car had travelled three miles! 'Never', declared Archer 'have I heard of a similar case'.*

The engine was sent to the Dublin agents and was returned after three weeks. But it refused to start. Archer opened it up again and found that the agents had fitted the crankshaft correctly but had timed the exhaust valves to open on a down stroke and the inlet valves to open on the up stroke. No time marks could be found so Archer and Hopkins set the timing by guesswork and were delighted to find the engine running better than ever before. This suggested to them that they might do well in the car business. They had enough knowledge, as Archer later remarked, not to assemble an engine to run backwards.

They found a small shed in Denzille Lane (off Holles Street) and opened up there in 1905, doing odd jobs on cars, motor cycles and bicycles, and 'just hanging on' as Archer recalled, until what was to be for them the momentous year of 1907. Archer visited the Motor Show and the first car he set eyes on after entering was the Ford Model N. He spent all his time talking to the man in charge. One thing in particular impressed him about the Ford. Some cars at that time had wooden frames which, not being rigid, allowed engine and steering to rock around alarmingly. The Ford had a rigid rectangular steel frame, braced by two diagonals, which gave it great strength. Moreover Archer believed the 15 h.p. engine developed far more power than the English and continental cars then on offer. So he signed the first Irish sales contract for Fords at the Show, being appointed sole agent for Leinster with a quota of six cars. Connaught was later added to his territory, his quota being increased to twelve cars.

Archer found it hard to sell the cars. 'The trade were absolutely solid in their opposition. They laughed, sneered, made jokes about building out of "scrapped sardine tins", and lost no possible chance of running down the Ford with their mouths because they could not do it with their cars.'† Archer wasn't fighting a lone battle in Ireland. The head of the Ford sales organisation in Britain, Percival (later Sir Percival) Perry, entered a Model N for the 1907 Irish Reliability Trials and won a gold medal. He repeated the achievement the following year. The car also won a Wicklow hill climbing test in 1908, getting up Altadore and Ballinaslaughter hills faster than 'cars of three times the power and four times the price, not only on formula, but on actual time'.** (Not quite true: one English car, a Crossley, made better time.)

In spite of these proofs of the Model N's capacity, sales resistance continued. Nevertheless nine cars were sold the first year, although

*Golden Jubilee: Archers 1905–55, foreword by R. W. Archer.
†Quoted in The First Sixty Years: Ford in Ireland 1917–1977, p.6.
**Ibid., p.7.

the sales graph rise wasn't to match the Ballinaslaughter climb. In fact hardly any Ford cars were sold in Archer's territory in 1909. But in the winter of that year Percival Perry's assistant arrived at Archer's garage with a new Ford model that had recently come to Britain from America. To Archer it seemed 'a new and perfect Ford'. It was the Model T. With the Model T Archer hit the jackpot at last. In 1913 some six hundred Fords were sold throughout Ireland, representing 10 per cent of total sales in these islands. The figure was impressive. With all Ireland's economic disadvantages as compared with Britain, sales here were in proportion to the respective populations.

By now Archers had moved to larger premises in Clare Lane (off Clare Street).

Naturally Henry Ford called to the Clare Lane premises during his 1912 visit. The two men got on well together, Ford inviting Archer to travel back to America with him and be his guest at the farm in Dearborn. Archer returned to Ireland with the Ford franchise for the entire South of Ireland (can Henry Ford have been so sapient as to forsee in 1913 the partition of Ireland?). The outbreak of war in 1914 brought the motor trade to a standstill but business revived for Archers in 1916 when the Ford tractor made its first appearance here.

4

It seems that since 1912 Henry Ford had been hankering after a factory in Cork but was energetically dissuaded by Percival Perry, who favoured developing the British branch. Perry argued that Ireland was too remote, that the steamship service from Cork was poor and that as a port Cork was inferior to Southampton, which moreover was nearer the continent. Above all, there was no tradition of mechanical skills in the Cork area. Perry was not only arguing for Britain as against Ireland but for Britain as against Canada where a Ford factory had been opened over ten years before with the object of making cars to sell in the British colonies. There may have been something in the Ford organisation at this stage of the left hand not knowing what the right hand was doing, for Perry seems to have been unaware that Ford had granted the Canadian company (of which he owned 51 per cent) exclusive sales rights throughout the British empire except for Britain and Ireland.

Henry Ford, autocratic by nature and the controlling shareholder in all his undertakings,* was in a position to override any opposition and also to alter or cancel his own decisions. But since this position

*He bought out the original stockholders in 1919.

The Fordson tractor of 1917, many thousands of which were manufactured at the Ford factory in Cork.

also entailed responsibility for any decisions at the top which might prove disastrous, Ford cannily sought advice from all quarters about a situation before he took action. Like Napoleon and other dictators he could dither for a long time, but once he had made up his mind and got going it was hard to stop him. He kept dithering over the question of making Model Ts in Cork until the outbreak of war shelved the matter for the duration.

But while war closed the door on motor manufacture it opened the door for the agricultural tractor. The wartime manpower shortage in Britain meant that a tractor capable of doing the work of at least half a dozen ploughmen was an attractive proposition to the government. Objection to a Cork site for a car factory, especially the lack of an adequate home market, did not hold good against a tractor factory. No matter where you made tractors you could never have an adequate home market: most of the vehicles would have to be exported anyway. There were several other attractions about Cork, politically and economically. For instance, by not manufacturing tractors in England there would be no further deflection of skilled labour away from the engineering industry, an industry whose whole energy was needed for the production of ammunition and war vehicles. Materials for the tractor would

The interior of the Cork factory in the early 1920s, showing the Fordson production line.

have to be imported from the USA and in view of the U-boat activities an Irish port seemed a safer bet than an English. Then of course, in the aftermath of the 1916 rising, there was the attraction to the British government of a new and important industry providing rebel (and idle) Cork with an alternative occupation to trouble-making.

Lloyd George, having recently displaced the worn-out Asquith as Prime Minister, was anxious to promote his own image as the man who could get things done. It didn't take him long to appreciate the advantages in having Ford come to Cork. He gave the enterprise his blessing: a special licence to Fords to manufacture agricultural tractors at Cork speedily followed (March 1917). A few months earlier Ford, acting through the Trafford Park Engineering Company, had negotiated the purchase of the Marina site from Cork Corporation and the Harbour Board at the giveaway price of a trifle over £160 an acre for 130 acres. Some of the good and great of Cork, including the owner of the influential newspaper,

88

the *Cork Examiner*, George Crosbie, helped the project along by making, in the words of the Prophet Isaiah, 'the crooked straight and the rough places plain'. Some help must have been very necessary because the site included two important public amenities, a park and a racecourse.

It's difficult to gauge sixty years later what Ireland's reaction was to the epoch-marking factory at Cork. One must presume that the man in the street would have welcomed, as he always does, any project offering secure and relatively well-paid employment. The doubtful factor is the extent to which the man in the streets of cities other than Cork was aware of the existence of Fords and the implications for Irish industry of their arrival. Indeed news of Ireland's rapidly expanding motor industry had not reached the schools even by the late 1930s, at least not the Christian Brothers school in Dublin I attended. The Brothers duly instructed me that Ireland's only manufacturing industries were ships and linen in Belfast, beer and biscuits in Dublin. Every other industrial venture had been crushed out of existence by 'the British' and a strange native sect referred to as 'the Wes' Brishish Proddissins'. Of the activity at the Marina in Cork there was no mention. Not that anything sinister need be read into this. Education in Ireland has always been somewhat behind the times.

Unless Henry Ford concentrated his attention on motor cars to the exclusion of everything else during his visit to Ireland in 1912 he must have heard something about home rule, one of the big talking points of the day. But Beddington-Behrens may have been right in his strictures about the narrowness of Ford's vision to the extent that the economic and financial implications of home rule hadn't registered with him. These should have been important considerations to anyone considering setting up in Ireland a new industry whose viability depended so much upon the tariff situation and upon the free interchange of goods within the United Kingdom. (Up to 1922 the whole of Ireland had been part of the UK.) But with the official birth of the Irish Free State on 6 December 1922 there was a radical change in the tariff situation. Parts manufactured in Cork for the Ford factory in England were to be subject to 22¾ per cent duty as from 1 April 1923. It seemed that Cork had become Ford's white elephant.

5

We must now backtrack a little to see how things had been getting along in Cork since the acquisition of the site. The plant proved harder to build than had been expected and wasn't ready to begin production until the summer of 1919. From May to September of that year, Sir Percival Perry was managing director of the Cork factory, which had hitherto been managed by Alfred Dugdale with Eugene Leonard Clarke, a future managing director, as secretary. But Perry was not a man to be happy to keep all his eggs in one basket or to be the salaried servant of a Henry Ford-type prima donna. The Bristol-born Perry, who by the age of forty had already been president of Britain's motor trade association, director of the war-time Food Production Department and director of the Agricultural Machinery Department of the Ministry of Munitions, was merely marking time in Cork while watching which way the cat would jump in the immediate post-war period. Quietly he formed a consortium to buy war surplus cars and lorries in France and sell them in vehicle-starved Britain. As soon as his harvest was ready for gathering in, Sir Percival resigned from the Cork job on the ground that life in Cork endangered his health. Although he was to remain a director of the Ford Motor Co. Ltd and later to make another guest appearance with it in a star part, he continued basically to be a freelance. He published verses and trade pamphlets, sedulously collected decorations from European royalties, plus a British peerage, and after a final stint of public service as business adviser to the Ministry of Food in 1939–40, divided his sunset years between London's West End and the Bahamas, dying aged seventy-eight in 1956.

Perry's successor at Cork was Edward Grace, an American who had formerly been a factory superintendent at Dearborn. Although the factory Grace took over wasn't yet complete it was producing a trickle of Fordson tractors. Grace's first full year in the Cork job was an administrator's dream. There was a booming demand for tractors. Cork produced 3,625 of them in 1920, Dearborn boasting that Cork would soon be producing 20,000 a year — and then the bottom suddenly fell out of the market. The unfortunate Cork sales manager, finding Marina awash with tractors he couldn't sell, took refuge in the elegant obliquity of diction which sends shivers down the experienced shareholder's spine: 'We are faced with the situation where our production is in danger of overtaking the British demands.'

And of course when troubles come they come not single spies but in battalions. In October of that wretched year a seamen's strike halted shipping, and in Cork itself, as in Ireland generally, the gun had replaced voice and pen as the medium of political persuasion. The Lord Mayor, Terence McSwiney, was arrested and brought over to Brixton Jail where, after a heroic seventy-four-day fast, he died. The city was in a continuous state of turmoil and presently was actually burned. Meanwhile Ford workers often had to make their way to the factory through the proverbial hail of bullets. One of Grace's assistants, the oddly named Mr Port Stewart, after lamenting to Dearborn that armoured cars were running

around the streets and machine-guns were going all night, reported that 'My wife and children and myself were held up the other evening whilst we were out for a drive; we were placed under arrest and made to drive to the Barracks between two truckloads of soldiers, with guns pointing all around us.' It is something of an anti-climax to learn that 'we got off all right without serious mishap'. Clearly there was more than met the innocent eye in Sir Percival Perry's stated reason for resigning: that living in Cork endangered his health.

During this frightful period a question, even if unspoken, must have been formulated in many minds in Dearborn: 'Who the hell brought us into Cork anyway?' No doubt if anyone less than the boss himself had been so actively concerned in the Cork adventure, heads would have rolled, and heavy capital investment in the Cork plant would hardly have continued. (During the first nine months of 1920 no less than a further £327,000 was spent on a machine shop, foundry expansion, new wharves and equipment.) Either Henry Ford was singularly obtuse, or he had the devil's own luck, or else, not scaring easily, he realised that the trouble in Cork was one of those little local difficulties that inevitably iron themselves out. Another possibility is that the Cork adventure ranked so low on the scale of his international activities that he knew little of what was going on there. At any rate Grace was allowed to develop a new use for Cork as a kind of supply factory for the great works at Manchester where the Model T was being made. Grace had already asked Arthur Griffith to negotiate for free trade between England and Ireland in cars and parts after Southern Ireland's departure from the United Kingdom, and later claimed that Griffith had given him satisfactory reassurances on the point. (In which case

The Model T was very popular with the army in the early days of the Irish Free State. This photograph shows a convey of Model Ts outside the Cork factory ready to be driven to various barracks throughout the country.

91

Griffith would have swallowed his principles about protecting Irish manufacturers by tariffs so as to defend the near two thousand Cork jobs.) On the basis of this understanding Grace now prepared his under-used machine shop and foundry to convert to Model T parts which Manchester would be able to import duty-free. Accordingly the tractor operation was run down and on 29 December 1922, after the 7,605th Cork-built tractor had come off the line, the tractor-making equipment was packed for shipment to Dearborn.

Cork was now supplying all Manchester's Model T needs, including the complete engine, and Grace was mentioning the possibility of an annual profit of £100,000. Even a threatened dispute with Cork Corporation over the number of employees at Marina had been smoothed over. Ford's lease of the site prescribed that not fewer than 2,000 were to be employed. Grace's replacement of tractors with Model T parts enabled him to get along with 1,600. The Corporation ordered Fords to comply with the terms of the lease or be evicted. Henry Ford dug his heels in and it momentarily seemed as if the Cork venture was about to end ingloriously. But a settlement was reached on the day that Michael Collins paid a surprise visit to the factory, cast four cylinders and, as an encore, took a turn on a tractor. Grace could now justifiably believe that his major troubles were over. But the announcement of the coming into effect of the 22¾ per cent duty as from 1 April 1923 heralded the most serious threat to extinction so far. Cork was ordered by Dearborn to stop making the Model T parts as soon as a suitable site for a factory in England was acquired. Grace accordingly went site hunting in England. The one he found and recommended was Dagenham.

Cork's new rôle was therefore to be as an assembly plant, producing for the home market. But pending the coming into operation of the new self-sufficient Ford factory at Dagenham, Cork would also continue making parts for the Manchester factory. In fact Cork was to continue making Model T parts up to the end of European Model T production in 1927, by which time Ireland had become relatively peaceful but had fallen under the rule of native Tories whose blueness reduced the British hue to a pastel shade by comparison. Irish breadwinners now had to concentrate on the problem of how to rear large families on a wage of between £2 and £3 a week. In the circumstances Henry Ford, speaking about his Cork factory, could be forgiven some public-relations humbug about his ancestors and about choosing Cork so as to start Ireland along the road to industry, since he could point to 1,800 men employed at a minimum weekly wage of £5. 'This', he said with perfect accuracy, 'is steady money, week in and week out — something that few if any of the men had every known before.'

It had been justly claimed that the Ford car contributed more to motorising the 1914—18 war than any other vehicle. However, it was probably all to the good from Ford's point of view that conditions in Ireland prevented Ford vehicles from becoming too closely associated in the public mind with military operations. That distinction was earned by the Crossley Tender, a vehicle built on a modified private car chassis and developed as a ground service for the Royal Air Force. The Crossley Tender was much used by the Black and Tans and as a consequence figured sinisterly in song and story. Even today its name makes sour music in Irish ears.

The Ford car had several rivals in popularity in Ireland in the early days. The Swift seems to have been held in great affection, partly so because it was a soundly designed little car. But as Howard Woods has pointed out, the company's shamrock-shaped badge may also have stirred some atavistic feeling in the motoring public's bosom. Mr Woods had also drawn attention to the fact that the Adler sold here in proportionately greater numbers than in the English market.

But it was mainly owing to Fords that the end of the 1920s saw the motor car established in Ireland as a popular method of private transport and one which could be afforded by many thousands more than could have afforded horse carriages. Indeed in those early days the two-car family was not at all uncommon, and some families ran three or four cars, plus a horse carriage for those invincibly conservative elders who have always been a feature of Irish life. The Waterford businessman, Sir William Davis Goff, whom I have already mentioned, had three cars and a chauffeur for each. The chauffeurs were heard lamenting that Sir William hadn't four cars since four drivers would be able to pass the vacant hours with a game of poker. Sir William often used all three cars on his holiday jaunts. One of the three went ahead with the luggage and the servants, the middle one carried himself and the more favoured members of the family. The third was partly for emergencies and occasionally for the transport of supernumerary relations. It is reported that on visits to Killarney the chauffeurs worked through the night to change the sprockets on the gears so that the cars could tackle the Kerry hills.

6

Henry Ford wasn't the only man to have an eye to the importance of the tractor in an Irish as well as a world context. It was inevitable that many people who worked on a farm and happened to have a mechanical bent must have speculated about how machines could be made do for farming what the Lancashire mills had done for cotton. Not many would have had the energy, the capacity and

the financial means to put their ideas into practice. However, on a farm at Growell, near Dromore, Co. Down, in 1884 there was born one Henry George Ferguson (but always called Harry) who had Henry Ford's engineering genius, who was to grow up and work on a farm as Henry Ford did and, like Ford, come to loathe its soul-destroying backbreaking drudgery. Harry's first objective was to get away from farming in general and from his father's farm in particular. Old James Ferguson not only believed in a vengeful God and a brimstone hell but was determined that his family should do likewise. At an early age Harry reasoned that the millions who were in hell could not have existed if God hadn't created them, and since God would have known they would end up in eternal torment when He created them it seemed distinctly odd of God to create them in the first place. Harry's conclusion was it would be sensible to become a sincere agnostic, the sincerity being an insurance against retribution in the next world since God could hardly punish you for your genuine beliefs. It didn't occur to Harry that his conclusion was based on two incompatible concepts of God, since a God who created people in full knowledge that they would go to hell was

94

hardly to be trusted where it came to drawing fine distinctions about sincerity. But Harry's failure to perceive this was understandable. He was too preoccupied with the importance of a second conclusion which flowed from the first. Namely, that the homestead of a militant and short-tempered Northern Irish Plymouth Brother wasn't the most comfortable place for an agnostic son who, though nearly eighteen, was the smallest and lightest male in the family.

Harry resolved to place the Atlantic Ocean between himself and the militant Plymouth Brother by emigrating to Canada.

Canada was the traditional place for the adventurous or necessitous Northern Irish to emigrate to, presumably because it helped to preserve the historical status quo by keeping Ulstermen well to the North of the feckless Southern Irish who tended to emigrate to the USA. But destiny intervened. Harry's eldest brother Joe had already fled to Belfast where, in a tiny premises on the Shankill Road which matched the size of the paternal financial backing, he ran a cycle and car repair shop. Just as Harry was on the point of buying his ticket for Canada, he received from Joe the offer of an apprenticeship in the repair shop. Harry, feeling the instincts of an engineer stirring within him, accepted the offer and that very evening accompanied his brother back to Belfast.

Harry Ferguson had found his true *métier* and, what is as important, had found the most propitious circumstances to exercise it. As Napoleon pointed out, talent is useless unless there is also opportunity. Harry could do wonders with engines, but the engines had to be there for him to do wonders with. As they *were* there his special talent for tuning engines was soon in evidence, causing his brother's repair shop to become increasingly well known in Belfast as an excellent place to bring an ailing car. Not that it was roses, roses all the way for Harry Ferguson. Like many another genius some of his early efforts suggested more ineptitude than the opposite. The first car he drove he skidded, with its driver, into a shop window.

Meanwhile he attended evening courses at Belfast Technical College and encountered John Lloyd Williams, later to be his business partner and intimate friend. According to his biographer Colin Fraser, Williams was the only intimate friend Harry Ferguson had and retained. For if you could not see eye to eye with Ferguson he tended to dismiss you from his life, unless you were likely to be so useful to him that, as when he was negotiating with Henry Ford, an attempt to convert you seemed worthwhile.

Ferguson had two valuable assets. In engineering he could perceive what were the really important issues, he could isolate them, and when unable to invent a practicable solution himself would insouciantly appropriate the solutions worked out by his employees. Second, he was above all a persuasive and imaginative salesman. It was his salesmanship which ensured his success when, in 1911, at the age of twenty-seven, he more or less dismissed his employer-brother from his life and set up his own business in May Street, Belfast.* The independence that May Street Motors gave him presently enabled him to devote himself to a darling project, the development of farm mechanisation. In this he may appear to have been Henry Ford's disciple, but the relationship was not that of master and disciple. Quite independently of Ford he had arrived at the same conclusion as the older man: that to improve the efficiency of farm machinery, by cutting costs, would increase the supply of cheap food and thus strike a giant blow at world poverty. He was determined to do something about it. Like Ford he had had personal experience of the more backbreaking forms of farm labour and like Ford refused to accept that this drudgery was inevitable. When, shortly after the outbreak of the 1914—18 war he became Irish agent for a large heavy American tractor with the off-putting name of Overtime, it can hardly have taken him long to realise that its design could be improved and that he was the man to do it. His objectives were twofold. To produce a cheap, lightweight, easily manoeuvreable tractor which would be an attractive proposition to the world's small farmers (the Model T of farm machinery) and to increase the tractor's versatility by developing a number of implements which could easily be attached to it.

The big difficulty in Harry Ferguson's way was the traditional Irish one, lack of capital. His local reputation had already secured him some financial backers but they could not command enough money to launch the large-scale manufacture of tractors. At first, therefore, Ferguson had to concentrate on the development of implements which could be used with existing models. His salesman-demonstration of what the Overtime tractor could do led to his being invited by the Irish Board of Agriculture to try to improve the efficiency of Irish tractors during the spring ploughing season of 1917. He and his technical right-hand man Willie Sands were supplied with a large car, adapted so that they could sleep in it if needs be, and with this they toured the country to inspect tractors. Ferguson preached the gospel of mechanisation, occasionally pulling on a pair of workgloves (he was almost neurotic about personal cleanliness and neatness) to help Sands make some adjustments. What they saw in the way of cumbersome, ill-designed, ill-made machinery confirmed Ferguson in his objectives. The Overtime at 2½ tons proved to be by no means the heaviest of tractors. For instance, the Omnitractor of London turned the scales

*Harry Ferguson was not sentimental about his family. Towards the end of his life he was asked what had happened to his brothers and snapped 'All dead! All dead!' in a way that inhibited further enquiry.

An early photograph of Harry Ferguson, taken when he was about twenty-three years old.

at 3¼ tons, the Harvester Mogul at over 4½ tons. These great weights were partly intended to secure stability when the tractor was drawing a plough, since there was a natural tendency for the front of the tractor to rear up when the plough encountered some sturdy obstacle like a big rock. For there was an ever-present danger of the tractor overturning and of the driver being injured or killed.

Ferguson accordingly conceived a new kind of plough which, when attached to a tractor, would become an integral part of it, another limb rather than an appendage like a man's briefcase or umbrella. By the end of 1917 Willie Sands had brought that concept into actual being. The new plough was specifically intended for use with Henry Ford's lightweight Eros tractor and not with any other. As Ferguson justly remarked, 'It is no more possible to design a plough which would be suitable for use with various sizes of tractors than it is to design a cart which can be drawn by a donkey or a Clydesdale . . .' The plough was also designed to be hitched not to the rear of the tractor, like a caravan to the towbar of the family car, but *under* the tractor body, thus ensuring that the 'pull' in drawing the plough would also pull the tractor towards the ground, avoiding the danger of overturning. Not alone had the design of this first Ferguson plough (perhaps we should call it Ferguson-Sands plough) the beauty of simplicity but it *worked*. It is not altogether fanciful to see in Ferguson's behaviour from now on a touch of the messianic. He caused one of his *dicta* to be printed and displayed on the walls of his engineering departments: 'Beauty in engineering is that which performs perfectly the function for which it was designed and has no superfluous parts.'

7

But Harry Ferguson's tragedy was that again and again the rug was to be pulled from under him just when the hour of victory was about to strike. No sooner had he designed a plough capable of working efficiently with the Eros tractor than Ford abandoned the Eros and introduced the Fordson, a lightweight tractor (under 1½ tons) of improved design. At a ploughing contest an Eros drawing a Ferguson plough easily beat a Fordson, but this was an empty victory for Ferguson. The Ford factory in Cork announced it would be making the Fordson (Fords, it will be remembered, had close connections with the British government), and that 6,000 Fordsons would be brought from America to help in the war effort until the Cork-built tractors began coming off the line.

Ferguson, however, knew better than to dismiss Henry Ford from his life in the lordly way he banished subordinates he could do without. So long as Ford could mass produce cheap and efficient tractors he would be useful to Ferguson. Every Fordson sold created the opportunity to sell a Ferguson plough. Ferguson accordingly sought ways to develop a personal relationship with Ford. This proved difficult. Ford was surrounded by lieutenants who took care that no one else got near enough to the Great Man to pose a threat to their own influence and consequently to their job security. When in 1920/21 Ferguson went to America and wangled a chance to demonstrate his plough to Ford, he was still kept far enough away for the Great Man to conclude he must be some kind of salesman, though a promising enough guy to be offered a job in the Ford organisation. It says something for Ferguson's self-control that he was able to turn the offer down politely.

On returning to Ireland Ferguson tried to get a foot inside the door at the Cork plant, but that portal was guarded by a redoubtable dragon, Patrick Hennessy, a Corkman able to beat the Co. Down man at his own game.

Hennessy, son of Patrick Hennessy of Ballyvodak House, Midleton, Co. Cork, and born in 1898, had joined Fords in 1920 after demobilisation from the Inniskilling Fusiliers, in which he had served during the 1914—18 war. He started on the shop floor in the foundry, working in the blacksmith's forge, in the machine shop and on the assembly line before being promoted to testing tractors as they came off the line. Next he was given the job of demonstrating tractors to foreign visitors to Henry Ford's farm. Then after a spell at Trafford Park to develop his sales technique, he was appointed representative for the whole Irish territory and, in 1923, came back to Cork as service manager. Eventually he was to become chairman of both Henry Ford & Son and of Ford of Britain, a knight, a member of the advisory council at the British Ministry of Aircraft Production, and president of the SMMT (1965—6). Such then was the man Ferguson tried his luck with in Cork. But his most effective weapon, his persuasive salesmanship, merely blunted itself on the armour of a fellow practitioner. Ferguson decided to reopen the fight on the American front.

He did this by establishing a sales organisation, Ferguson-Sherman Inc. of Evansville, Indiana, with two brothers, Eber and George Sherman, who were already agents for Fordson tractors. Ferguson-Sherman were to distribute Ferguson ploughs throughout the United States, the ploughs being manufactured by relatively small-time American firms. Eber Sherman was, in addition, reputed to be on very friendly terms with Henry Ford, and no doubt Ferguson banked on one thing leading to another. But just when Ferguson-Sherman began to get on its feet the rug was once again pulled away. Production of the Fordson tractor was halted in America and was concentrated in Cork in 1928. This arrangement continued until the complications of the Economic War between Britain and Ireland, which broke out after Fianna Fáil first gained office in 1932, made it advisable to transfer the whole operation to Dagenham the following year.

The blow to Ferguson-Sherman by the stoppage of Ford's tractor production in America in 1928 was followed by another, probably heavier, blow: the start of the 1929 world depression. It was not in Ferguson's character to shoulder any blame he could foist on someone else. Acrimonious letters passed between Ferguson and the Shermans about the falling off of business. As one would expect, such exchanges led nowhere. But the indomitable Ferguson had meanwhile changed his strategy. If he could not rely on a supply of tractors from Ford, these tractors moreover being by no means perfect in design, then he would design his own ideal tractor and is alleged to have asked the Northern Ireland government for $4m. to enable him to manufacture it. He was refused on the ground that Northern farmers would never replace horses with machines.

Ferguson's prototype tractor of 1935, the mechanical basis of his famous partnership with Henry Ford.

He now tried working with the Craven Wagon Works of Sheffield but dismissed them from his life when they wouldn't give him his own way in everything. His next affair was with the David Brown engineering company of Huddersfield in 1938 and resulted in production and sale of well over a thousand tractors. But the partnership ended, ostensibly because David Brown was going ahead with a heavier tractor of its own design but also, it had been hinted, because Ferguson wished it to end. Another opportunity had arisen to develop a Ford-Ferguson collaboration. Ferguson had invited his old American partner Eber Sherman to watch a Ferguson-Brown tractor in operation. Sherman, much impressed, arranged that Ferguson should bring a tractor and various implements to Henry Ford's farm in Dearborn. Ford was most favourably impressed. There followed the famous and unfortunate gentlemen's agreement by which the 75-year-old Ford, on the basis of a handshake with the 54-year-old Ferguson, agreed to make the tractors for Ferguson to sell.

100

Ferguson-Sherman rose phoenix-like from its ashes with the aid of an advance of $50,000 from Ford and set about production. Before long Ferguson was taking much the same attitude to the Sherman brothers as Dunlop had taken to the Booths over their share of the tyre profits. What had the Shermans actually *done* to entitle them to hold their bucket under the coming shower of gold? By 1942 the Shermans had been got rid of (for their 'lack of drive') and joined the swelling ranks of those whom Harry Ferguson dismissed from his life. At the time all seemed set fair for the success of the Ford-Ferguson handshake enterprise, and Ford sank some $2m. in tooling for the tractor. The beauty of the agreement was that there were no written words for lawyers to wrangle over. But trouble began when one of the handshakers suffered a stroke and his grip on his organisation slackened. Ford's first stroke came in 1938, the year of the agreement. His second followed in 1941, when he was 78. He was now obviously no longer fit to be commander-in-chief of so huge and complicated an organisation as the Ford Motor Company. Trouble deepened in 1943 when his only son and heir, Edsel, died suddenly at fifty, and a 26-year-old grandson, Henry II, had to be pulled out of wartime service in the navy in the hope that he could reduce the growing chaos in the company to some kind of order. The position as regards the gentlemen's agreement was, therefore, that the more important of the gentlemen could no longer answer his helm, and none of his lieutenants liked the agreement. They had persuaded themselves that because of slack sales and steel supply difficulties in wartime they were actually losing money on every tractor they sold. It now seemed they would be only too happy to do unto Harry Ferguson what he had done unto the Sherman brothers.

The first shot fired across Ferguson's bows was Henry Ford II's proposal in 1944 that his grandfather's handshake agreement be replaced by a written contract. Further proposals made it clear that Fords wanted absolute control over design, manufacture and sales and the dropping of the Ferguson name. The inevitable parting of the ways occurred on 11 November 1946. The president of Ferguson's American company Roger Kyes, (later a Deputy Secretary of Defence), congratulated Ferguson on 'achieving his freedom', which may have been an intentional rubbing of salt into the wound. A relationship of sorts was kept up between Fords and Ferguson for a year or so, but Ferguson now pinned his hopes on getting his tractors manufactured in Britain since Fords were obviously going to squeeze him out of America sooner or later. He didn't go without a fight, however. In 1948 he sued Fords in the New York courts for $251m., a sum made up of treble damages in respect of their alleged conspiracy to destroy his business and $5m. for infringement of patent rights. Fords must have seen that Ferguson had some chance of winning because the following year Henry Ford II came to London with a peace offer of an out-of-court settlement for $10m. Ferguson unwisely refused. He seems to have persuaded himself that he was not just fighting for himself but for the rights of all inventors, and in such Joan-of-Arc moods a man can become foolishly intractable. The case dragged on, Ferguson now developing the suspicion that the Ford lawyers were deliberately stalling so that the time limit on the patent rights might well run out before the case ended. Settlement negotiations were concurrently being carried on behind the scenes but without much success. At one point Fords were offering $1.5m. to settle Ferguson's claim for $15m. Finally both sides agreed on a consent judgment for $9.75m., or $250,000 less than Ferguson could have got from the Ford offer of three years before. He also had to pay much of the swollen legal costs of some $3.5m. out of his award, so that all in all he had suffered defeat except in the technical sense. But to newspaper reporters he maintained it was a famous victory, and since he cunningly stressed the 'human' angle of the lone little man taking on the giant corporation in defence of inventors' rights, the reporters swallowed his version and gave it gratifying publicity.

It is a commonplace observation that as people grow older their various characteristics tend to get more pronounced. In Harry Ferguson's case his autocracy increased, even at the expense of common-sense. His American business interests (manufacture and sales of tractors) prospered chiefly on paper, partly because of unfavourable world conditions in the early 1950s but also because he tried to run things by remote control. He had bought a charming manor house, Abbotswood, in the Cotswolds and was loath to leave it because here at last he had surrounded himself with a little kingdom in which not only was he absolute monarch but rich enough to impose his idiosyncrasies on everything and everyone. His liking for neatness and precision had now become neurotic. Staff were employed to hurry forward and pick up any leaf that happened to fall on the manicured lawns. Round-shouldered trees were forced with guy ropes to stand with soldierlike erectness, and the sheep which were permitted to graze his parkland (provided they didn't shed any tufts of wool), were compelled to proceed through ever-changing wire-fenced corridors in case their feet wore the grass down into a track in any one place. As he Rolls-Royced around the countryside he would order a halt whenever he spotted a badly running or ill-kept Ferguson tractor, go into the field with a spanner and either make the required adjustment himself or lecture the driver on the importance of keeping the tractor spick and span.

The wonder of it is that no sturdy British farmer knocked him down for such impertinence (at least his biographer cites no instance of this). One can only conclude that in those days the sturdy British farmer was as liable as the rest of us to be overawed by expensively dressed men with authoritarian manners, issuing from immaculate Rolls-Royces. He was also to overawe the management of Claridges, the London hotel sacred to crowned heads and millionaires, into permitting him to drive a Ferguson tractor down its main staircase for the benefit of press photographers.

When Henry Ford II visited Ford's Cork plant in 1977 he took the opportunity to sit on the oldest Cork-built working tractor in Ireland.

Yet such gimmicks were not simply to gratify a younger son's psychological urge to draw attention to himself, or the small man's need to compensate himself for his lack of inches. Ferguson had an economic gospel to preach and sought to catch the public eye in order to be able to catch the public ear. The post-war inflation of 5 per cent a year alarmed him. He launched a one-man campaign for stabilisation of wages and profits as the first step towards a real rise in living standards, and he practised what he preached. The prices of Ferguson tractors and implements were kept steady, Ferguson cutting his already small profit margin so as to absorb the rising costs of his dealers. He could not persist on this course indefinitely. To add to his difficulties, the day of the one-man band was ending in areas which were becoming the preserve of the multinational orchestra. A merger was inevitable.

9

In 1953 the now 69-year-old Ferguson entered into a partnership with the Canadian firm of Massey-Harris which had a century of experience in manufacturing farm machinery behind it. Professor John B. Rae saw in the Massey-Harris-Ferguson merger the realisation of Ferguson's 35-year dream 'whether he thought so or not', and that 'he left an indelible imprint on it, far more than just his name. The firm is genuinely Massey-Ferguson, not simply Massey-Harris with the Ferguson enterprises added.'*

But Ferguson stayed only a year in the partnership. His remaining five years were passed mostly at Abbotswood where he occupied himself with designing a 'people's car' with a four-wheel drive. His frequent visits to his native Ulster, especially to the country places he had known so well in boyhood, seemed to knock years off him until their effect wore off. In 1957 he and his wife took a winter holiday in Jamaica during which an armed burglar entered his hotel room. In his account of the incident for journalists Ferguson said, 'I told him to go. He did. He didn't get away with a single damned cent.' But before he went the burglar had shot Ferguson in the leg. Fortunately it was only a flesh wound and didn't appear to have had any effect other than passing inconvenience. In fact for a man of his years Harry Ferguson was uncommonly spry both in body and in mind. His only bother was increasing insomnia, for which he took sleeping pills. On the morning of 25 October 1960 he failed to join his wife for breakfast in her room at precisely 8.30 a.m., as was his unvarying custom. After a few minutes she went to find out what was keeping him. He was lying submerged in his bath, and when taken out was found to be dead. He was just seventy-six years of age.

The inquest jury returned an open verdict after being told that he had died from an overdose of barbiturates (the estimate was 114 tablets), with no evidence to show whether they had been taken accidentally or intentionally. Speculation is pointless. One can argue on good grounds that it was quite in character for him, an agnostic, to put an unfussy and efficient end to a life that had become burdensome. On other good grounds one could argue that Ferguson's death had to be an accident, common enough with elderly people, because it is unthinkable that so doughty a fighter would throw in the towel when he still had a well cared for and serviceable body, a loving and beloved wife, and no money worries.†

*Harry Ferguson and Henry Ford by John B. Rae, Ph.D., Professor of the History of Technology, Emeritus, at Harvey Mudd College, Claremont, California (Ulster Historical Foundation 1980), p.23.

†He left £598,889 2s. 9d.

There remains, of course, the possibility that behind the spry and optimistic manner was a heart gnawed at by self-doubt and a sense of failure. The shattering of his high hopes for the Ford alliance must have been searingly painful for so proud a man and may have left him more depressed than Ferguson-watchers thought. Call no man happy until he is dead is depressing advice but it is also sound. We are astonished to read of Beethoven and Shakespeare, both of them men of great preeminence and awesome achievement in the world's eyes, returning a sad verdict on their own careers, the musician with his 'so little done, so much to do', the dramatist with his 'and my ending is despair'. Harry Ferguson's self-judgment in his seventy-sixth year, could we know what it really was, might astonish us too.

Ford workers leaving the Ford factory, 'down the Marina', Cork, early 1920s.

7

The Trade Organises

1

Until the setting up of the Irish Free State in 1922, the Irish motor traders belonged to one or the other (or both) of two English-based associations: the Motor Traders Association and the Society of Motor Manufacturers and Traders, the latter being the more important. The SMMT had been founded in 1902 and in an introductory article to its first circular to members the Society acknowledged that it 'came into existence at a time of great difficulty and dissension in the Trade'. The allusion was to the formidable looking barriers to development which had been put up by the ring of patent monopoly holders. As mentioned in Chapter 1, the syndicate hoped the wholesale buying-up of patents would lead to eventual control of the motor industry. No vital part of the car would be manufactured except under licence and the cost of the licence would not be just what the market would bear but, as with petrol and oil in the 1970s, the market had to learn to bear whatever those in control demanded. A graphic instance was the Maybach float-feed carburettor.*

The monopolists, who held the patent rights, planned to charge for the carburettor a royalty of 10 per cent on the cost of the entire engine and chassis, thus creating the possibility of the carburettor alone costing, in today's values, £400–£500.

The monopolists launched a scare campaign to protect what they believed to be their legal rights. Intimidating advertisements appeared and writs were showered on offenders. Had the situation been allowed to continue, the effect on the motor trade and on motorists would have been catastrophic. The industry decided to stand and fight. One of their defensive bodies, the Automobile Mutual Protection Association Limited, backed a court action in the name of a member, challenging the validity of Maybach's 1893 patent on the ground that it had been anticipated by other inventors' patents in 1889 and 1890. It was much the same kind of situation as had existed over Dunlop's patent, only in this case

*Wilhelm Maybach was the friend and partner of Gottlieb Daimler.

106

the monopolists had no Harvey du Cros to recognise defeat while it could still be kept at arm's length and parleyed with. The monopolosists lost their case and truculently lodged an appeal before the could bring themselves to face the facts and cut their losses. They continued to fight on other fronts but their spirit had been broken in the law courts in July 1901 and presently the British Motor Traction Company,* as they called themselves, faded from the scene.

Another worry to the industry was the proliferation of motor shows organised by 'outsiders'. The industry's nominal objection to these shows was that almost everything about the show was subjected to the organiser's personal profit. Their real objection was to see the handsome profits which almost automatically accrue from such shows going outside the industry. If the motor men agreed about nothing else they were at one over the need to clip the outsiders' wings. The obvious solution to their problems was to have only one motor show a year and that the one officially sponsored by the industry itself. The indispensible preliminary was to establish some kind of association which, amongst other things, would organise such an exhibition.

A few associations had already been formed, but as they were mostly intended to deal with one or two specific problems their objectives were narrow and once these had been achieved, or had been seen to be impossible to achieve, the association was let run out of steam and out of existence. Most people in responsible positions in the industry must have felt that what was required was a broadly based and fully representative association which would take care of the interests of the industry as a whole. But as generally happens in such situations, what's everybody's business is nobody's business. Matters might have dragged on for years were it not for the intervention of a consulting engineer who also happened to be a born initiator. This was Frederick Richard Simms, he who had been the first to import into Britain 'a high-speed internal combustion engine with self-timing tube ignition'. Simms went about the job of founding what was to become the Society of Motor Manufacturers and Traders so cautiously, almost so deviously, that one would be pardoned for wondering whether he was fully aware of what he was doing or was merely responding to some vague instinct. He had already (1897) founded the Automobile Club of Great Britain and Ireland to combat the authorities' active opposition to, and the general public's resentment of, the motor car. He had been an early member of the patent-buying syndicate, resigning when he discovered the way they were going. Perhaps

*They had abandoned the original name of the company, the British Motor Syndicate Limited, as too red in tooth and claw.

it was his experience of the latter body which made him approach the founding of the SMMT in such a roundabout way, considering every step as if treading on mined ground. Perhaps it was something in his character. But he could hardly have proceeded more circumspectly if he had been organising a branch of the Fenian Brotherhood in Buckingham Palace. One develops the feeling that his first recruits cannot have been sure what exactly they had been asked to join when, in February 1902, he convened a meeting of some of the eminences of the industry and asked their views on his idea of a corporate body to guard their interests, which would include the institution of a monopoly in motor shows. Those who themselves have had experience in founding an association will know how necessary it is in the early stages to *appear* to be outlining a detailed constitution while in fact only proferring vague generalities which nobody can argue against, and to *appear* to be wishing to involve everyone present in the organising process while in fact making sure everything will be left to oneself. Only in this way can the organiser generate by the end of the meeting the bonhomous atmosphere in which a majority of the meeting warmly encourage him to press on and be assured of their warmest support. This

108

enables him to cite the approval of the meeting when he turns up subsequently with articles of association he has himself produced, and with cut and dried plans to establish the association officially. By then the presidency is his for the asking and he should have little difficulty in planting his own nominees in the important offices.

This is precisely what Simms did. Yet he still moved with great caution. Some six weeks before registering the Society he produced a deed of covenant by which the covenanters undertook not to exhibit motor cars in any unauthorised show, under a penalty of £250. With this approved his next move was to have the Society of Motor Manufacturers and Traders registered (July 1902) as a company without capital, limited by guarantee, the maximum liability of each member being £1. One of the original subscribers was S. F. Edge, winner of the 1902 Gordon Bennett Race. Simms organised a celebratory luncheon for Edge at the Cecil Hotel six days after the registration of the SMMT. After luncheon, when the atmosphere was extremely jovial, Simms invited the Society members present to join him in another room in the hotel for the first general meeting of the newly fledged body. At 3.30 p.m., with Simms in the chair, the six others present briskly elected themselves first members of the council and then adjourned until 4.00 p.m. when, at a more leisurely pace, and presumably with eased bladders, they considered who else they should let on the governing body. It was at this resumed session that the familiar names of Austin, Lanchester, Singer and Thornycroft were added to the Society's first council. Although Harvey du Cros was never on the council he, as head of the Dunlop Pneumatic Tyre Co. Ltd, was a member of the Society. A selection of his sons represented various car companies (Ariel, Panhard and Levassor, and Mercedes), but when elected to the Council and to the management committee they proved to be bad attenders and were eventually dropped.

2

One of the Society's first jobs was to make Simms's motor show covenant, slightly modified, a Society covenant. The signatory undertook not to support or exhibit at any show within twenty miles of Charing Cross other than the Society's own show at the Crystal Palace. The covenant was strengthened year by year until 1907, when a printed bond was substituted, obliging the signatories to exhibit only at the Society show: a matter that was to have repercussions in Ireland later on. In order to get supplies from the manufacturers the trader had to sign the bond: it was a case of no bond, no supplies. Thus the very monopolistic practices which had roused the anger of the industry when operated by the British Motor Traction Company were soon officially adopted by themselves, although they could fairly claim to be operating them more in the interests of the industry at large than of private profit.

Naturally the privateers didn't give up without a fight. When Charles Cordingley, proprietor of a motoring weekly and organiser of one of the three annual shows with which London was being regaled, saw that the Society, originally twenty-one in number, reached a membership of ninety in a year,* he sought to join what he couldn't beat. He offered £1,200 a year for five years for the concession to run the show on the Society's behalf, but was refused. He carried on with his own show, but it was a hopeless contest and the 1907 bond finished him off. The Society further strengthened its show position by securing the support and official recognition of the RAC which, it will be recalled, was another Simms foundation.

Meanwhile in John Bull's other island the local branch of the Automobile Club of Great Britain and Ireland had been formally established at a meeting on 22 January 1901 at which a committee was elected,† and R. J. Mecredy appointed honorary secretary *pro tem*. But although in effect a branch of the ACGBI, they called themselves the Irish Automobile Club, becoming Royal in 1918 with the English parent body.

The Club's officially stated policy was to encourage and popularise the motor movement in Ireland, to engender feelings of consideration and toleration between motorists and the public, to prevent inconsiderate driving and to protect motorists' interests, but it can hardly be said to have achieved marked success in most of these laudable objectives. However, the newborn club did succeed in one early undertaking. It organised the first Irish Motor Show, which was held in January 1907 in the large exhibition hall of the Royal Dublin Society's premises at Ballsbridge. Although several Irish dealers declined to participate, alleging it 'would not be in our interests' to do so (probably meaning that they didn't see any point in spending the money), a large range of cars was on display and R. J. Mecredy's *Motor News*, having given the public a hearty come-on ('the motorists will see what they want at the Show'), added a tempting bait to potential buyers:

The local agents also will give instruction gratis, tune up the car, and carry out many little adjustments which otherwise would be charged for.

The show was successful enough for another to be held the

*By 1906 the membership was nearly 400. In 1981 it had reached 1,750.

†Members were: Lord Louth, W. G. D. Goff, Lieut Colonel H. Irvine, Colonel Magrath, Captain H. R. Langrishe, E. O'Coner, Dr Pryce Peacock, Dr J. F. Colohan, E. C. Herdiman, G. S. Perry, R. J. Mecredy, A. J. Orr, the Hon. Leopold Canning, J. Smithwick, W. B. Jameson and J. Grogan.

The scene at the Irish Automobile Club's 1907 Motor Show at Ballsbridge.

following January at the same place, but it was to take that splendidly remote body, the governing council of the Royal Dublin Society, many, many years to realise the significance of the motor shows held under its roof. It was perhaps understandable that there should be no mention of the shows in the official RDS history by Henry F. Berry, a venerable Victorian barrister and antiquary, published in 1915. But as late as the RDS *Bi-Centenary Souvenir* of 1931 the existence of the motor show was still unnoted, the society's attention remaining agriculturally riveted on cock and bull. Nonetheless the *Souvenir* contains eight and a half pages of motoring advertisements compared with only five for tractors and agricultural machinery.

The two shows at the RDS organised by the Irish Automobile Club had not been officially recognised by the SMMT. Recognition for a show to be held in 1909 was applied for but was refused. Similar applications from Scotland and from Manchester were also refused: only the Olympia Show was to be sanctioned. The Scottish Motor Trade Association showed fight, declaring that the planned show at the Edinburgh Exhibition would be gone ahead with. But the Scottish Association had the traders solid behind it. In Ireland opinion was sharply divided as to the benefits claimed to flow from such shows. The prevailing opinion seems to have been that no Dublin show was likely to change the mind of those whose practice was to buy their cars in England and that those who bought in Ireland would go on doing so anyway. A show therefore served no useful purpose, was a costly nuisance to the trade, and at the end of the day merely swelled the funds of the Automobile Club.

The truth is, opposition to an Irish show was a side effect of the trade's general hostility to the Irish Automobile Club. Traders found that membership of the club was being used to secure special discounts on cars and accessories bought abroad by members for direct import by themselves. It was alleged that one member, using his chauffeur as a 'front', had directly imported six cars, securing 20 per cent discount on chassis and 10 per cent on bodies.* As some if not all of these cars were clearly for re-sale in private deals the risk to the motor traders' livelihood was alarming. It will be remembered that Dr Colohan changed his cars with suspicious frequency and, although a director of Huttons, seems not to have availed of their professional sales services. Sir William Davis Goff, owner of the first car to be registered in Co. Waterford, was the behind-the-scenes owner of Waterford city's first garage, managed for him by an employee named Peare. Both Colohan and Goff were prominent members of the Automobile Club, as was the person living in Paris who, though not in the trade, allegedly supplied most of the cars delivered in Carlow in the period 1906—8. A sore point that continued to exist for many years was the practice of certain tyre and oil companies of allowing full trade discount to every private purchaser. In the light of which it was rather stingy of the member of the august Kildare Street Club, a peer of the realm, who flogged Dunlop tyres to his friends at only 5 per cent off list price.

Another grievance of the trade against the Irish Automobile Club was the club's garage in Dawson Street with its resident mechanic. In a somewhat lofty reply to a complaint from the trade, the club's Hon. Sec., Edward White, a solicitor, pointed out that competition between the club and other garages could hardly be classed as unfair since the club charged for cars left more than two nights whereas the others made no charge no matter how long the car remained on the premises. Mr White did not seem to realise he was merely rubbing salt into the wound.

The situation was exacerbated by the big recession which hit the trade in 1908. A very popular explanation of the recession, and one

*The Motor Trader, 11 March 1908.

112

smacking of sour grapes, was that a lot of people with notions beyond their means had bought cars and were now finding they could not afford to run them. No doubt there was some truth in this, but the fact is that the recession had hit England, Germany, Italy and America as well, and even in motor-mad France at least forty-eight firms had gone to the wall during the first two months of 1908. In short, a motor show in 1909 was about the last thing the Irish traders wanted, so that few voices amongst them were raised against the SMMT decision to refuse recognition.

The Irish Automobile Club for its part could only complain that it was being poorly rewarded for its efforts to develop the sport and pastime of motoring to the benefit of the trade. It had used its funds to protect the interests of motorists and prevent irksome restrictions being imposed. It had put up warning signs throughout the country. Above all it had inaugurated the Dublin Show, making it a success, for people preferred to see the latest models in Dublin instead of having to traipse over to Olympia. When the Scottish Society had defied the SMMT, the SMMT climbed down and sanctioned the Edinburgh Show. Dublin still had to bow to London's veto, for the SMMT bond permitted manufacturers to exhibit only where the SMMT said they might.*

It may well be that the crack about Dublin's having to knuckle down made itself felt. The Irish traders began to feel that at least they should have their own local branch of the SMMT. The SMMT was applied to and conceded the point. Ireland was given a local section, the secretary being an accountant, William Houghton Baskin, who had an office in Star Life Buildings, 12/14 College Green, Dublin. Either Mr Baskin hadn't much to do or was prepared to accept a modest remuneration, for the total Irish salaries and expenses for 1911 came to £50. (This was the same as the London section, and twice the figure for the English Northern Counties section.) But by 1913 the Irish figure had sunk to £15 14s. 8d. and the following year, like all the other sections, it was closed down because of the outbreak of war.

After the war, Mr Baskin reappears as secretary of the Irish Midlands Division of the Motor Traders' Association, apparently having abandoned the SMMT. But it is evident that amongst the Irish members of the SMMT and the Motor Traders' Association the feeling was growing that these essentially British bodies regarded them as second-class citizens. Besides, one had only to be moderately farsighted to realise that the impending establishment of an Irish Free State with control of its own taxes and customs duties would inevitably affect business relations between the Irish motor trader and his English suppliers. So during the Olympia Show in

*See p.109.

F.M. Summerfield. He was a founder member of the IMAA in 1921 and remained a stalwart in all succeeding trade associations until after the war.

November 1921 a group of Irish traders convened an informal meeting at the Clarendon Restaurant in London and, under the chairmanship of S. L. Hutchinson (of the Hutchinson Tyre Co. of Golden Lane), the Irish Motor Agents' Association was formed, with membership restricted to agents and with its headquarters in Ireland.

The confusing succession of motor associations, which were

114

intended to perform much the same kind of service for the trade, makes it desirable to pause here to enlarge a little on the matter. The Irish Motor Agents' Association combined the functions of a trade union and of a protection and professional association, but the lawyers advised that these functions be kept strictly separate and be dealt with by separate bodies. Two new bodies were therefore set up. The Society of Irish Motor Traders Ltd, the professional association, was incorporated on 22 October 1926 and the Irish Motor Traders' Association was registered as a trade union on 12 July 1927, the parent body (the Agents' Association) being dissolved on 7 July 1927. In theory all was now set fair. The presence of manufacturers, oil companies and wholesalers in the SIMT made it imperative for the Society not to take any part in industrial disputes, as this would divide the Society against itself. The IMTA, intended to be mainly a retailers' protection body, would be a largely autonomous grouping. But what had been plausible in theory proved cumbersome in practice. The root of the trouble was that both bodies had the same office and the same paid staff and since the SIMT council nominated the IMTA council, inevitably with several men serving on both, boundaries became blurred and council members often did not bother to change their hats when strictly speaking they should have done so. From time to time the suggestion was floated that each body should have its own separate premises and staff but it was realised that the advantage would not justify the heavy additional cost. Eventually the necessity for two motor trade bodies no longer existed. Both were merged as from 1 January 1968 in The Society of the Irish Motor Industry.

Let us now return to November 1921 and the newly formed motor agents' association.* In the course of the next few weeks delegates were appointed to an all-Ireland central council, and these gathered at the Dawson Street Club, Dublin for the inaugural council meeting of what was now to be called the Irish Motor Agents' Association. The date was 16 January 1922, nine days after the Dail had ratified the Treaty with Britain. And while the new association was electing its officers and drafting its constitution in 42 Dawson Street, across the road in the Mansion House the Provisional Government of the Irish Free State was being formed.

The Association unanimously elected as chairman Leo Callow of the old established coachbuilding firm in Westland Row and Upper Kevin Street. F. M. Summerfield, car importer, Lower Baggot Street, was asked to act as secretary *pro tem*. Among the decisions taken were: affiliation to be sought with the Motor Traders' Association; local executive committees to be formed in every county,

*Which, let me record with mischievous conscientiousness, was first called the Irish Motor Trade Association.

riding and city, delegates from each forming the central council;* the annual subscription was to be five guineas (£5.25), members with branches in more than one city paying an additional subscription for each branch; and, importantly, that only traders with garages staffed by skilled mechanics were to be eligible for membership, irrespective of whether they were already members of an English association. Eligibility was to be decided at local level, but the rejected could appeal to the central council.

F. M. Summerfield, having been moved into the temporary secretaryship at the beginning of the meeting, adroitly moved himself out of it by the end. Accordingly an invitation had to be sent to our old friend Mr Baskin to fill the gap — again, temporarily.

There were several reasons why Mr Baskin trod warily as he entered the councils of the IMAA. In the first place, British employers were reputed to be more open-handed (less close-fisted if you prefer) than the Irish species, and if the SMMT could measure his salary and expenses for a whole year at £15, the mind boggled at what remuneration the IMAA might propose.† As against that, the political situation in the Ireland of 1922 was such that no one knew which way the cat would jump, or if it would jump at all, so that an Irish-based association could conceivably turn out a better bet for a Dublin accountant than a British-based one. Finally, there was always the possibility that the age of miracles was *not* past and that the Irish scale of remuneration might rival the British. Indeed it might even surpass it now that the foreign yoke had been taken off Kathleen Ni Houlihan's neck and instead of being obliged to wistfully window-shop in her rags, she could boldly enter and purchase the garments of *haute couture* with the profits of independence.

But whatever thoughts may have been entertained by Mr Baskin as he attended his first meeting of the IMAA, a speculative glance around the assembled motor traders enabled him to make up his mind. At the meeting of 13 February he asked 'to be relieved forthwith'. To those skilled in the interpretation of minutes that *forthwith* speaks volumes. It was decided to advertise for a general secretary, Mr Baskin agreeing to stay on until the next meeting. In the event he stayed on until 7 March, when out of a shortlist of eight candidates Mr James Moore of 51 Lower Beechwood Avenue, Ranelagh, was selected for the post. His salary is not stated but was probably not far off £500 a year, which would have been fairly good pay for the times.

*But the Dublin and Belfast committees were to have special representation with four delegates each, and Cork city to have two.

†I can testify, as the person involved, that as late as 1938 Huet Motors Ltd of Mount Street Bridge paid their assistant costing clerk a starting salary of five shillings (25 pence) a week.

116

Mr Baskin, however, didn't completely cut the cable. He agreed to become the Association's auditor and at the next meeting a cheque was made out to him for £26 2s. 6d. (£26.12½) for office equipment and for £20 petty cash in advance, payments which in the circumstances are rather puzzling. Finally, the secretary was authorised to engage a typist at not more than £2 a week, and this resulted in the employment of Miss M. Quinlan.

3

The IMAA now seemed set fair to get down to serious business. The matter of holding a motor show was deferred until more propitious times politically, and negotiations were started with the wholesalers and with the British associations with a view to establishing a useful and harmonious understanding on the delicate subject of stop lists (i.e. black lists). The British associations were naturally anxious to be sure of the legal implications of any arrangements of this kind they might enter into with a group based in an area which was no longer part of the United Kingdom. They were, of course, quite right to be so. But the Irish temperament is impatient of other people's cautious desire to be sure of their bearings in an altered situation. We are eager to cut red tape, but only so long as it is to our advantage. Once we stand to gain a penny by retaining the red tape we are like Shakespeare's Hotspur: ready to cavil at the ninth part of a hair. So the IMAA tended to view the caution of the SMMT and MTA as foot-dragging, and since rumblings were coming from the 'grass roots' about the IMAA appearing not to be doing very much, negotiations developed a touch of acerbity. The view was expressed that IMAA members who also belonged to the MTA should resign from the latter body to show the Irish members 'intend to adhere to their own organisation'. After this letting off of steam it was decided that legal opinion should be sought about whether Irish agents were eligible to be members of the MTA, but at the next meeting, nine days later, temperatures rose again. It was alleged that 'much harm was being done by the competition of the MTA', and the point was reached when there was talk about a delegation being sent to London 'at once' to request the MTA to recognise the IMAA and to return the balance of subscriptions not yet expired. The council rounded off a lively meeting by refusing to let motor cycle agents into the Association — for the present.

Meanwhile the losses suffered by the motor trade as a result of civil disorder engaged the council's attention. Their vehicles had been stolen or commandeered by the opposing forces and it had been virtually impossible to get insurance cover for these vehicles. A deputation was ordered to be sent to the 'Minister of Trade'

Cartons of Bunclody, Co. Wexford were typical of the retail outlets represented by the IMAA. This advertisement dates from the autumn of 1923.

(officially Minister for Industry and Commerce: the IMAA hadn't yet got used to Saorstat Eireann departmental nomenclature), but the meeting was not to take place for some considerable time. This may have been partly because the followers of President Cosgrave and President de Valera hadn't yet reached agreement as to which of their parties was the government and which the opposition, and were conducting their argument with guns. But after the delegation had at length chatted about their difficulties with the Minister, Mr Joe McGrath (later of Irish Hospitals Sweep-

118

stakes fame), the IMAA had little joy. Mr McGrath's official reassurances were not followed by pecuniary action, and the association had to keep dunning the government even to the point of threatening court proceedings.

4

Now the Irish Motor Agents' Association had been started as an all-Ireland body. The inaugural meeting of the central council in Dublin on 16 January 1922 was attended by three Northern Ireland delegates* and at a meeting on 13 February of what was specifically called 'the All-Ireland Council' Harry Ferguson of Belfast was elected the Ulster vice-president on the proposal of P. F. Quinlan of Limerick, seconded by H. Thompson of Wexford. The other provincial vice-presidents — R. W. Archer of Dublin (Leinster), John F. O'Gorman of Clonmel (Munster) and J. White of Ballina (Connaught) — attended council meetings fairly regularly, but Harry Ferguson, after sending apologies once or twice, eventually didn't bother to do even that and except for a letter of advice to the council, took no further part in its work. The very few Northern Ireland traders who had joined the IMAA presently dropped out, without, so far as I can gather, ever formally resigning. The only instance mentioned in the minutes of a Northern Ireland trader's interest was in May 1922 when a letter was read from the Bann Cycle Company of Banbridge, Co. Down, asking the association's help to recover a motor-bicycle stolen in their district. The council, with rather tactless haste, resolved by majority vote that if any member of the association were interested in tracing a car he should be entitled, on payment of an expenses fee of a guinea (£1.05) to have all members circularised on the matter. This is the kind of thing which causes members of any association to wonder what they are paying their annual subscription for, because, when not on the finance committee, they fail to realise how much money the preparation and posting of a simple circular can cost. Nonetheless, it might have been better policy for the council not to have 'instituted a charge' immediately on getting just one request for help. But then councils everywhere tend to react like the waiter who begged the diner not to mention the fly in the soup in case everyone else wanted one.

At any rate, before its first year was out the Irish Motor Agents' Association had effectively become a twenty-six county organisation only. An attempt to maintain the old link was made by sending delegates to a meeting of the MTA in Belfast. The delegates were received with a cordiality and hospitality that has

*P. Roberts of Londonderry, and C. Pakenham-Walsh and James Boyd of Belfast.

misled many a deputation from South to North. The Dublin delegates described what the IMAA was doing to advance agents' interests and expressed the hope that some members of the Belfast organisation would attend the next IMAA council meeting in Dublin. But they didn't, and a proposal to exchange minutes of meetings doesn't appear to have come to anything. Organisations on both sides of the border were at last beginning to grasp that partition really meant what it said and that in many areas the Irish Free State would be going it alone.

This fact was rubbed in by the result of the delegates' meeting with the Motor Agents' Association* in London and with a section of the SMMT. The MAA announced that on legal advice it would no longer act for its members within the Irish Free State, nor could it have any function in regard to Irish trade questions. Moreover, it could not enter into any agreement with the IMAA or with any other such Irish association. The Irish delegates found all efforts to negotiate an agreement — any agreement — were repulsed, and they had to report to their council that any moves to protect prices in Ireland would have to be taken by the IMAA itself. However, the delegates were able to bring back some comfort. They had received an unofficial undertaking from the SMMT that British manufacturers would be glad to co-operate with the Irish association in price maintenance. Or, as they put it, 'for the purpose of maintaining the principles of fair trade in Ireland'. In the circumstances it was inevitable that the IMAA should request members who also belonged to the MTA to resign from the British body.

Once the air had been cleared in this way about the trading consequences of the Irish Free State's ceasing to be part of the UK, the IMAA settled down to tackling problems in a business-like manner. Many matters soon became routine. Instances of traders trying to cut corners at each other's expense recurred constantly (they still do), and were dealt with firmly yet humanely. A typical case was that of a firm in Bagenalstown, Co. Carlow, which had been deprived of petrol supplies because of price cutting. The council agreed to ask the oil companies to lift the ban provided the firm undertook to sell only at the fixed price. Action was also taken to stop a Dublin trader from advertising his cars from the Wicklow Hotel in Wicklow Street, although it required more than one rap on the knuckles to get the offender to curb such enticing hospitality.

But the most urgent matters coming before the council arose from the continuing civil strife. Apart from the impeding of the

*Originally the agents' section of the SMMT, it became a separate organisation c.1909. Incorporated as a limited company on 31 December 1913 as The Agents Section Ltd., it changed its name to Motor Agents Association Ltd. on 14 February 1928.

120

work of organising, there was the difficulty of getting the government to pay out compensation for loss or damage to cars seized by the rival forces, a grievance exacerbated by the point-blank refusal of the Minister for Finance (Ernest Blythe) to waive payment of the outstanding road tax for 1921, which had been impossible to collect because of the chaotic administrative situation, or make any concession in the 1922 demand. The council held that demands for road tax under existing conditions were unjust, and that some relief ought to be given to traders in their personal taxes, seeing the frightful conditions under which they were trying to do business. Then the Cork members reported the rumour that Lloyds of London planned to replace destroyed or damaged cars insured with them with new cars bought directly from the makers. Lloyds were successfully expostulated with, and the Cork dealers' commission was saved.

While Ernest Blythe was playing the association along with philosophical discussions about whether to substitute a petrol tax for road tax (not then revealing that the department was planning a tax assault on both fronts), a further complaint was laid about the government. It appeared that the Department of Defence was running up bills for vehicles, petrol and repairs but not paying them; and that the Minister, General Richard Mulcahy, was being dunned in vain. Since the motor traders were not able to get any

Motor cycles were popular in Ireland, as elsewhere, from an early date. This photograph shows a Triumph 2¼ h.p. two-stroke of 1914.

121

change (in any sense of the term) out of Ernest Blythe, Joe McGrath, and Dick Mulcahy, they appealed to President Cosgrave and arranged for the every-obliging 'Alfie' Byrne (later the hand-shaking perpetual Lord Mayor of Dublin) to ask a question in the Dáil. Meanwhile some militant members of the council carried a motion authorising a confrontation with Ernest Blythe himself over the unpaid bills. In the event the Minister remained in his lair and subordinates were sent out to discuss the matter. They counter-attacked with allegations of overcharging, and on being assured that only the normal retail rates had been charged, replied that the government should be given a cut. The only consolation the delegates got was a promise to take 'immediate steps' to collect all motor agents' accounts at one office and have them 'examined, checked, and paid'. That was in February 1923. In March the council, in a bout of irritation, ordered that a letter be sent to President Cosgrave telling him that unless the accounts were paid within a week, they would advise their members to set the law on his administration. Since President Cosgrave and his colleagues, like all successful revolutionists, had achieved their first steps to power by breaking the law, the threat appears not to have disturbed him. He showed no outward signs of panic. By September the unfortunate dealers still hadn't got their money. The council accordingly directed that a solicitor's letter be sent to the government, and at the beginning of December the council learned 'with satisfaction' that 'some progress was at last being made in dealing with these accounts' by the Department of Finance.

5

The council also tried to get the Department to lighten the tax burden on the motorist. In a transient mood of determination they instructed the secretary to ask President Cosgrave to meet them for a discussion on tax reform, the use of trade plates, and the granting to the IMAA of representation on the Roads Board. Once again the President waited for their aggressive mood to evaporate, which it did. But the Minister for Local Government, Mr James A. Burke, set them raging again with a boast that his Department was in a position to get cars below the list prices by direct purchase from manufacturers or concessionaires. Here was a striking example of the Irishman's tendency to regard paying the proper price for anything as a sign of personal inadequacy, with even a government minister bragging in public about how he could cheat a trader out of part of his livelihood. R. W. Archer undertook the task of sorting out the Minister.

Burke's statement had highlighted the ever-present problem of how to achieve closed-shop conditions in the motor trade for the benefit of those already established in it, without drawing unwelcome public attention to the move. In this aspiration the motor dealers were no different from carpenters and electricians, doctors and dentists, pub owners and playwrights. Most of the trades and professions had been able, over the years, to establish what they called their 'mystery'. The carpenter did not become officially competent to drive a nail or saw or plank until he had completed a seven-year apprenticeship. The doctor and the surgeon had to undergo his period of drinking and skylarking with hospital nurses, relieved by brief intervals of more academic study of human anatomy, before securing his licence to kill. The problem in the motor trade was how to create a convincing mystery which would make the exclusive preserve of its priesthood the job of selling a car, tightening a nut in accordance with the instructions in a maintenance manual, and handing a motorist a two-gallon can of petrol in exchange for three and sevenpence.

A daunting difficulty in creating such a mystery was that from the earliest days of motoring the driver had of necessity to be his own mechanic, for running repairs at any rate. The driver who couldn't coax back to life an engine which had conked out, risked being immobilised in the middle of nowhere every time he went for a spin in the country. Moreover, as already related, many laymen had actually built their own cars from bits and pieces, and almost welcomed breakdowns for the challenge these offered to skill and ingenuity. Garage charges had therefore to be modest. One could dine out a few times on the story of the invoice sent by a Mullingar garage to a J. McCreevy, c/o Boyd-Rochfort of Middleton Park. It runs::

> *December 12, 1913*
> Repairs to Rolls-Royce   5s. 8d. (28p)
> Material   4d. (1⅔)

A total of just under thirty pence for repairs to a Rolls-Royce, and no doubt the garage owner had to explain to the expostulating owner that he could hardly expect the job to be done for less.

Clearly the man trying to make a living out of a garage, especially down the country, must have had his work cut out for him. It must have been galling to set up your little friendly neighbourhood garage, only to find that the Irish-American Oil Company (among others) had agreed to supply petrol to the local hotelier, or publican, or even greengrocer, as well as to you. If ever there was unfair competition in a trade still in its infancy, this was it. Small wonder that the early records of the IMAA are dotted with representations and protests to the various oil companies about petrol supplies to non-traders. The oil-companies' reply was that since they were in the petrol selling business they were entitled to sell to anyone

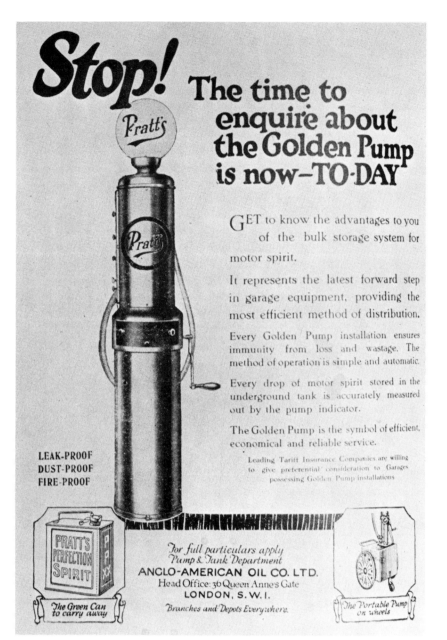

Stop! The time to enquire about the Golden Pump is now—TO-DAY

GET to know the advantages to you of the bulk storage system for motor spirit.

It represents the latest forward step in garage equipment, providing the most efficient method of distribution.

Every Golden Pump installation ensures immunity from loss and wastage. The method of operation is simple and automatic.

Every drop of motor spirit stored in the underground tank is accurately measured out by the pump indicator.

The Golden Pump is the symbol of efficient, economical and reliable service.

Leading Tariff Insurance Companies are willing to give preferential consideration to Garages possessing Golden Pump installations

LEAK-PROOF
DUST-PROOF
FIRE-PROOF

PRATT'S PERFECTION SPIRIT

The Green Can to carry away

For full particulars apply Pump & Tank Department
ANGLO-AMERICAN OIL CO. LTD.
Head Office: 36 Queen Anne's Gate
LONDON, S.W.I.
Branches and Depots Everywhere.

The Portable Pump on wheels

In the years after the First World War, automatic petrol pumps became increasingly common. This advertisement from The Motor News *of March 1921 illustrates an automatic pump similar to the type first installed in Dublin around that time.*

anywhere. In January 1923 the IMAA arranged for a delegation headed by R. W. Archer and Leo Callow 'to wait on the petrol companies with a view to ascertaining whether any agreement could be reached which would have the effect of regulating the distribution of petrol on principles more just to Agents than the

124

present system.' The danger of enabling co-operative societies to obtain supplies was particularised as a point for discussion.

The association had also to campaign against indiscriminate tyre distribution. The tyre companies, like the oil companies, took the view that they were entitled to sell to anyone and everyone in a position to meet their terms. It was reported that, apart from commonplace examples like the non-trader in Foxford, Co. Mayo being supplied by the manufacturer with Avon tyres for re-sale, in Dublin a firm of *wholesale ironmongers* was supplying tyres to their retail customers for re-sale. Protests were at first of no avail. The petrol companies for their part airily replied that they were not yet in a position to reply. The tyre companies didn't bother to reply at all. Presently there were signs of an outbreak of common-sense in both tyre and petrol companies. It began to be realised that the IMAA was here to stay, that it was steadily increasing its influence and should therefore be conciliated. Early effects of this wind of change included a letter from the Michelin Tyre Co. to say they had now decided to remove from their list of agents a person in Cashel who had been objected to by the association. But they asserted their independence by declining to remove a person in Dungarvan who had also been objected to. The Irish-American Oil Company had referred to the association a number of applications to have kerbside petrol pumps installed. The association expressed disapproval of most of them, which caused the oil company to protest that the association was taking an impossible attitude. The association in its turn gracefully conceded that on reconsideration of the matter they could approve the granting of certain applications. These wise face-saving exchanges paved the way for further co-operation and helped to soothe the fears of some IMAA members that the association might have no legal right to interfere with the discretion of the wholesale traders and car distributors in granting trade terms*. Nevertheless several major companies continued to drag their feet about coming to an agreement with the association, especially Dunlops and BP. Eventually these agreed to play ball but don't appear to have stuck scrupulously to their undertakings. For a long time complaints continued to come before the council with regard to alleged irregularities by Dunlops, and in March 1924 the council threatened that if BP didn't mend its ways† all IMAA members would be informed how it had not kept its promises and was not inclined to respect the association's views.

*A solicitor was instructed to obtain counsel's opinion on the matter, which was meanwhile quietly dropped.

†It had gone on to instal a pump for a general merchant in Kilcock, Co. Kildare, despite IMAA disapproval.

6

The point about the manufacturers not being inclined to respect the association raises the question of whether it was yet formidable enough to command respect. In almost every case where an organisation is run by a paid full-time secretary working to an unpaid voluntary management committee, the success or otherwise of that organisation depends largely upon the secretary. Unless the secretary's powers and responsibilities have been carefully specified they can become, conveniently for the secretary, rather vague. Since chairmen and committee members tend to come and go, and secretaries to remain, the secretary can become like the constitutional monarch *vis à vis* the prime minister. The monarch, even when of very ordinary capacity, by being *there* eventually gets to know the ropes at least as well as the shrewdest party leader, and is often better placed to advise the politician than to be advised by him. A secretary can similarly manipulate the committee, even when it has a powerful chairman, because the secretary can determine which way the information given to the members shall be slanted, or even whether information shall be given at all. The records of the IMAA show that the secretary, James Moore, had quickly taken the measure of his council and had learned how to handle it. The minutes of the monthly meetings *appear* to inform without actually doing so. As a result the council members, when confirming the record of what had taken place the previous month, would not have been re-possessed of the details of the several matters they had dealt with. In effect, many urgent problems were being swept under the carpet while details of routine business like the payment of accounts, travelling expenses, and office salaries were meticulously recorded and followed through. In short, James Moore's performance as the association's first secretary suggests that he was hardly the best man for the job.

It was a job which called for a man of uncommon energy, one whose impetuosity might lead him into the occasional mistake but whose drive would energise the infant association and generate the power which makes third parties feel that here is a body to be reckoned with. The minutes of the council meetings do not suggest a press of business that would keep a reasonably well organised man busy five and a half days a week. On the contrary they suggest that the said well organised person should have been able to dispatch the week's desk work in a day or two, leaving plenty of time for expeditions hither and yon, to recruit new members and pay inspiriting calls to the hon. secs. of local branches. There are no signs that James Moore did this, or any indication that in his dealings with manufacturers and wholesalers he made them take him and the IMAA very seriously.

Again, he did not ensure that there was a proper follow-through with council decisions, so that you had the by no means uncommon situation of a council laying down the law at its monthly meetings, with the secretary taking careful notes, and nobody doing anything further about anything. Presently the country members began to complain that the IMAA didn't seem to be getting anywhere. Old grievances remained unredressed, unqualified garage staff were still carrying out repairs, price cutting was still rife, and non-traders still seemed to have little difficulty in getting supplies from manufacturers and wholesalers.*

The secretary countered criticism after the fashion of his kind. He explained that the requirements of members could be met only if he were provided with assistants. This was done. But while an 'outside organiser' justified his wage packet by inducing several more traders to apply for membership, existing members found no significant change in the general situation. They must have viewed with some cynicism the association's move to a suite of offices in No. 31 Upper Merrion Street, although the rent was hardly exorbitant: £85 p.a. (A brass plate was acquired for the halldoor.) The secretary's supervision of his staff was not above reproach: in some cases he seems not to have made their conditions of employment absolutely clear to them. For example, there was some confusion about the outside organiser's travel allowance. The organiser, a Mr Wisdom, hardly lived up to his name by presenting a committee of motor traders with a bill for £75 wear and tear on two motor cycles used in their service. Not surprisingly Mr Wisdom and the association soon parted company.

One infers from a later proposal to have Mr Baskin invited to return as secretary or director, that if certain council members had had their way James Moore would have followed Mr Wisdom. One who knew the late W. J. Lemass recalls that he often mentioned that when acting as Moore's assistant he was obliged to do all the work the secretary himself should be doing. The reason James Moore survived was that as from 1927 he had become Seamus Moore, TD for Wicklow in the Fianna Fail interest. In the August

---

*I can mention here that my father, who had been apprenticed to a pharmacist in Cork, was induced by a friend who had served his time in a haberdasher's, to join him in opening an unusual kind of car showrooms in Dublin's Dawson Street, which would surely make their fortune. The idea was that while in one corner of the showrooms the former haberdasher would try to sell Daimlers to gentlemen, my father in another corner would try to sell perfume and toiletries to their lady wives. When the weeks passed and the only sale was one achieved by my father (a tin of expensive talcum powder to a typist from across the street), the haberdasher fled, leaving the dispirited partner to spend what was left of his patrimony on paying the firm's debts, thus preserving the family's honour. The business survived, however, just long enough for me to be driven to my christening in what was, for a mad moment, technically my father's own Daimler, and for his profession to be truthfully inscribed on my birth certificate as 'company director'. One learns from this to sympathise with the problems of the Irish Motor Agents' Association.

of that year he and his colleagues had ceased to ostracise the Dail, had sworn the Treaty Oath and had taken their seats. Since the Fianna Fail opposition were bound to come to power sooner or later, the IMAA council deemed it prudent to allow Mr Moore to go on ambling in and out of 31 Merrion Street instead of replacing him with the really efficient executive they so badly needed.

James Moore was certainly not the man to put the fear of God into the oil and tyre companies. There was a series of conferences and concordats between the association and the companies but the companies paid only lip service to agreements. An attempt was made to enlist the support of the Irish Motor and Cycle Wholesale Traders' Association by inviting their co-operation in stamping out trading abuses. But as the abuses profited the wholesalers as much as delinquent dealers, the Wholesalers' Association stalled. When pressed for a definite answer they proposed yet more conferences. As complaints kept pouring in from IMAA members that the oil and tyre companies were still going their own sweet way, tempers on the council began to simmer, and a proposal was made that the IMAA should dissolve itself and reform as a society open to all degrees of the motor trade, manufacturers and wholesalers as well as dealers. The proposal may have been floated by R. W. Archer; at any rate it won his early support. Nevertheless it was rejected, and there the matter rested for a while.

Meanwhile the Michelin Tyre Company were becoming notable for their persistence in supplying unapproved dealers ('dabblers'). Their supply at trade terms to dabblers in the Kenmare district, reported to the council in April 1926, brought matters to a head. Michelin was warned in separate letters by P. F. Quinlan of Limerick, that year's president, and F. M. Summerfield, that a continuance of their supplies policy would bring unpleasant consequences. When Michelin, heartened by the lack of co-operation between the Irish wholesalers and the dealers, exhibited no signs of repentance let alone reform, the association circularised its members with a proposal to ban sales of Michelin tyres and to return all sale-or-return stocks. Michelin promptly asked the SMMT in London to request that the ban be removed, and for the next several months the Pneumatic Tyre Section of the SMMT found itself bedevilled with the Irish tyre problem.

7

Since James Moore was now required to embark on a correspondence with London he appears to have abandoned the keeping of IMAA records as too taxing for his strength, so that we depend upon SMMT records to inform us of the progress of events. The fact is, matters were progressing along two separate but related

A Difference.

Clerk—How much shall I charge for this ¾-inch clip screw?
Manager—For a bicycle, I suppose? Oh, a penny.
Clerk—No; it's for a motor car, sir.
Manager—Eh! Charge half-a-crown.

As the trade became more organised, public suspicion of motor traders' charges increased, as this cartoon from the 1920s illustrates.

lines and there was clearly a lot of behind-the-scenes manoeuvring of which we have no written record. First, there was the attempt to resolve the conflict over the Michelin ban, concerning which the IMAA had dug their heels in and for which, to their gratified surprise, they were getting some tardy support from their wholesaler colleagues. Second, there was a move to revive the proposal to replace the IMAA with a broader based body which should include manufacturers as well as dealers.

The SMMT, having its own problems to deal with concerning price maintenance, had circularised tyre manufacturers with compromise proposals which were also notified to the Dublin body. Dublin had a special meeting on 24 June (unrecorded by Mr Moore) and a letter was sent to London the following day saying the council had full authority to negotiate but was not prepared to lift the ban on Michelin. London replied that if Dublin lifted the ban by 3 July, a conference could ensue, but if the ban were not lifted then all British tyre manufacturers would stop supplies and demand that sale-or-return stocks be sent back. The SMMT felt they could take this strong line because the IMAA had fallen victim to that traditional inevitability, a split. F. M. Summerfield had written to London to express his strong disapproval of the Michelin ban, and a group described in the SMMT minutes as 'the main Car Distributors in the Irish Free State' told London that having withdrawn from the IMAA it desired London's help in setting up another organisation.

Faced with the threat of a complete stoppage of tyre supplies to the Free State, and with the split in their own ranks, the IMAA caved in. They first proposed to London that the SMMT should nominate two of its members, not connected with the tyre trade, to come over and inspect for themselves the Kenmare district premises which had been objected to. They added that they believed the SMMT was unconstitutional. And this is where the differences in calibre between the SMMT secretary, Colonel Hacking, and James Moore became very evident. The colonel replied stiffly that it was always open to members of any section of the SMMT to take any action necessary to protect the general interests of the industry, and that in any event the facts should have been placed before the SMMT council by the two Irish representatives, R. W. Archer and F. M. Summerfield.

At this the IMAA threw in the towel.

Colonel Hacking was told that the ban would be lifted on condition that negotiations to solve the underlying problem began within a month, and London agreed to this. In passing on this information to the SMMT council the colonel added that he had been in correspondence with Dublin about the new car distributors' organisation and that he desired SMMT sanction to go over the following week and help things along. Sanction was given, all the more readily, one feels, now that London saw a prospect of getting rid of the Irish and their little local difficulties. The colonel, having temporarily struck camp, departed from the sister island.

130

8

Harmony Restored

1

The Dublin upon which Colonel Hacking descended on a June day in 1926 was by his standards more of a run-down provincial town than a capital city. The place, shabby genteel at the best of times, hadn't yet recovered from the bombardments and depredations of the 1916–22 period. In 1916 a gunboat, sent up the Liffey to help reduce the GPO, had instead helped to reduce virtually every building in Sackville (O'Connell) Street *except* the GPO. Six years later, at the start of the Civil War, the troops of the Irish Free State borrowed British field guns to bombard the Four Courts; during the War of Independence the IRA had already burned and severely damaged Dublin's other classical masterpiece, the Custom House. The slums of Dublin were of course proverbial and five years of self-government hadn't done much to improve the situation. Every visitor remarked upon the number and the persistence of beggars, and on the hordes of barefoot children. The only notable industries in the city were Jacob's biscuit factory and Guinness's brewery. The Guinness barges on the river and horse-drawn drays on the streets, each neatly loaded with big oaken barrels, seemed to make up a large proportion of the city's traffic.

The main streets were cobbled (sometimes only in the middle strip which carried the tram rails), or paved with wooden blocks which became quite slippy in rainy weather. The principal footpaths were paved with large oblong granite slabs or concrete sections. Motor traffic was still largely governed by the Motor Car Act 1903, which had imposed an upper limit of 20 mph on public roads. But rules and speed limits were generally ignored, especially on country roads, and there was little the police could do about it as they were not themselves motorised. (Besides, the stopping of cars was still connected in the police folk-memory with republican fusilades from behind hedges or from rooftops.) Although only some 11,000 motor vehicles had been registered in Dublin city and county in 1926 (as against 5,000 in 1914), and these were not used by their owners as much as cars are nowadays, traffic was heavy and jams not infrequent. The song which tells how sweet

Motor vehicles had their military as well as their civilian uses. This photograph, taken during the civil war in 1922, shows the Free State's armoured car known popularly as 'The Big Fella' after the Free State's commander-in-chief, Michael Collins.

Molly Malone wheeled her barrow through streets broad and narrow, was factually correct as to street widths. The trouble was that the generous breadth of O'Connell Street, Westmoreland Street, Dame Street and St Stephen's Green was feeding traffic into meanly narrow Henry Street, Grafton Street and Nassau Street, and there was a preposterously narrow entrance to South Great Georges Street. Moreover, the traffic mix of mechanised and horse-drawn vehicles, including 600 outside cars, cabs and phaetons, 300 job carriages, 207 taxis, 103 buses and 22 charabancs, seemed specially designed for snarl-ups. Add the complication of 265 rigid-railed team cars whose set-down and pick-up points were in the middle of the street, and one can see how Dublin's continuing rush-hour jams are nothing new.

The 1925 Return of Accidents for the city showed that 30 persons had been killed in motor traffic accidents (57 in 1935), 112 (80) seriously injured, and 546 (1,536) had suffered minor injuries. In 1925 four persons contrived to get themselves killed by horse drawn vehicles and 101 injured (the 1935 figures were 2 and 78). Injuries from motor vehicles increased steadily from the mid 1920s onwards, mainly in urban areas. The pattern of the future had become set. The part played by drink in accidents can only be guessed at, but one feels that in the mid-1920s the drunkenness was more on the pedestrians' side than on the drivers'.

The city's 316,471 inhabitants* were served by some 750 pubs, roughly the same number as ten years previously, but the number of arrests for drunkenness had halved in that period to 1,400. Which might suggest that British rule in the old days had driven twice as many Dubliners to drink as home rule was doing. The likelier explanation is that the Free State police were more easy-going about drink than their predecessors.

Veterans in the motor industry are apt to tell you that car salesrooms in those days were all in either Dawson Street or South King Street. The statement had some truth in it, for a lot of important dealers had premises in the area,† not many favouring the then unfashionable north side. But when all was said and done, an appearance of concentration of the premises of the various motor interests in one area was inevitable since central Dublin in those days was itself so small. Once you had crossed the canals you were decidedly in the suburbs, and you were in the sticks before you had quite reached the top of Rathgar Road.

As Colonel Hacking made his way to the IMAA offices in 31 Upper Merrion Street he might have noticed Ireland's first kerb-side petrol pump, a hand-operated machine attached to a 500-gallon tank, which the Irish-American Oil Co. Ltd had installed outside a garage in Nassau Street in 1923. But he would certainly have passed through a Georgian area which had provided an eighteenth-century writer with reason to say of Dublin that 'there never was so splendid a metropolis in so poor a country.' Upper Merrion Street was built from the 1750s onwards as town houses for the nobility.** A century later it had come down a bit in the world and was lived in by lawyers and doctors. The association shared No. 31 with a dentist, whereas the colonel's organisation had a mansion in Pall Mall all to itself,†† and in measuring himself against his opposite number Mr Moore, the colonel would have had little reason to feel inferior. Nevertheless, he must have already realised that the council members he was about to meet on their own ground were a tough bunch. They had brought the Michelin Company to heel with the Irish speciality, the boycott, and although this had now been lifted the Irish dealers had shown themselves in no hurry to return to the

*1926 Census.
†In Dawson Street were Crawfords, Express Auto, R. E. Grady, Hupmobile, McLysaght & Douglas, and Peugeot; in South King Street: A. J. Doyle, A. F. Nolan, S. T. Robinson, and Swift Motor Co.; while in or just off Grafton Street were the Grafton Motor Co., Wayte Bros., and Fiat. In St Stephen's Green were John O'Neill Ltd and Rudge-Whitworth Ltd, with Lincoln & Nolan Ltd, the Central Service Motor Co. Ltd, and F. M. Summerfield not far away in Baggot Street.
**The Duke of Wellington had been born a few doors away in No. 24, now the Land Commission offices. No. 31 however, was not built until early in the nineteenth century and had no notable aristocratic connections.
††It now occupies Forbes House in Halkin Street, former London residence of the Earls of Granard, who owned two castles and 20,000 acres in Ireland.

133

Michelin fold. Of the sixty-four dealers who had sent back their stocks, only ten had spontaneously re-ordered, and the honeyed words of the Michelin travellers had been able to recapture only another twenty-seven. To make matters worse, the British tyre industry had been passing through a bad patch, and Dunlops in particular had been feeling the breeze. The displeasure of the Irish dealers was therefore to be feared.*

Colonel Hacking's objective was probably to bring about the establishment of a new organisation which, like the SMMT, would include representatives of all branches of the industry in Ireland, manufacturing and wholesale as well as retail, and would resolve disputes around its own table in Dublin, thus keeping out of the SMMT's hair. He may not have been aware that there had already been a strong move the previous year in this direction.

2

As already mentioned, in June 1925, R. W. Archer had floated the suggestion that the IMAA merge with the Irish Motor & Cycle Wholesale Traders' Association. No doubt Archer had seen the benefits accruing from the broad base of the SMMT. The following September he circulated a draft constitution for 'a new Association to include all grades of Motor Traders'. The document was discussed by the council, and while some members held that any proposal to disband the IMAA would be resisted by many agents, and might leave them without any organisation, others maintained that the association 'had proved powerless to cope with the main evils of the trade', and that co-operation with wholesalers would prove a great asset to the Garage business'. The council's final decision was:

> That a further Conference with representatives of the Whole-salers' Association be requested, at which the formation of a new IMTA, to be based on the continuance of the IMAA as the Agents' Organization, would be proposed. At the Conference, the promise might be given that at the end of the twelve months the necessity for the further existence of the IMAA would be considered by its members.

Clearly the secretary's job was now to push ahead with plans for the conference with the wholesalers, but it does not appear that James Moore bothered to lift a finger about it. He seemed to be more concerned about securing the council's authorisation to have an electric bell installed 'for communication within the offices'

---

*When Dunlops were caught supplying an unauthorised dealer in Ballinasloe, they did not reply *de haut en bas* as they probably would have done before the Michelin boycott. The recently appointed Irish Dunlop managing director was conciliatory. He wrote that he 'would be glad to attend a meeting of the IMAA to discuss the question'.

P.F. Quinlan, last chairman of the IMAA and a founder of the SIMT in 1926.

and thus save himself the bother of going out to summon the lady clerks by word of mouth.

The council did not meet between September and mid-December. Business was transacted by the standing committee, whose minutes have disappeared without having been incorporated in those of the council. As a result we have no details of the row that caused R. W. Archer to resign as president of the IMAA, and three other council members with him. One suspects that it was the foot-dragging over his proposal to found the new society, culminating in a definite decision by the remaining members of the council to oppose such a society as 'unnecessary and based on the false hope that a stop list would be a successful means of combatting the evils of the trade'. Naturally the keep-things-as-they-are brigade knew they must make some gesture to reduce the general dissatisfaction with the state of affairs. So there was a further decision to have the powers of the association 'used to the full for the protection of the members' and a proposal was to be made at the general meeting the following day that members be obliged to sign an undertaking to obey the orders of the executive council under a penalty of £10 for each and every failure to do so.

There had of course been a long discussion of the problem posed by the resignation of the president and the three council members. A Mr O'Gorman (whom the secretary hadn't recorded as being present) read a resolution of which the minutes give no details but which seems to have been about the resignations. Mr O'Gorman said he wished to submit his resolution to the general meeting on the morrow, and the council said it was content he should do so. Meanwhile it declined to accept the resignations but requested Archer to preside at the general meeting. Whether he did or not I cannot say, as the minutes of that meeting do not appear to have survived.

Before concluding, the council arrived at a few more decisions. First, they would in future meet at provincial centres. But as need hardly be said, the secretary did nothing to implement this decision, merely continuing to follow Frederick the Great's idea about power-sharing with his subjects: 'I let them say what they like, they let me do what I like'. Mr Moore did, however, more conscientiously put before the council the lady typist's application for a rise. It would not have been absent from his mind that when a secretary warmly recommends an 'increase for his hardworking staff' and the council succumbs, it behoves him to suddenly fall dumb and stare exhausted at his papers until the council recollects that its next move is to request him, with nods and becks and wreathed smiles, to leave the meeting for a few moments while his own rise is discussed.

But at that particular meeting, although Christmas was only ten days away, the council, having just voted a £10 honorarium to Mr J. F. Walsh of Limerick, had exhausted its impulses towards distributing largesse. The financial position, they said, did not admit of any increase at present, although they added a Yuletide assurance that they would consider the matter again in the new year. Thus the meeting ended and those with experience of secretaries won't find it hard to believe that Mr Moore took himself and his armful of papers out of the room with the stricken expression of King Lear bearing away the dead Cordelia. The council was not to meet again until 8 April 1926, when Archer was present though not in the chair. He had been replaced as president by P.F. Quinlan.* It was

*Archer's predecessor, F. M. Summerfield, had served for two successive years, and it is

at this meeting that the matter of the Michelin Company first came to the council's attention, the decision being that F. M. Summerfield and P. F. Quinlan should write to warn Michelin of the consequences of their policy. Meanwhile another consequence of the secretary's dilatoriness was that the position *vis à vis* the Irish Motor & Cycle Wholesale Traders Association was still confused. The minutes refer to their having 'apparently declined' to co-operate in the operation of a stop list, and the secretary was directed to write to them 'for a definite statement as to whether representatives of that body would confer with representatives of the IMAA for the purpose of preparing a list of persons and firms eligible for trade terms'. This then was the position when Colonel Hacking arrived.

We have two accounts of the ensuing meetings, Colonel Hacking's report to the SMMT, and what appears in the IMAA's own minutes. The differences in emphasis between the two versions have their human interest.

The SMMT Version

83, Pall Mall, S.W.1, on Monday, 26th July, 1926, at 2.30 p.m.

Irish Free State

The Secretary reported interviews in Ireland with representatives of the Distributors, Wholesalers and Dealers, individually and collectively, as a result of which it had been agreed to set up a society, not a trade union, to be called 'The Society of Irish Motor Traders, Ltd', into which the existing organisations in the Free State would be merged. The Society would be under the control of a council representative of all three branches of the trade, and the Memorandum and Articles of Association were now being prepared. It was proposed, subject to the consent of the council of the SMMT, to deal with exhibition questions and to have a bond somewhat on the lines of the SMMT bond.

Subsequently an Irish Motor Trade Association would be formed as a trade union to deal with such matters as might be delegated to it by the council of the Society of Irish Motor Traders Ltd.

The IMAA Version

Executive Council meeting of 21st July 1926 [held presumably at 31 Upper Merrion Street.]

Conference with Colonel Hacking

In connection with the ban which had been imposed by the Association on the sale of Michelin products, Colonel Hacking, Secretary of the Society of Motor Manufacturers & Traders Ltd, attended.

Having been invited to make a statement Colonel Hacking said that he had been sent over by his council to see if some agreement could be arrived at by which a recurrence of such disputes as had arisen would be obviated. He fully explained the constitution and powers of the SMM&T, and the method employed in Great Britain of operating a stop list and stated that the Society was anxious to see *one* association in the Irish Free State built up on its lines and to which it could delegate its powers. This would be impossible, however, unless the Society was satisfied that the new organisation represented all interests and had the support of all

---

probable that the pattern could have been followed in Archer's case if he had been willing. But the practice started in 1926 of an annual change of president, although some were re-elected after an interval of a few years. This practice has continued to the time of writing (1982).

In the circumstances it was felt that the conference proposed between representatives of this committee and representatives of the IMAA when the boycott had been removed was not necessary.

Consideration was given to any recommendations to be put forward to the Management Committee in connection with the new society, and it was unanimously resolved to recommend that the proposed bond should be subject to the approval of the council of the SMMT.

Resolved to request the IMAA to remind their members that the boycott had been removed and that trading relations be resumed.

sections of the motor trade in the Free State.

At the request of the chairman, Colonel Hacking proceeded to outline the probable machinery of such an organisation. A long discussion then ensued on the question of representation on the council of the proposed new association; its powers to approve of exhibitions, speed trials and races in the Free State; the compilation of an agreed list of Motor Agents and other matters.

The Chairman stated emphatically that any scheme which would involve the disruption of the Association would not be acceptable to the members. Mr O'Neill then put forward the suggestion that, as the new association would require a trade union behind it to enforce its wishes, the IMAA would be recognised as that trade union.

Finally Colonel Hacking asked permission to have these proposals drawn up in skeleton form and to submit them for further discussion on the following day when he invited the agents' representatives to meet the car distributors' and wholesalers' representatives at luncheon.

The chairman thanked Colonel Hacking for his invitation and pointed out that such proposals could only be tentative as they had no power to agree to them without the sanction of the general meeting of the members.

A vote of thanks to Colonel Hacking for his presence was proposed by Mr J. A. Cross, seconded by Mr A. F. Nolan, and passed unanimously.

Colonel Hacking having replied, the meeting terminated.

3

The inaugural meeting of the Society of Irish Motor Traders Ltd took place at the Central Hotel, Exchequer Street, Dublin (of which Arthur H. Huet was a director) on Wednesday, 8 December 1926. Huet moved P. F. Quinlan, chairman of the IMAA, to the chair, from which Quinlan stated that their first business must be to co-opt Colonel Hacking, secretary of the SMMT, and two of his colleagues also present as representatives of that body, to the council of the new society. This done, the colonel presided over the election of John O'Neill as the Society's first chairman. Arthur Huet was later elected vice-chairman.

While the Society was a nominally autonomous body operating in a nominally Free State, its relationship with the SMMT resembled that between the Free State and the UK. Certain important powers were reserved by the SMMT: for instance, the power to withhold sanction of trade participation in motoring rallies and other events and, above all, in motor shows. Motor shows were lucrative enterprises for the organisers, the SMMT's own annual shows in London having over a few years shot its reserve fund from hundreds of pounds to tens of thousands. The IMAA from its inception had been making noises about holding its own shows in Ireland, but put off a definite decision because of the unsettled political state of the country in the early 1920s. Perhaps they were glad of so good an excuse to avoid raising what might prove a thorny question.

Meanwhile if Mr Moore, who had been appointed secretary of the SIMT at £500 a year, thought he could meander along in his usual fashion with the eye of A. H. Huet on him, he had another think coming. Huet screwed the fullest value out of every penny spent and kept a sharp watch on how employees filled their time. He also wanted proof that orders had been carried out and council decisions implemented, or else he wanted to know why. Actually implementing decisions would have proved far too heavy a burden for Moore's back. For years he had happily and meticulously recorded council decisions without doing anything further. Now faced with doing the job or losing it, Mr Moore, TD, made a politician's choice: he would and he wouldn't. He intimated to the council that he would not be able to devote all his time to the secretaryship *in future*, so a sub-committee recommended that his salary be cut to £300 p.a. The sub-committee further recommended that since the Society could not afford to pay an organiser £400 p.a. plus travelling expenses, the organiser should be sacked and a new post be created, combining the duties of organiser and assistant secretary, at £250 p.a. One infers that the lady clerk-typist, Miss Thompson, was to find herself saddled with extra duties and responsibilities as the sub-committee recommended that her salary be increased to £3 10s. 0d. (£3.50) a week. Alas, for poor Miss Thompson, this modest recommendation was rejected, although the other two were accepted. Thus the organiser, a Mr T. J. Loughlin, joined the long roll of IMAA/SIMT organisers who hadn't Moore's skill in the art of surviving. But although it may have been tough luck on Mr Loughlin the motor traders had done themselves a better turn than they realised, for at their meeting of 30 March

The RIAC organised the Irish International Grand Prix of 1929, which was run over a course in the Phoenix Park. This photograph shows cars passing the grand stand during the first day's race.

1928, Huet in the chair, they chose from a short list of five candidates, W. J. Lemass of 35 Percy Place, Dublin, to be their new assistant secretary-cum-organiser. He was to be given 'his actual expenses when travelling' (significant phrasing!) but after three months the council would consider whether a fixed amount should be allowed 'or other method adopted'.

The council's apparent stinginess probably owed something to its precarious finances. Its chief source of income was entrance fees and subscriptions, and as need hardly be said it wasn't always easy to extract money from members. In February 1927 a Ballymote trader had written to say he would not pay more than two guineas (£2.10), although he admitted he had an agency for cars, which made him liable to pay five guineas. The council ordered his two-guinea cheque to be returned with an intimation that he could not be elected. At that same meeting seven other subscriptions were returned because the applicants had refused to pay the entrance fee. One rather surprising case was that of the Avon India Rubber Co. Ltd which right from the foundation of the Society fought vigorously to defend its bawbees. It began in December 1926 by

140

maintaining that the wholesalers' subscription of ten guineas (£10.50) was too high, that in the opinion of their London office it should not exceed five guineas. The Society stood to its ten-guinea guns and Avon had to capitulate. But Avon didn't immed-iately part with its cash. In September 1927 it was enquiring whether a reduction could be made in view of the late period of the year. A full year's subscription, argued Avon's Major Coningsby, seemed too much to pay for a mere four months' membership. The council retorted that it had no power to grant this request.* The major paid up in November and when reminded in February that his 1928 subscription had been due since 1 January replied indignantly in March that Avon was not prepared to pay up yet again. The council retorted that it had no power to depart from the terms of the articles of association.

In May 1929 the still battling major was besieged by Willie Lemass, as he was now called by everyone in the trade. The major, however, made an overnight flit to new ground. He would not renew, he declared, 'because he was dissatisfied with the manner in which the Society was working'. The big guns were now brought into play. Arthur Huet, reinforced by C. W. Murphy, was trundled in the direction of the major, but the major's evasive action was so effective that several months later his £10.50 still hadn't been captured. Nevertheless the council hesitated to strike Avon from the approved list, and instead sent off the Lemassian light infantry in pursuit once more.

With so much ado to get a £10.50 subscription out of the Avon India Rubber Co. it is hardly surprising that the Society was obliged to plead with Colonel Hacking for some crumbs from the SMMT table. The colonel's response was more heartwarming than the major's. The SMMT, he announced, would give a grant of £1,000, and he archly enquired whether the Society would like it all at once or in two instalments of £500 each. Not that this was to make military titles as henceforth a sweet smelling savour in the nostrils of the Society. A Dublin trader angrily reported that a Free State army officer was purchasing tyres for his private car on army order forms. Moore reported that he had *phoned* the O/C, Contracts Department, to protest, but he was instructed to *write* to the Department to request investigation of the matter.

The civilians were just as bad. Complaints kept coming in that wholesalers were continuing to supply on trade terms to retail customers, and there was documentary proof in many instances. The difficulty was that the operations of a few black sheep made it very difficult for the white sheep to remain white. Arthur Huet (who, it will be remembered, was managing director of Dunlops)

*But the rules were altered in 1930 to meet this objection.

Arthur H. Huet was for many years one of the most formidable and efficient characters in the Irish motor trade.

pointed out that when his firm obeyed the Society's regulations concerning whom to supply and on what terms, they ended up by losing business to their rivals. During a later discussion on ways and means to detect price-cutting, Huet described one method practised by the Northern Ireland traders' association — the rewarding of informers. But Arthur Huet, a Newry man, hadn't grasped the Southerner's formidable powers of doublethink on subjects like informing. It had long been known in Dublin Castle that probably nowhere else in the world had the art of informing been brought to such perfection as in Ireland, where one distinction between the honourable and dishonourable is that whereas the dishonourable will inform for money, the honourable will inform for the mere fun of it. But although this, as Hamlet remarked in another

142

connection, he most powerfully and potently believed, yet he held it not honesty to have thus set down.

Although the council members can hardly have doublethought themselves out of recognising that every complaint they got about price cutting and so forth was informing, and that the investigation of a complaint was tantamount to rewarding the informer, they suavely recorded that 'an offer of a reward for information might not be successful in the Free State'. Nevertheless they tried to pacify Huet, not a man to yield a point easily, by agreeing that council members would write to him 'giving their definite opinions'.

As to which it is quite safe to say that if Arthur Huet were alive today he would still be waiting on those definite opinions in writing.

Again, when a proposal was made that Willie Lemass be provided with a camera to take pictures of premises which did not accord with the descriptions sent by applicants for membership, the council turned it down. Incidentally the minimum requirements to make a premises suitable were reasonable enough. The council had defined them in 1927 ('after a long discussion') as:

(1) separate premises devoted solely to the sale and repair of motor cars, the minimum size to be 500 square feet of floor space, under cover, and capable of accommodating four cars at any one time.
(2) the premises to be devoted solely to the repair of motor cars and accessories.
(3) the garage to be open to the public at all reasonable hours and, while open, to have an assistant or assistants in attendance to give service to the public.

The checking of suitability of premises and the investigation of trading complaints did not of course constitute the whole of the Society's activities. Attention was also paid to racing events, trials, and such like, with a view to imparting an official blessing to them. There were many such events: for example, the Dunlop Cup Trial, the Leinster Two-day Trial, the Twenty-Four Hours' Trial, the Cork Motor Club's Twenty-Hour Trial, and the famous International Grand Prix Races in the Phoenix Park.

9

National Assembly

1

In the early 1930s the general feeling in the trade was that car assembly in Ireland did not in itself make economic sense. Among the reasons put forward were that there was no traditional engineering industry in Ireland, at least outside Belfast, to provide the impetus and the manufacturing skills. Nor was there much of a home market. The population of four million or so was mostly too poor to have the minimum £200 needed to acquire a cheap car, not to mention running costs. Lack of capital was inevitably mentioned, although in the early days the chief requisites for making cars were engineering skill, a modicum of organising ability and only a relatively modest financial backing. Austin had been started in England with a mere £4,000, the infant enterprise taking off with a vengeance when the seemingly ubiquitous Harvey du Cros injected a further £20,000.

As already mentioned, some attempts were made before Ford opened in Cork to launch Irish car factories, the most significant being Chambers of Belfast. None survived for very long, their fate showing that whatever money was to be made in this country out of cars it certainly would not be out of manufacturing them. The main obstacle to success, apart from the smallness of the home market, was the invincible reluctance of Irish people to buy anything Irish except butter, meat, potatoes, whiskey and stout. In the matter of cars it took acts of the Dail to get around this reluctance, although the acts failed to remove it.

Where money *was* to be made was in importing cars, and it is surprising how long it took engineering firms to grasp this. Some however were quick off their mark. R. W. Archer had in 1907 become Fords' first European contracting dealer. Then in 1919 the first Irish Leyland franchise was secured by a small Dublin firm, Ashenhurst Williams & Co., then located in modest premises in Talbot Place, near Amiens Street. (Later it was to move to larger premises in the Bluebell industrial estate.) Ashenhurst Williams, which sold Dublin Corporation its first Leyland fire engine, and also provided the Leyland straight-eight tourer in which

Michael Collins was travelling when killed in 1922, remained in business until 1982, when it went into voluntary liquidation. In 1924 a near neighbour of Ashenhurst Williams in Talbot Place, Alexander F. Buckley (No. 6) was appointed dealer for Hillman and Singer, the former model becoming one of Ireland's best sellers in the 1930s. In 1923, Fiats, which had sold their first car in Ireland twenty years before, opened an Irish subsidiary, Fiat Motors (Ireland) Ltd, at 8 South Anne Street. They had a service depot and a stores in premises they shared with S. N. Robinson & Co., coal merchants and steamship owners, at South Gloucester Street (now Sean MacDermott Street) and City Quay. The Fiat connection resulted in Robinsons sprouting a related company, S. T. Robinson & Co., automobile engineers, with premises in South King Street.

Austin were handled by Lincoln & Nolan, a firm in whose formation R. W. Archer had played a parental part.

When General Motors introduced their Chevrolet to Ireland Archer became interested in the agency and asked Fords if they would object to his opening another firm to handle that car. They gave him the all-clear, so he founded the Lincoln Motor Co. in 1923 at 4–7 Lincoln Place (formerly the premises of L'Estrange & Hay Ltd, consulting automobile engineers). Meanwhile over in 33–34 South King Street, Andy F. Nolan was operating as sole

Ford's enterprise in Ireland continued to prosper during the 1920s. This photograph shows some of the senior management team at that time. Edward Grace is fourth from the left, and his successor as managing director, E.L. Clarke, is second from the left.

145

concessionaire for another General Motors model, the Buick. Presently General Motors came up with the suggestion that the two agents should amalgamate, which they presently did as Lincoln & Nolan of Lower Baggot Street, soon adding the distribution of the Austin car as another string to their bow.* G. A. Brittain, already in Hatch Street and in Dawson Street, moved into the former Lincoln Motor Co.'s premises in Lincoln Place,† from where the Morris Irish franchise was exercised.

2

For the better part of a decade Ireland's car importers enjoyed golden times. Between three and four thousand fully assembled cars were imported annually, the importer having little to do but pocket his percentage. The only fly in the ointment was that Ministers of Finance had already developed the habit of regarding the motorist as an easy prey. Tariffs on imported cars were built up steadily until danger point for the trade was reached in 1932. In that year Fianna Fail were elected to government and came in determined to 'whip John Bull' and his lucrative exports to Ireland. A dispute over the payment of land annuities led to the Economic War with the UK, each side bombarding the other with new tariffs. The Irish car trade seemed bound to suffer.

At this juncture Fred Summerfield approached the Minister for Industry and Commerce, Seán Lemass, with a beguiling proposition. There were certain operations in car assembly, he pointed out, for example fitting the upholstery, which could easily be done here instead of at the factory, thus providing some much-needed employment. Surely *partly* assembled cars would attract a lower duty? Lemass took the point, agreeing to permit the import of motor body shells at the special rate of 26⅔ per cent *ad valorem*.**

Thus was conceived the plan to import only CKD (completely knocked down) cars for assembly in Ireland. For Seán Lemass was to better his instruction, taking the line that there seemed no insuperable difficulty to having the whole assembly process carried out here. He accordingly ordered that from 8 November 1934 the import of assembled cars was to be strictly limited, not more than 420 between that date and the end of the following

*When Lincoln & Nolan brought over an Englishman, Mr Martin Brierly, as manager he proposed to reduce dealers' discounts and must have been taken aback by the unexpectedly vigorous opposition. Oswald Barton Snr, a leading Austin agent, recalls that he took pleasure in informing Mr Brierly 'as a fellow Englishman who had lived in Ireland for twenty years', that he had learned one might hope to lead an Irishman but never to drive him. Mr Brierly dropped his plan.

†As can be seen, Dublin's car dealers had a habit of moving in and out of one another's premises as if taking part in a game of musical chairs.

**See Appendix 2 for correspondence between Lemass and Summerfield.

R.W. Archer, photographed in 1925. Nearly twenty years earlier, he had been the first Irish agent for Fords, and now he was one of the founders of Lincoln & Nolan Ltd.

June. Contrary to popular belief the trade was not immediately made jubilant at the prospect of making vast profits from screwing together a box of loose parts to make a motor car. The importers were shocked and angered by a move so undeniably taken in the national interest. Nor was the general public captivated by the Lemassian ideal of a self-sufficient Ireland. From Lemass's point of view it seemed eminently sensible to stop paying outsiders to do what unemployed Irishmen in their own country could easily be trained to do. The trade saw things differently. It is convenient

147

to look at assembly through the eyes of one who was to become a very well-known assembler, Vincent Brittain of G. A. Brittain Ltd.

3

It has been said of Ludwig II of Bavaria that he was so very sane he was bound to be called mad. In much the same way George Alfred Brittain and his son Vincent held such commonsense views about running their business that a low opinion was bound to be formed by a certain kind of people of their administrative ability. Moreover, since Vincent Brittain was not the man to be easily deflected from a path he had decided was the right one for him, he was inevitably criticised as too rigid.

The father, George Alfred Brittain, founder of the firm, was born in 1878. He had a laundry and dry cleaning business in Belfast which he ran so well that for lengthy periods it could run itself while he toured Ireland on a bicycle. In due course he transferred to the new-fangled motor car, in which as he liked to relate he spread terror throughout the West of Ireland. He claimed that one Clare farmer jumped over a hedge to escape from him and, more credibly, that he was a steward in the Gordon Bennett Race. It was an easy step for him to enter the motor business as a side line. G. A. Brittain Ltd became main dealers for the Unic model, the Lancia and the Bianchi, taking for a showrooms what used to be a skating rink in Hatch Street, opposite the university building (now the National Concert Hall). Brittain had opened a branch of his laundry business on the north side of the city.

The Royal Flying Corps borrowed the Hatch Street premises during World War I to mount an exhibition of planes and apparently could not be got to leave when the exhibition was over. Vincent Brittain says his father had to fight through the courts as far as the House of Lords to regain possession. The post-war years saw Brittains back in business in Hatch Street, but they had also taken over a piano warehouse at 40 Dawson Street and were later to take over yet another premises in Lincoln Place from R. W. Archer. During the 1920s George Alfred conducted his Dublin business by remote control for, not liking the way things were shaping in the new Irish Free State, he moved to England with his family, settling in Hove. Here he got the Morris franchise for a large part of South Sussex. Towards the end of the 1920s he decided that the Free State had now made itself fit for Brittains to live in, so he returned, bringing with him the Morris franchise for Leinster, Munster and Connacht. He reported that W. H. Alexander had beaten him to Morris's office by twenty-four hours, otherwise he could have secured the franchise for the whole of Ireland.

George Alfred Brittain was amongst those opposed to assembling cars in Ireland. His view was that assembly in a country of such small capacity to consume as Ireland's was simply not a practical proposition.* There was also a lack of the traditional engineering skills required for successful assembling.

Naturally the British manufacturers were opposed to the idea too. But it was also clear that the Minister for Industry and Commerce, Seán Lemass, meant business and that assembly in Ireland would soon be a fact. Brittain's opposition met Lemass's irresistible force, so Brittain prepared to assemble cars. The first move was to acquire a big builders' yard on the banks of the Grand Canal at Portobello, where Samuel Bolton's firm (timber mills and ironworks) had been based on a house and grounds supposed to have been occupied at one time by Henry Grattan. The Bolton

The Irish motor assembly industry was established under the Fianna Fáil governments of the 1930s. This photograph shows the Taoiseach, Eamon de Valera, at the Ford plant in Cork. He is talking to John O'Neill, managing director of Fords since 1932.

---

*Matt McQuaid, who was employed by Brittains, was made redundant by the threat of compulsory assembly. In his letter giving notice to Mr McQuaid, George Brittain remarked that he would not commit financial suicide by assembling cars.

occupation lasted three-quarters of a century, the Brittain for about a quarter.

George Alfred's son and successor Vincent entered the firm from Trinity College, Dublin, in 1934 at the age of twenty-one. Although born and bred in Dunmurry, Co. Antrim, his teenage sojourn in Sussex and adolescence in Dublin removed so much of the Northern gravel from his accent that the unwary tended to underestimate the amount of Northern stubbornness in his character.

The year that Vincent joined the company, G. A. Brittain Ltd became the first firm outside the main factory at Cowley to build Morris cars. In Vincent's view the government regulations about assembling constituted a recipe for total chaos. For example, the chassis assembled at Cowley had to be dismantled again before it could be sent to Ireland, and the back of the car, having been welded together, had to be cut into three parts before crossing the Irish Sea. This added heavily to the costs, but the general public being unaware of the wasteful duplication and reduplication of labour, naturally concluded that the significant difference between the price of a car ex factory in England and ex assembly works in Ireland was extra loot in the assembler's pocket. Moreover the lack of technical skill in Ireland in the early days of assembling showed in the car, especially in the finish of the upholstery and paintwork. The protection given to the infant industry by the combination of high tariffs and prohibition obviated what otherwise would have been a heavy pressure to improve workmanship. As things stood, it was not uncommon to find people willing to pay twice as much to get an English-assembled car.

Vincent Brittain's career in the Irish motor industry wasn't a voyage on smooth waters. The old craft unions, as was only to be expected, were traditionally hostile to mass production, and were not going to be any friendlier to car assembly in Ireland. In 1936 Vincent Brittain, now the twenty-three-year old managing director of the firm, found himself confronted with a union dispute which led to a strike. With his father's concurrence the strike was converted into a lock-out. Vincent's crisp summary of the affair is that 'We had a lock-out on Thursday and started recruiting on Monday.' The Irish unions in those days had neither the strength nor the resources (and perhaps not the will) to put up effective resistance to such treatment. So when the Dublin dockers refused to handle consignments to Brittains, the firm merely had them re-consigned to Drogheda and thence borne to the Portobello works on what Vincent describes as 'many an exciting run'. When difficulties arose Brittains bought a coaster and had the consignments landed at Dun Laoghaire from Avonmouth. This operation lasted from 1936 to 1939.

Brittains remained effectively a non-union house until 1948.

150

Industrial unrest was avoided by keeping wages slightly above union rates, usually 2d. an hour more (something less than 1p). But the repercussions of British Labour's post-war welfare state were felt too strongly in Ireland for G. A. Brittain Ltd to remain non-union indefinitely. The management foresaw trouble and prudently decided to forestall it by inviting a union in. They decided to pick the lucky union themselves. As Vincent Brittain describes it, there was a certain cloak-and-dagger atmosphere about this operation. Representatives from three unions were invited to meet at a secret rendezvous, and the result was an invitation to the National Union of Vehicle Builders to unionise G. A. Brittain Ltd and so establish industrial peace.

4

But in following the relationship between Brittains and the unions we have bypassed the incidents of the 1930s. Vincent's entry to the firm in 1934 was marked by a lively exchange between the firm and the IMTA. At the council's meeting of 3 May it was reported that Brittains were promoting a competition at their filling station at Mount Merrion. Purchasers of four gallons of petrol and/or oil at the station could enter a guessing game competition for which the prize was a 1934 Morris Ten Four saloon. The council decided that this was unfair trading, equivalent to price cutting. Brittains were requested to desist, the Petrol Distributors Committee was informed of the request and was asked to help the IMTA to get the competition discontinued. Since the letter could be presumed to arrive at Brittains on the morning of Friday 4 May, the council decided to reconvene at 11.30 on the following Monday morning to consider what they knew would be Brittains' prompt, and guessed would be negative, reply.

When they met again on Monday morning they found Brittains had fulfilled both expectations.

The secretary, Seamus Moore, read out the letter he had sent as instructed to the Petrol Distributors Committee which, he added, was probably that moment in session over the Brittain crisis. But in an effort to restore sweetness and light he had also drafted a letter to be sent to every member of the trade, asking them to use their influence with Messrs Brittain to get them to drop the competition. This merely had the effect of stiffening the IMTA resolve to fight to a finish. The Petrol Distributors Committee was phoned up on the spot and requested to receive a deputation. The Committee agreed to this, so the IMTA appointed their deputation and accorded them plenary powers.

The next meeting of the IMTA council was held on 16 May. The crisis seems to have gone off the boil because not enough members turned up to form a quorum to consider the report of the plenipotentiaries. The chairman, M. P. Mahony, pointed out to the three members present (who included the redoubtable A. H. Huet) that no business could be transacted. Nevertheless he proceeded to do business, although calling it just a 'conference', with the Association's solicitor, Arthur Cox.

Mr Cox said he had examined the Association's rules and in his opinion the only action the Association could take against Brittains was to expel them. He ventured the further opinion that the guessing competition undoubtedly amounted to price cutting. The chairman now respectfully raised the question of whether or not to seek counsel's opinion. He hastened to point out that the Association was in no position to spend 'a very large figure' to obtain such an opinion. Mr Cox's reassuring reply was that an opinion might be had for ten guineas (£10.50). One can almost hear from the minute book an echo of the sigh of relief which greeted this example of legal moderation. It was unanimously agreed to speculate the ten guineas on an opinion. Before leaving, Mr Cox bestowed on the members the bonus of his own opinion that if the attorney-general's notice were drawn to the matter, 'it was quite possible' that he would take action to stop Messrs Brittains' competition on the ground that it was a lottery.

Much heartened, and now positively warlike, the members requested Mr Cox to bring the matter to the notice of the attorney-general.

In due course counsel opined that the competition was a breach of the distributing companies' conditions of sale. It was decided to forward a copy of the opinion to the petrol distributors and to circulate their reply, together with copies of the opinion, to all members. Earlier in the meeting the secretary, Mr Moore, had depressed the council by reminding them of the general financial situation of the IMTA, a situation the council sought to alleviate by a bargain offer to non-member traders. They could enter the fold for the remaining half of 1934 on payment of £1.05. Mr Moore now proceeded to fan the council's flickering flame into a warlike blaze at the expense of the Petrol Distributors Committee. He reported that there were many complaints about the Committee's refusal 'to take any or insufficient action regarding irregularities' (he meant *sufficient* action). The council ordered a list of cases to be drawn up and a memorandum of grievances in relation to petrol business prepared, for consideration at the next meeting.

Meanwhile Brittains must have dropped the competition, for no more was heard of it at the council meetings.

5

Early in 1939 Brittains, in expectation of a big increase in business, moved its service department to Ringsend, to the old Dublin United Tramways Company depot. With hindsight we may regard this as an odd thing for businessmen to do with the war clouds looming. To a later generation looking back to 1938—9 the signs of impending war were all there. Those who lived in Ireland through the period can only reply that the signs and symptoms, well known to those perambulating the corridors of power, were not allowed to get into the newspapers. The public at large accepted Neville Chamberlain's 'peace in our time' statement at face value and in August 1939 was buying its new cars with as little foreboding as in August 1937. In any event a European war was not connected in the mind of the Irish public with any particular shortage except white flour. Even to those who had lived through World War I, the return of war (in which Ireland would be neutral and life would accordingly go on as usual) would at worst involve no more than a return of 'black bread' and a mildly inconvenient shortage of tea. Brittains' expansionist move to Ringsend in 1939 seemed entirely sensible in the

This photograph, taken in May 1939, shows Captain St G. Harper, managing director of Irish Shell Ltd, wearing a gas mask at the company's Air Raid Precaution practice at their East Wall depot in Dublin.

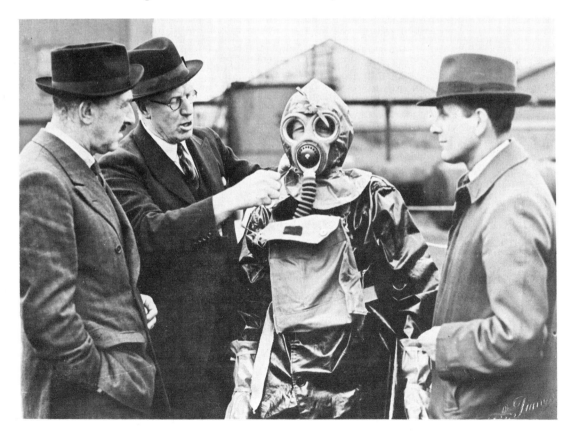

prevailing circumstances. The effects of the war on motoring didn't begin to strike home until the introduction of petrol rationing in October 1939. Only then did garage owners and car assemblers fully grasp the implications of what would appear to be merely a truism: that the public's attitude to buying a car depends upon the ready availability of petrol.

Nevertheless the assembly business in Ireland didn't die the death as quickly as might be expected. It was not until early 1940, nearly six months after the outbreak of war, that the last car 'for the duration' was assembled by Brittains. The Portobello premises was used for storing the now immobilised private cars of customers who could afford to pay to have their vehicles cared for by the skeleton staff Brittains maintained, until the return of happier times. To this extent at least Portobello wasn't a dead loss until early in 1947 when Brittains started reassembling Morris cars once again.

6

The Irish assembly of cars wasn't intended to be just the putting together of the bits and pieces in Ireland. The intention was also to have manufactured in Ireland as many as possible of those bits and pieces, leaving for importation only those parts which could not as yet be made here. John O'Neill Ltd of Pleasants Street in Dublin, the assemblers of the American Dodge car,* opened a factory in Wexford for the manufacture of car body springs, and once Irish-made springs became available a protective tariff was immediately applied to the imported article. Brittains, supported by Morris, refused to accept the Wexford springs on grounds of suitability and quality. They applied to the Department of Industry and Commerce for permission to import Morris springs on the old terms. Predictably this was refused. There followed what Vincent Brittain describes as 'a falling out with the government' and Brittains temporarily closed their works. The impasse was broken only when Brittains started to make springs themselves. It was now clear that

*The Dodge agency for certain Southern counties was however vested in P. J. O'Hea & Co. Ltd. of St Patricks Quay, Cork, from 1923 until 1950 when the devaluation of the £ put an end to Dodge assembly in Ireland. Mr J. J. O'Hea, son of the original agent, recalls that a Mr and Mrs Dodge visited their home around 1924 or 1925. In pre-assembly days the Dodges arrived in separate cases at the Cork quays and apart from releasing the springs, connecting the batteries, pumping the tyres and filling the petrol tank, the agent had nothing else to do to prepare the car for driving off. Irish assembly of the Dodge started in 1934. The cars arrived at Cork in 'knocked-down' condition, usually in batches of thirty. In 1947 O'Hea's biggest consignment, seventy-two cars being carried in the SS *Irish Plane*, was destroyed when the vessel was driven onto the rocks as it entered Cork Harbour during a storm. It was a particularly unfortunate loss, demand being very heavy at the time and some of the cars actually sold before arrival.

Mr O'Hea adds that relations between his company and G. A. Brittains were very friendly during the period, starting in 1925, when O'Hea's held the Southern agency for Morris as well as for Dodge.

any attempt by Brittains or any other firm to evade the letter or the spirit of Seán Lemass's car assembly policy was unlikely to succeed. This wasn't the only difficulty in the path of Brittains, or, if you like, the only irritant to men who were so essentially autocratic as George Alfred and Vincent Brittain. They regarded as appalling the supply position with Morrises. They had calculated that with a reasonable expenditure of energy by the workers, coupled with reasonable efficiency in workshop supervision and administration by management, it should take no more than three weeks for the car components to leave Cowley and be assembled complete to the last detail at Portobello. In fact they found the process was stretched out to ten weeks, with inevitable bad effects on Brittains' profits and on the cost to the purchaser. It wasn't simply a matter of finding ways to hustle the workmen. Another trouble was common to most Irish assemblers because somewhere between the beginning of packing operations in the UK and unpacking in Dublin, a greater number of component parts were missing that could be accounted for by human error. Generally speaking the parts were small but they were vital, their loss entailing expense and delay. A man connected with the trade (*not* Vincent Brittain) believes that many a Morris engine must have been constructed in the Oxfordshire area from parts earmarked for Portobello which never reached there.

The founder of Brittains did not live to see the post-war reconstruction of his firm. George Alfred Brittain died in Hove in October 1943 at the age of 65, bequeathing control to Vincent.

10

The Mergers

Many of the problems besetting Brittains at Portobello were also experienced by Booth Brothers in Stephen Street when in due course the evolution of their business brought them to the assembly of Wolseley cars. Like almost every other motor agent Booths were reluctant to go into the assembly business. The prospect of heavy capital investment, the almost total lack of skilled labour, and the worry of a venture into the unknown were inhibiting. Moreover there was the stubborn opposition of the English manufacturers to the idea. At first Wolseleys, for whom Booths had been agents, refused point blank to permit assembly in Ireland. 'I can only suggest,' said the Wolseley chairman to an afflicted Booth, 'that you go into the drapery trade.' Booths started discussing an assembly deal with Fords and believe they nearly came to terms, although it is hard to imagine Fords handing over a slice of their profitable cake to outsiders.

Fords had planned to import fully built-up cars from their English factory but, confronted with the government's *force majeure* on the assembly question, they surrendered. In view of this the English car manufacturers had little choice but to do likewise. So Booths sent men over to the Wolseley factory to learn how to assemble, how to weld without buckling, how to pre-treat metal so that the paint would stick, and so on. It was a considerable change from the previous disciplines of Irish mechanical engineering, where the basic tools, as Lionel Booth dryly remarks, were a screwdriver, an adjustable spanner and, in moments of desperation, a hammer.

The Booth Brothers' operation was much more modest than Brittains'. Brittain was selling between 200 and 300 Morris Minors a week. Booth sold between 30 and 40 Wolseleys and MGs a week, but regarded the assembly of such a number as something of an achievement in view of the difficulties besetting them. For the supply situation from the UK had the flavour of Charlie Chaplin farce. As Brittains had found in their own case, there were shortages even in sealed containers, and deliveries seemed to be based on madness without method. For example, you could find yourself

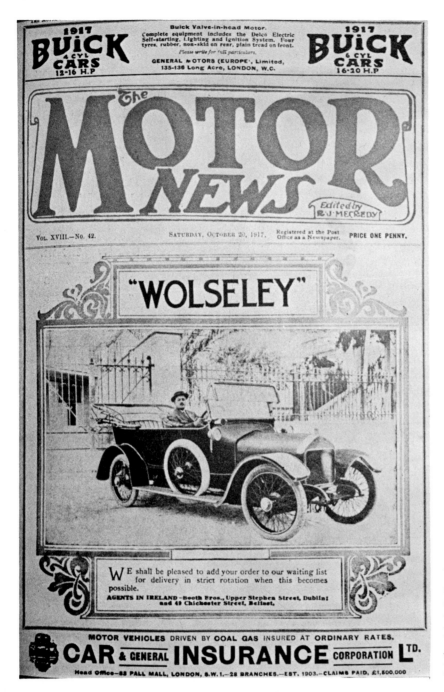

For many years, the Wolseley range of cars was one of the principal lines represented in Ireland by Booth Brothers. This advertisement is taken from the front page of The Motor News *of 20 October 1917.*

with a hundred sets of right-hand doors and no left-hand door. Worst of all was the absence of some small but vital component for the innards of a vehicle, so that assembly ground to a halt because

157

some particular section could not be covered in until the missing item arrived. There were other headaches. Lionel Booth recalls that the firm sold a new car to a conscientious but literal-minded bank manager who read in the service book that the engine oil should be drained after 500 miles. Presently the bank manager came in to complain that the car wouldn't move. Booths went to his house and found the engine sump bone dry. When the aghast mechanics asked where the oil was, the bank manager replied belligerently that the service manual said nothing about *refilling* the drained sump with fresh oil.

During World War II Booth Brothers went into Nuffield tractors, which they imported fully built up. The British authorities gladly facilitated these imports since Ireland, both North and South, was a vitally important food supplier. After the war they continued with the Nuffield tractors, as well as Wolseleys and MGs. But in 1954 they were approached by Nuffield with a suggestion that they merge with W. J. Poole & Co. Ltd of 43–4 Westland Row, distributors of the Morris-Commercial, Foden and Dennis vehicles. It was a move towards rationalisation, the cutting out of wasteful duplication and as such was welcomed by both Booths and Pooles. The merger took place the following year: a new premises for Booth, Poole & Co. Ltd being opened at Liffey Bank, Islandbridge. Booth Brothers reverted to the tool business: for them the wheel had come full circle, except that their old premises in Stephen Street having been badly damaged by fire, they now operated from 15–17 South King Street. (In the then best Dublin tradition the move was not far away.)* Booth, Poole & Co. meanwhile rejoiced in no fewer than three joint managing directors: 'Billy' Poole, who was in charge of sales, Lionel Booth in charge of service, and William Stirling who acted as financial controller. Billy Poole is said to have conducted most of his business in Kennedy's pub in Westland Row and to have promoted his sales wonderfully by stopping every Morris-Commercial driver he encountered on the road and tipping him £1, a sum well worth having in the 1950s. The drivers became very enthusiastic about the Morris-Commercials.

2

Booth, Poole & Co. were getting themselves nicely established at Islandbridge when they received another merger proposal. This was from Lincoln & Nolan, the prime movers appearing to be Martin Brierly, the managing director, and Jack Freeman, the chairman. Here again the proposal had a lot going for it. Austin and Morris

*The Stephen Street premises was rebuilt for sales and service and another premises was acquired in North Portland Street.

158

in England had joined forces to become British Leyland, and, under Lord Stokes, were forging ahead.

A similar merger in Ireland seemed sensible. Both companies appeared to be flourishing, Lincoln & Nolan being regarded in the trade as fortunate in having Mr Brierly as managing director and Mr Glover in charge of assembly. Steps towards the merger were taken quickly and the point at which the parties would be signing on the dotted line was drawing near when suddenly Lincoln & Nolan began to alter their already agreed conditions. At first Booth, Poole & Co. were prepared to accept these alterations but when further alterations were proposed, which were quite unacceptable, the deal fell through.

An observer might have been puzzled by the apparent lack of interest displayed in the merger negotiations by Vincent Brittain, a shareholder in Lincoln & Nolan. It was out of character for Mr Brittain to remain so detached, he being a man who usually insisted on his right to have a say in all matters affecting him and his business interests. It was assumed in the trade that Mr Brittain was merely a minor shareholder, and that the possibility therefore

Con Smith, the dynamic founder of the Smith Group.

existed that he was not aware of the merger moves with Booth, Poole & Co. However it presently transpired that Vincent Brittain was *not* just a minor shareholder, and that the Lincoln & Nolan merger would be not with Booth, Poole and Co. but with Brittain & Co., the latter being decidedly the dominant partner. This dominance was emphasised by the abrupt disappearance of the old Lincoln & Nolan stalwarts from the scene. The new enterprise did not achieve the tremendous success that many people assumed it would. An impression was formed that the Austins were not selling as well under the new dispensation as formerly. Nevertheless, towards the end of the 1960s Vincent Brittain started negotiating another merger: one with Con Smith of the Smith Group, which originated in Cavan, the Renault assemblers and proprietors of a garage chain. The bringing of that garage chain within Vincent Brittain's sphere of influence seemed bound to make him a power to be reckoned with by British Leyland should they at any time feel disposed to voice criticisms of his policy or performance.

3

Two unlikelier partners than Con Smith and Vincent Brittain it would be hard to imagine. They had little in common except the autocratic temperament and even then that temperament manifested itself in very different ways. On first acquaintance you would probably classify the ebullient, eupeptic Con Smith as the volatile one and Vincent Brittain as an uncommonly staid and stolid character. The reverse would be nearer the truth.

Con Smith, founder and chief architect of the fortunes of the Smith Group (two roles not always united in the same man), was born in Cavan, son of a local motor trader and an Austin main dealer. After a couple of false starts in architecture and in the law Smith was led by his instincts back into the motor trade. Being located in a country town the firm was naturally interested in agricultural machinery. In the 1950s it imported Ferguson tractors from England for rebuilding. Marketed as Smith's Rebuilt Tractors, the machines sold well, gave good service and enhanced the Smith reputation. When the motor trade went into the doldrums Con Smith shrewdly began raising capital to buy up garages, thus launching on its career what would become the group which perpetuates his name.

Around this time he established contact through friends with a young Dublin chartered accountant, Leo P. Booth, then working in a tractor firm in Laois. He offered Booth (no relation of the Booth brothers) the post of financial controller. Leo Booth accepted without hesitation. 'The most dynamic man I'd ever met' was to be his later verdict on Con Smith. Smith was of medium height, plump, exuberant, mesmeric, tending to become the focus of attention when he entered a room. But although colourful he seldom lost a certain elegance of style. He gave the impression of relying heavily on instinct, which is another way of saying he was a quick thinker. He could work out deals on the back of an envelope, tossing the envelope to his financial aides for the ironing out of complications, the fashioning of details. The ability to delegate, although usually more an expression of self-confidence than of trust in others, earned him the regard and loyalty of his associates. His popularity was to survive his untimely death. Yet he was not an easygoing man. His mind was concentrated on his enterprises to the exclusion of most of the traditional recreations of his kind, for he was one of those who find no interest in sport. Many a Saturday as the clock crept towards 1.00 p.m., he would keep chatting with colleagues whose agitation was painful as they thought of Lansdowne Road. His response to a sledgehammer hint about The Match was often a genuinely unaffected 'What match?' He was regarded as one who merely played *at* golf without believing that excellence in ball-hitting is a major achievement in life, and was never discomposed to be chosen as what golfers call 'the lady'.

In 1964, with about twenty-five garages at his command, he looked around for his own franchise. To the dismay of his associates he returned from a visit to France and announced that henceforward Smiths would be assembling the Renault, then an unpromising vehicle so far as Ireland was concerned. It had previously been handled by Stephen O'Flaherty's firm Motor Distributors Ltd, but their franchise had now expired and either O'Flaherty was not interested in a renewal or Renault declined to continue with him as his sales had been very low. Nobody in Smiths shared their leader's belief that Renault had a future here. There were hazardous interludes when, as Leo Booth recalls, 'we had sleepless nights'. Assembly began in 1965 on a five-acre site on the Wexford town waterfront of a number of models from 'completely knocked down' components. Output rose from an initial 400 units, about 0.5 per cent of the market, to a 10 per cent share in a strenuously competitive area. Wexford had come into the Smith catchment area because of the acquisition in 1963 of three agricultural machinery firms, Pierces of Wexford, Corrys and Star. The interest in agricultural machinery, always there, has been maintained to this day. The Smith Group holds the franchise for Renault tractors. It has other interests nowadays in the construction industry, in property, finance, and department stores.

The establishment of the unexpected, improbable and short-lived partnership between Con Smith and Vincent Brittain came in 1969. It is not only in hindsight that the union can be seen to have been

The Renault franchise made Con Smith's fortune in a manner similar to that in which Volkswagen made Stephen O'Flaherty's. This photograph shows the Renault 8S, 1970 model.

doomed from the start. Even at the time there were many who received news of the merger with incredulity. It was not that the objectives were unattainable but that the chances seemed remote that two authoritarian types, each accustomed to presidential style rule in his own patch, could ever settle down to work harmoniously in tandem as joint managing directors. Vincent Brittain was deemed the more rigid of the two, but Con Smith's flexibility proved more apparent than real when it came to adjusting differences. As we have seen, it was Con Smith's practice to make the broad decisions and leave the details to his aides. Vincent Brittain's temperament led him to prefer involvement at virtually every stage of a transaction, even at the risk of finding himself in a head-on collision with his partner's aides on a relatively minor matter, which could raise protocol problems and affect his own status. There were also the inevitable jealousies and rivalries between the Smith men and the Brittain men, each side determined to uphold the leader's dignity and position, since loss of face would affect them too. Thus there was the ever-present risk of friction all along the line, the rival aides scorning each other as yes-men and tending to view the other side's every action as calculated to promote its own interest at the expense of a nominally united enterprise.

What the secret hopes and objectives of Con Smith and Vincent Brittain may have been we can only guess at. Presumably each thought he would eventually become the dominant partner. If so they both miscalculated, Smith over-estimating the persuasive effect of his polish and bonhomie, Brittain under-estimating the Southerners' power to stand firm in the face of Northern drive and intransigence. A man who pounds his desk may expect to intimidate, but the intended victim may be clever enough to perceive in the pounding evidence of impotent frustration and play his cards accordingly. On the other hand Con Smith may not have intended or expected the merger to last. He may have been using it merely as a stepping stone. But one or other of the partners, if not both, had yet another merger in mind, a merger with Booth, Poole & Co.

The situation with Booth, Poole & Co. was that the Wolseley had been taken off the market and the MG's prospects of survival did not look particularly rosy. British Leyland accordingly let it be known that they favoured a merger with Brittain. But Con Smith and his Renault line being now in partnership with Brittain, it seemed highly unlikely to Lionel Booth (who it will be recalled was a joint managing director of Booth, Poole & Co.) that British Leyland could agree to a perpetuation of the Renault connection. Con Smith, however, who seemed to be taking the lead in the merger negotiations, gave the prospective partners to understand that British Leyland had no objection to this. Lionel Booth, still sceptical on the point, wrote to BL chief, Lord Stokes, who promptly invited Booth to a meeting at Longbridge, during which the office copy of a letter to Brittain-Smith was shown to him. Lionel Booth recalls that the letter made it clear that an end to the Brittain-Smith merger was required by BL. When he taxed Con Smith with the true situation, Smith replied, 'Ah — so you know about the letter.'

The upshot was that in 1970 Smith and Brittain 'demerged'. Con Smith would appear to have come out stronger than he had gone in. He went in as a private company; he came out a public one, having used the merger to cut corners on the road to the coveted stock exchange acceptance. (His admirers maintain he had the best of it both going in and coming out.) Vincent Brittain for his part came out with the stake he wanted in the agricultural area. He was also freed to proceed with the merger with Booth, Poole & Co. on his own account.

The new combination, the constituent parts of which were the former G. A. Brittain & Co., Lincoln & Nolan, Booth Brothers and W. J. Poole & Co., was known as the Brittain Group. Jack Freeman was chairman, but it was the vice-chairman Vincent Brittain who wielded real power. Billy Poole and Lionel Booth retained their old posts as managing directors in charge of sales and of service respectively and it seemed that Fords and the Brittain Group would be the Gog and Magog of the Irish motor trade, with none to say

The Smith Group's ultra-modern garage at Wilton, Co. Cork, in the closing stages of its construction.

them nay. Success would have been inevitable and defeat impossible if it were not that in Ireland, as we know, the impossible always happens and the inevitable never. Why this proved to be the case with the Brittain Group cannot at the moment be stated for there are too many people still around who know too much of what led to the Group's collapse for opinion to have matured into fact. But today Vincent Brittain lives in elegant retirement in Scotland and the name of his once important company is a fast fading memory in Dublin. Con Smith died, along with a dozen prominent Irish businessmen, in the Staines air disaster of 1972 but the company he founded has lived on to flourish and to display every outward sign of impregnability.

4

After the break with Brittain, Con Smith planned other mergers. But there would be no more power sharing: Con Smith would be in sole command. In 1972 everything was set for a merger with the long established fertilizer firm, Gouldings, headed by Sir Basil Goulding, Bart. The commercial energy and drive which had brought the Gouldings from pawnbroking and a small chemical works in Cork to titled gentility and a flourishing business in the capital, had been reduced to a feebly flickering flame by the time it reached Sir Basil. His heart was in art collecting and in gardening, his soul soaring above acids and fertilizers. The old firm seemed to roll on through the momentum developed in an earlier generation, operating narrowly from a broad asset base. Since Con Smith's situation was the reverse, the merger with Gouldings was rich in promise. The arrangement was that Smith would be chief executive, Sir Basil's face being saved by a limited period as chairman, at the expiry of which he would surrender the position to Smith. The documents were ready for signing when Con Smith died. There was now no point in proceeding with the merger. Sir Basil went back on the hazard where he was soon picked up by Mr A. J. (Tony) O'Reilly. The Smithless Smith Group was presently bought by the Waterford Glass Co.

Con Smith was only forty-one when he vanished from the tide he had taken at the flood and which led him on to fortune. But his Group had not been left drifting aimlessly. As full financial control had remained firmly in his hands he did not have to fear rivals near the throne and could therefore afford the luxury of really capable aides instead of yes-men. Thus the Smithless Smith Group never lost momentum but kept going from strength to strength while ownership was transferred from Con Smith's family to the Waterford Glass Co. Smiths' headquarters are on the Naas Road; the garages are spread all over the country. In 1977 the Group expanded its motor section once more, taking over CRV Engineering Ltd in Dundalk to give itself the distribution of Leyland trucks, and in September 1980 opening at Wilton in Cork a £1m. garage, built, according to the locals, on the most expensive bit of grass in the county. The Group regards Wilton with special pride as a kind of flagship, claiming it to be the most up-to-date garage in Ireland.

The Smith Group employs 1,400 people, of whom 750 are involved in the Renault section of the business. The chairman is Patrick W. McGrath. The managing director, Leo P. Booth, operates from 28 Fitzwilliam Place, formerly town house of the legendary Christopher Palles, last chief baron of the exchequer division at the Four Courts. The chief baron's piety caused him to have a private chapel erected at the back of the house to facilitate communication with the only judge he acknowledged as his superior. Today the chapel's dim religious light has retreated before the full light of day, plain glass having been substituted for stained except in a few tiny roof windows. The apartment now gives sanctuary to computers.

11

Petrol, Oil and Batteries

1

In the early years it was customary to find three or four different brands of petrol on offer at any reasonably sized garage. Although this added to the bookkeeping and general administration it had the advantage of giving traders a certain independence. Consequently there was resistance in the trade (although by no means unanimous) to moves towards monopoly in supply. Oswald Barton argued that monopoly might result in petrol pumps being erected outside shops and pubs to the detriment of the legitimate trade. His special interest in the petrol sales position caused him to be elected to the council of the SIMT, but on the question of trading independence he could not carry a majority of his colleagues with him. In the 1930s the petrol companies were accordingly able to introduce semi-monopolistic conditions into petrol sales. Using subsidies and loans for the improvement of service stations as bait, they induced traders to surrender their small measure of independence by undertaking to carry only one brand.

The first kerbside petrol pump in Ireland was installed outside 25 Nassau Street in Dublin in 1923 for the Nassau Motor Company, a firm owned by William Doyle.* The pump, an Avery Hardall hand-operated with chains, was installed by the Anglo-American Oil Company Ltd., now better known as Esso.

The Anglo-American, an associate of Standard Oil (the initials of which were spelt out to form Esso), began to market oil in Ireland towards the end of the nineteenth century. Their Dublin terminal, built in 1898, was equipped with storage tanks, a boiler house, automatic machines for filling wooden barrels with paraffin, and a factory which could turn out 800 wooden barrels a day. There was a large warehouse for stocks. In short, a little bit of the USA, its methods and manners, was to be found at Dublin's East Wall.†

The Anglo-American was probably the most important of the score or so of oil companies operating in the country during the

---

*Mrs Doyle was godmother to Owen Hayes (see biographies).

†So prestigious was the Anglo-American name that it was used for a car company in Dawson Street and even for a dental company in Harcourt Street.

BE PREPARED!

or

THE PACE *of Industry after the war will leave* YOU *behind*

Order your

STAR
COMMERCIAL
VEHICLE

IF YOU WOULD ATTAIN AND KEEP THAT PACE.

The
STAR ENGINEERING
Co . . Ltd
WOLVERHAMPTON.

LONDON Showrooms:
The Star Motor Agency, Ltd., 24, Long Acre, W.C.2.
EDINBURGH—The Scottish Motor Traction Co., Ltd., East Fountainbridge.
MANCHESTER—Lookers, Ltd., Hardman Street.
DUBLIN—H. S. Huet, 6, Glover's Alley.
BRISTOL—Harris and Hassel, Ltd., 141, Victoria Street.

Colonial Experience.

From
THE MIDHURST CO-OPERATIVE
DAIRY CO., LTD.,
NEW ZEALAND, July 11th, 1917.
Dear Sirs, "STAR" LORRY:
Regarding the "Star" Lorry we purchased 12 months ago from Messrs. Inglis Bros. & Co., Ltd., I have much pleasure in stating that it has given me entire satisfaction.

During the 12 months we have run nearly 20,000 miles, and it has not cost us anything for repairs—never a stoppage. I find she averages a gallon of benzine to 12 miles.

She has carried 870 tons of butter to railway station, besides 200 tons for our general store, and brought in the cream from our creameries, besides other work.

THE "STAR" SUITS THIS COMPANY. WE ARE QUITE SATISFIED.
Yours faithfully,
(Signed) F. KLEEMAN, Manager.

Commercial vehicles established the importance of road haulage from the early days of the internal combustion engine. This 1917 advertisement from The Motor News *for Star lorries is typical of the period.*

first two decades of the century.* In fact its Dublin terminal was able to cater for the country's needs until the establishment of the Irish Free State.

Other depots however had been erected at Cork (first on a relatively small site at Albert Quay, and later moved to Centre Park Road), and at Limerick, Sligo and Derry. Until 1912, when the Anglo-American started to use motor transport to distribute its products, the amusing situation existed that essential fuel for

*Dubliners will remember the Greenmount Oil Refinery at Harold's Cross, the managing director being Louis le Brocquy, father of the painter.

167

the car was distributed by a fleet of horse-drawn tankers. (The Anglo-American stable had 200 horses.) The spirit was retailed in two-gallon green cans from an astonishing variety of sources including pharmacists, whose cans were held to contain an especially pure petrol, although of course it all came from the same refinery. It was customary for cars to carry one or two spare cans of petrol strapped to the footboard; nevertheless it was a common occurrence for the motorist to be stranded fuel-less in the middle of nowhere.

On the establishment of the Irish Free State in 1922 the Anglo-American became the first major company to register itself with the new authority, its name being changed to Irish-American Oil Co.

Shell did not appear on the Irish scene until about 1907. Under the name Asiatic Petroleum Co. Ltd (the Shell marketing organisation) it leased a site at Alexandra Road, Dublin, where the Shell terminal now stands. The marketing of the products was entrusted to British Petroleum Co. Ltd (BP) and the career of both companies was intertwined for more than half a century. During their first decade in Ireland Shell did a good trade in paraffin for illumination and gas-making spirit for private plants. They were also of course building up a national network of petrol retailers and found that the two-gallon can trade remained an important element of their business up to the mid-thirties. Horse-drawn tankers were used up to that period too, and even later in Cork because of its narrow streets and steep hills.*

The growth of the retail network was governed by the distance a horse and cart could travel from depot to delivery point and back in one day. A journey from the Dublin depot to, say, Dunlavin in Co. Wicklow (a short hour nowadays) involved an overnight stay. Nevertheless Shell managed to supply fuel to remote areas like Arranmore, the island off Burtonport, Co. Donegal. Up to thirty barrels of petrol and oil would be left in the care of the stationmaster at Burtonport to await a boat from the island. A Shell inspector, evidently not an Irishman, expressed alarm at this arrangement when he discovered that the stationmaster was not under contract to the company. 'He just does it to oblige me' was the driver's explanation.

Paraffin and motor spirit continued to be imported in barrels until the erection at Foynes, Co. Limerick by the Consolidated Petroleum Co. of the first bulk storage installation. Bulk storage naturally reduced costs for all companies and improved efficiency. But Shell have a rueful tale about the two farmers who had a contract with them for the supply of paraffin in oak barrels. The farmers insisted on their contract being fulfilled to the letter. They

*Shell records show that a Mr Young and a Mr McIlroy were awarded £2 2s. 0d. in 1918 for having the best-kept tank-wagon in Clones, Co. Monaghan.

168

were able to cut the empty barrels in two to serve as troughs. The Consolidated Petroleum Co. therefore maintained a cooper at Foynes to make barrels exclusively for these astute customers.

Shell and BP became separate companies in 1916 but this was little more than a bookkeeping manoeuvre. Political proprieties were observed by the opening of a Belfast office staffed by Dublin employees. (The world has had ample opportunity to see how the more things change politically the more they remain the same for oil companies.) Shell and BP competed with each other within their multinational framework for a decade, then came together again in 1932 as Irish Shell Ltd. BP was dropped from the title because of its too obvious British connotation, but in 1961 the onset of milder political weather enabled the company to bloom once more as Irish Shell and BP Ltd. The resemblance to turbulent matrimonial life was again emphasised in the mid-1970s with another separation. Heaven knows what the situation will be at the time of reading but at the time of writing it is this: BP Ireland Ltd, with a head office at Setanta Place, Dublin 2; and Irish Shell Limited Petroleum Distributors, with a head office at 20 Lower Hatch Street, Dublin 2.*

In the 1920s other now familiar names first became prominent: the Texas Oil Co. (later Caltex, now Texaco), Russian Oil Products, McMullan Bros (now Maxol), and so on. Lubricating oils came from several local companies, Esso (as the Irish-American became in 1952) claims to have been first in Ireland to market bottled motor oil and first to offer 'ethyl' petrol.

Petrol prices remained remarkably stable for more than fifty years. Veterans claim to recall when petrol could be bought for 9½ or 10½d. (4–4½p.), representing about a quarter of a day's wage for a Dublin labourer. But officially the best petrol was retailing in these islands in 1914 at 1s 9d., a gallon (including 3d duty), or about 9p. in modern money. Conditions during World War I drove the basic price of a gallon up to about 19p., the price remaining relatively high until 1922, when it returned to the old level. Which, taking inflation into account, meant a price drop in real terms. Only in the 1970s did petrol prices really take off, partly because of the OPEC retaliatory rises following the 1973 Yom Kippur war, but chiefly because of taxation intended as much to reduce consumption as to raise revenue.

---

*Shell actively markets several petroleum-based products. In 1952 its then managing director Mr Crawford Young organised the establishment of a bulk bitumen plant, the first in the world not attached to a refinery. Up to that time bitumen was barrelled and in Dublin was handled by a squad of up to 120 dockers.

For many years there was friction between the Society* and the oil companies. The companies were largely indifferent to the price at which retailers sold petrol and were therefore not as perturbed by price cutting as the Society was. Each company wanted the largest possible number of outlets regardless of whether or not these were at garages conforming to the Society's rules. The companies were prepared — eager in fact — to supply hotels, public houses, even village shops, a policy the Society saw as open encouragement of price cutting. Warrens of St Stephen's Green, the chief suppliers of petrol pumps, being vigorous upholders of Society policy, were in a delicate position when disputes arose with the oil companies, but Charles Warren's diplomacy seems to have prevented alarming confrontations. Where it came to applications to have pumps installed at premises with no servicing facilities, Warrens took the inflexible line: no facilities, no pumps.

The Society, however, was having difficulties over petrol suppliers, not just with the companies but with some of its own members. This was part of a general resistance to the Society's rules and regulations, human nature disliking having to obey rules if they conflict with long-established and easy-going ways, even when the rules will clearly benefit everyone in the long run.

There is also the human being's natural resistance to compulsion, a resistance which Irishmen tend to carry to extreme lengths. With the serenity of old age the late Denis Dennehy, chairman of Dennehy's Cross Garage Ltd, Cork, could recall with amusement his own part in the petrol disputes of the 1930s with the Society, which he had recently joined. The story is worth re-telling because it was typical of what the Society had to contend with in those days.

In 1936 Dennehys carried two brands: Shell BP and ROP (Russian Oil Products). ROP, according to Denis Dennehy, was a great petrol, very strong, and moreover could be sold cheaper than less potent brands. One night a Society member in Cork city bought a gallon of the cut-price petrol. The next thing was a letter from the Society to Dennehys, warning them that their petrol supplies would be stopped forthwith. Dennehy ordered supplies from Irish-American, enclosing his cheque with the order. The cheque was returned. He now approached a man named Joyce who bought large supplies from the oil companies which he resold to the smaller traders, using two small tankers for delivery. For the next several months Dennehys got their pumps replenished surreptitiously in the middle of the night. But in the end Mr Mahony of the Avon Tyre Co. in Dublin, a member of the Society

*For the reader's convenience both the SIMT and the IMTA will from now on be referred to as the Society.

council, recommended Denis Dennehy to present himself to the Council and 'face the music'. Facing the music entailed a £25 fine and an apology in the trade magazine, but supplies were restored.

Most of the offending traders seem to have been able to accept defeat gracefully like Denis Dennehy. But there were also the 'no surrender' types. These were dealt with by having *all* their suppliers notified that they were *non grata*, so that they couldn't officially get as much as a nut and bolt let alone a tankful of petrol.

Garages received a nasty knock in 1938. On 30 November the Petrol Distributors Committee notified the Society that from the following day the 2½ per cent discount for cash on delivery would be discontinued. A high-powered deputation (Summerfield, Archer, Huet, Braine, Barton and Hudson) were sent to the Distributors and

Henry Ford in old age, with his ill-fated son Edsel on the left. Ford's V8 engine, also shown here, was first introduced in March 1932 and brought sports car performance to the family saloon market. It remained a feature of Ford cars for three decades.

171

the matter was argued all through December. But on the 29th the deputation could only report failure. London, on having the protest referred to it, replied that the old discount could not be restored, claiming that the companies had been obliged to withdraw the discount because of 'the economic position in this country', whatever that might mean. Like an Irish government minister forty years later, the Society tried sabre-rattling with the oil companies, but with no more success than the minister. The companies were unimpressed by rattles like a threat that the Society would advise members to order no more than 200 gallons at a time and, where possible, only from subsidiary companies, and to hide petrol company signs away from the public gaze. Although the old hands must have known the cause was lost, the council had to fight on, particularly when Brendan J. Cross, having been asked what the feeling down in Cork was, vigorously replied that Cork was 'incensed' and would immediately put into effect whatever counter-measures the Society decided upon.

A fortnight later the position was that the Petrol Distributors Committee stood firm on the discount decision but offered traders an extra halfpenny profit per gallon, the halfpenny being passed on to the motorist. Since this, if implemented, would not have restored the *status quo*, the talk about taking strong action continued. But the search for an escape route continued. A tentative enquiry as to how the provinces were now feeling was met with the bellicose response that the provinces were 'looking for results' and expected the Society to take 'any and every action in support of their demand for a restoration of the 2½ per cent discount'. In view of this the council conscientiously began to fan the flickering flame of its indignation. There was talk of 'proceeding to London to interview the joint managers,' but by March the joint managers were cynically admitting that while the abrupt manner of withdrawing the discount was 'unfair and ill-advised' they were not going to do anything about it. They desired to return to the credit system and were prepared to 'make a concession to the trade concerning the future erection of pumps for users owning commercial vehicles of which the total carrying capacity is six tons and less'.

The council made a counter-suggestion. That the oil companies undertake not to sell petrol direct to any commercial consumer unless he had more than 6 tons carrying capacity. They also decided to set up a petrol committee to settle all matters still at issue between the two sides. Presumably the withdrawal of discount was still an issue but by now it had been lost sight of. As 1939 advanced so did greater threats to survival than the loss of 2½ per cent off for cash.

3

The declaration of the 1939 war naturally changed the face of Irish motoring. But the change was not an overnight one. When, twenty-four hours after the declaration, the sun was still in the sky and water still came from the urban domestic tap, Ireland began to feel that life in a neutral country would probably go on pretty much as before. This was wishful thinking so far as most people were concerned. Those who had spare money to hand took steps to ensure that life would continue much the same for *them*. They bought in large stocks of coal, bags of white flour, and enough tea and coffee to keep them going for years. Petrol and paraffin, not being so easily storable, couldn't be much stockpiled by the ordinary motorist; nevertheless most motorists kept a few cans and containers of the stuff stashed away, or tried to do a deal with a garage whereby a quantity of petrol would be earmarked for them, withdrawable on demand. Those in a position to do so arranged to sell or lay up their gas-guzzlers, replacing them with smaller models. The petrol distributors were eager to fill garage tanks to the brim to gain more storage space at their terminals and depots which in turn were refilled as fast as the oil tankers could tie up at the docks. It was accepted of course that a measure of rationing would be inevitable, and ration books had been issued. The order introducing petrol rationing was made on 16 September 1939, to take effect in October, and the government announced that the value of each petrol coupon would change according to the supply position. Few in the motoring world, motorists or traders, realised how quickly that position would deteriorate. Yet when Ireland's petrol supplies, which were channelled through Britain, were abruptly cut to virtually nothing, so that the promised ration had to be cancelled, Seán Lemass, now Minister for Supplies,* unaccountably delayed the announcement for several hours, with tragi-comic consequences for one well-known Dublin garage, Huet Motors at Mount Street Bridge.

On the morning of Cancellation Day the rumour ran through Dublin that Britain was cutting off Ireland's supply of petrol completely: that not another drop would enter the country until the war was over. There was an immediate rush to the petrol pumps but every garage in Dublin turned the private motorist away, coupons or no coupons, irrespective of appeals, hard luck stories, mothers dying down the country and even offers of bribes. There was one exception. Huet Motors, which like every other garage had brim-

*Lemass became Minister for Supplies on 16 September 1939, with Seán MacEntee taking over Industry and Commerce. This arrangement lasted for less than two years: on 18 August 1941 Lemass returned to Industry and Commerce, but without relinquishing Supplies. He held both portfolios until the Department of Supplies was wound up on 21 July 1945.

ming tanks, decided to give every comer two gallons of his monthly ration. The decision was taken by Percy Huet, elder of A. H. Huet's two sons and titular managing director. Titular because his authority extended only to the day-to-day running of the firm, important matters being reserved for his father as chairman. Percy took the view that there was no reason for panic as the government had made no announcement and a phone call to Lemass's Department elicited the assurance that nothing was known there of any impending change in the petrol situation.

Percy's line of reasoning was that by obliging everyone they would sell a lot of petrol, which would of course be replaced on foot of the official coupons collected, the increase in the motoring public's goodwill towards Huet Motors being incalculable. Arthur Huet had phoned Percy in alarm on hearing that theirs was the only garage in Dublin open for petrol. Percy must have persuaded his father that everything was all right, for Arthur did not arrive at the garage until the afternoon was well advanced. His arrival coincided with the Department of Supplies announcement that the ration for private motorists was cancelled and their coupons worthless. Somebody must have given Arthur the news before he entered the showrooms for, massive and menacing, he tramped straight over to the pale, quaking Percy. I, then the firm's junior costing clerk, happened to be in the showrooms at the time and although I could not distinguish what words Arthur addressed to his son through clenched teeth, it was easy to guess their import. Percy cannot have been far off forty at the time, but he was whimpering excuses like a guilty schoolboy and backing away from the ham fist being flourished in his face. I saw he was backing into one of the potted palms that were an essential part of the decor of every motor showrooms, and as every personal tragedy has its comic side for the uninvolved spectator, I fled towards the lavatory before the inevitable catastrophe. As I reached the door Percy fell over the potted palm and I heard his unsympathetic sire yelling at him to get up and not be lying there like a bloody fool.

Luckily Percy had stopped selling the petrol before the last tank was broached, so that Huets did have a few hundred gallons in hand to see them through the five years of war. But like the Ghost in *Hamlet*, Percy was doomed for a certain term to walk the earth instead of driving around in one of the firm's choicer stock cars. This paternal chastisement for his folly was all the harder for him to bear because he lived in Bray and was thus at the mercy of wartime public transport. How long the penance lasted I cannot say, for shortly afterwards I accepted Arthur Huet's offer of a transfer to another of his business interests, the Central Hotel.

The petrol situation during the war turned out to be not quite so awful as had been first rumoured. Britain released enough of the precious fluid to meet the country's essential needs, and the great objective of all dealers was to get their hands on it. Indeed this was the objective of virtually everyone who was allowed to keep a car on the road. The clergy and doctors enjoyed special rations and were observed to be called with astonishing frequency to golf courses to render spiritual and medical aid to persons who regularly collapsed there. The Society drew up an approved list of dealers throughout the country who were recommended for special allowances for genuine trade use. The dealer, to qualify, had to have at least the prescribed minimum space for carrying out repairs and to be in the hireage business. More than one dealer tried to cheat by doing up some wreck of a car and pretending it was for hire. Another trick was to get hold of an ancient tractor that would never move and claim an allowance for it. Culprits when detected were removed from the Society's approved list, the government greatly appreciating the vigilance of the policing.

Joseph Lucas, the founder of Lucas and Son, photographed shortly before his death in 1902.

Many efforts were made during the war years to find a practicable alternative to petrol. McCairns tried to keep commercial vehicles on the road by improvising gas converters which made gas from coal fed from a hopper fixed to the truck. The improvistime some private cars could be seen travelling around with vast rectangular canvas bags of gas affixed to the roof. These vanished when shortage of coal made gas scarce. It was alleged that in some cases the gas bags were only hoaxes, the car in fact being driven on illicitly obtained petrol. For a surprisingly long time the manager of at least one firm which obtained a petrol supply to carry out essential services drove his Austin 12/6 with a token tin cylinder, about the size of a fire extinguisher, attached neatly to the rear bumper.

It was not until 17 December 1951 that the ending of petrol rationing from the end of that month was officially announced.

5

The Birmingham-based firm of Joseph Lucas & Son can fairly claim to have been the pioneers of car lighting. They had also branched out into starting and ignition sets, for many years sharing the market with CAV (run by C. A. Vandervell) and Rotex. In 1926 they took over their rivals, thereby achieving a virtual monopoly of lighting, starting and ignition sets which lasted until after the end of World War II. Up to 1926 they had done business in the twenty-six counties through a long established firm of agents, Taylor Bros of 41 Middle Abbey Street. In that year they took over from Taylor Bros, acquiring the premises as well.

The firm had been founded in the middle of the nineteenth century by Joseph Lucas (1834–1902), the son of a Birmingham electro-plater. Joseph married early and fathered a larger family than he could afford to keep. Finding the pressure too much for them, Joseph Lucas and his wife took to heavy drinking, going down hill rapidly. In the nick of time Joseph pulled himself together and made a fresh start as a street seller of paraffin oil, which he pushed around in a container in a handcart. He added buckets and shovels to his stock-in-trade, and, presently, lamps. The lamps, which bore the odd name of Tom Bowlings, were the foundation of his fortune. These ship's lamps had not been invented by Lucas. The credit belongs to one Isaac Sherwood, who also manufactured the lamps in small quantities. It is not known whether it was Lucas or Sherwood who named the lamps Tom Bowlings* but it was

*The name was borrowed from the famous sentimental ballad by the eighteenth-century composer Charles Dibdin about Tom Bowling whose
Heart was kind and soft,
Faithful below he did his duty,
But now he's gone aloft.

Joseph Lucas's son Harry, who succeeded his father as head of the Lucas company.

Joseph Lucas who exploited them in much the same way as Harvey du Cros exploited Dunlop's tyre. With the invention of the bicycle, Lucas marketed the King of the Road hub lamp, and when the motor car came on the road it too was provided with King of the Road lamps which were designed to give motorists 'sufficient light to show up the hedges or borders of the road, but with a broad beam of the greatest intensity straight ahead, so that the path of the car is strongly and evenly illuminated.' Soaring into capital letters the 1908 proclamation claimed that

177

THE DRIVER CAN ACTUALLY SEE light objects, such as light-coloured cottages, walls, gates, posts etc., fully 200 yards away and vehicles, pedestrians and cyclists at about 150 yards.

Lucas was also producing individually tuned horns, one instrument being acoustically so correct that 'the resulting tone, while not too loud, reaches the slow traffic in time to allow of its clearing the road before being overtaken, and is especially useful at cross-roads and corners.'

Just before the outbreak of World War I the firm completed plans for a dynamo lighting system for cars. Eventually the Lucas Motoralities, as they were called, comprised a dynamo, switchbox, accumulator (now being called battery), a pair of projectors (head-lights), side lights, tail lamp, set of sundries (cable, clips, screws) and a Vee driving belt. Prices ranged from £32 10s. for relatively small cars (12 h.p.) to £49 10s. for Rolls-Royces.

Joseph Lucas died at Christmas 1902 in Naples from typhoid fever, apparently contracted by drinking the local water instead of the customary wine, so conscientious was he in keeping his pledge. For several years his son Harry had been the real force in the firm, so much so that he was continually lecturing — hectoring, in fact — his sire on everything from business methods to spelling. ('The name of the house is The Firs, you have written The Furs.') Harry survived until 1939, having developed the firm into a large and prosperous concern, but he never shed his Victorian passion for small economies, constantly urging his staff to untie not cut the string on parcels, and to save envelopes for re-use. In 1882, when he was twenty-seven, he and his brother ventured to Ireland on a three-week holiday which began with a visit to the spot in the Phoenix Park where the chief secretary, Lord Frederick Cavendish, son of the Duke of Devonshire, and the under-secretary, Thomas Henry Burke, had been knifed to death by the Invincibles two months previously. What stirred Harry even deeper were the prices he and his brother had to pay for their lodgings in Killarney: four shillings (20p.) for a bedroom, 'the furniture of which could all be bought for the price of a month's lodging at this exorbitant rate'. Teas at a shilling a head and breakfasts at two shillings caused him similar grief, but the last straw was being charged a shilling each entrance fee to view the ruins of Muckross Abbey, 'this mean charge made by the proprietor, Mr Herbert — an MP too — who we all agreed was no gentleman'. At Galway the train was joined, hardly surprisingly, by 'Irish men and women'. Harry found the place 'full of country women bending under their loads of market stuff — eggs, butter, poultry, etc. — which they carry in baskets on their backs under a thick black woolly cloak of Spanish mantilla pattern, which reaching over their heads also takes the place of a

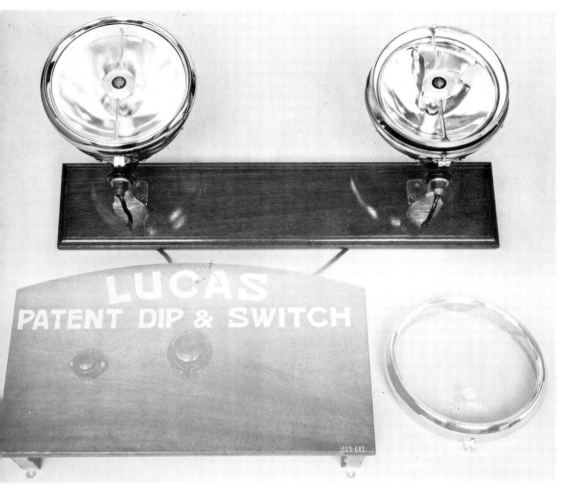

bonnet. Under this black cloak they wear a coarse sort of thick flannel petticoat of a bright red colour, but no shoes or stockings and evidently little or no underclothes to encumber them.' He calculated that the women 'must be about three women-power at least' to endure their occupation of beasts of burden, for although he and his brother had seen many weight-carrying women, 'not a single man did we see encumbered with a basket or a bundle.* At Limerick, where the train was joined by emigrants bound for America, the pathos of their last farewells to family and friends brought tears to Harry's eyes, 'although my sympathies are not easily moved by scenes of this kind'.

After Lucas's took over in Dublin from Taylor Bros the first

Lucas dip switch lamps of 1931. Up to the Second World War, Lucas's virtually controlled the market in car lighting.

*Quoted in Harold Nockolds, *Lucas: The First 100 Years*, David & Charles 1976, pp. 49–50.

179

local manager was L. A. Taylor, one of the previous owners. R. W. Penrose was in charge during the war years and, as in other areas of the trade, was faced with a daunting challenge to managerial ingenuity. After the war Lucas started making batteries here. Today Lucas continue their Irish operation as auto-electrical and fuelling specialists in North Portland Street, Dublin, and Bachelor's Quay in Cork. Frank Mooney, whose father used run the Cabra Garage, and who joined the firm as a sales representative in 1956, is now general manager.

Tourism became a major growth area in the Irish economy from the late 1950s onwards. CIE's modern fleet of touring coaches has proved popular with sightseers.

12

Stephen O'Flaherty

1

From the 1930s onward it seemed that the Irish motor world was in a recurring state of chaos, motorists and traders alike being called upon to suffer one thing after another. Hardly had they accommodated themselves to Mr Lemass's home assembly policy than World War II broke out. Even then the restless Mr Lemass would not allow them to suffer their war hardships in peace. It became known that he was planning a revolutionary reorganisation of Irish transport, one which appeared to threaten the citizen's ancient privilege of choosing his own mode of travel.

In fact what Lemass was trying to do was to solve the problem created for railways by the rise of motorised transport, a problem compounded by the concurrent rise in rail labour and fuel costs. Ireland's railways had been built in the nineteenth century on the assumption that ever-expanding industry and commerce would demand a nationwide freight service, of which it would make considerable use; and that the ever-growing population would avail itself of a uniquely quick and efficient passenger service which was also relatively cheap. The realities turned out to be that trade did not expand as expected, the population kept dropping because of emigration, and country people did not regularly refresh themselves by rail journeys for change of air and scenery, being obliged to stay put to fodder their livestock, milk their cows and dig their potatoes. The rivalry of the motor car really began to be felt in the 1920s. In a fight for survival twenty-six different Irish railway companies amalgamated to save costs, forming the Great Southern Railway Company in 1925. But hopes were frustrated by the inexorable swing to road transport of both freight and passengers. Small bus companies and haulage firms mushroomed all over the country, competing savagely with each other by cutting fares and freight charges to the bone. So many corners were cut in the literal and metaphorical sense that public safety was threatened. The government had to move. The Road Transport Acts of 1932 and 1933 made it an offence as from 25 July 1932 for any person to carry on a passenger road service save under and in accordance with a

licence. Fare lists and timetables had to be published, accounts had to be kept and returns made as prescribed by the Minister, and the carriage of merchandise and mails was prohibited. In short, everything possible was done to drive the fly-by-night road operator out of business. The 1933 Act also empowered the railways to acquire the licences of private operators, so that within a few years the GSR had a virtual monopoly of road passenger and freight business. But railway revenues continued to decline. In 1938 a tribunal was set up to inquire into the whole question of public transport. In general it favoured the railways, for it recommended further restrictions on road transport. The outbreak of war and the consequent petrol shortage would have been a godsend to the railways if only they had the coal to run the trains.

But at best the reprieve could only be temporary, for the war would not last for ever. In 1942 Lemass began his kill-or-cure remedy for railway ills. In that year the government assumed the power to appoint the chairman of the GSR, a move which was interpreted by the motor trade leaders as the thin end of the wedge. It seemed wise for the trade to secure some kind of representation at decision-making level where at least an eye could be kept on

182

Lemass's legislative activities. The obvious first move was to secure a seat in the Seanad, which then seemed a more influential body than it was later perceived to be. The trade in general, however, showed itself lackadaisical about getting Seanad representation. F. M. Summerfield complained that in the 1943 Seanad election three approved motor traders who had votes did not, or because of party ties would not, give a Society candidate (of whom he was one) their No. 1 votes. With a little extra effort on the part of the trade, he said, his own success could have been assured. The secretary was directed to draft a letter to the Taoiseach (de Valera) protesting against his failure to nominate a representative of motor transport interests to the Seanad. Meanwhile the Cork traders felt that the Society council up in Dublin was letting things slide. A deputation was despatched to urge that some signs of life be exhibited in the capital city, the indignant Dubliners retorting that the council's provincial members hadn't bothered to come up as often as the situation required. But ranks quickly closed when it was mentioned that the coming monopoly might entail restrictions on private motoring when this was resumed after the war. A transport committee was set up to fight the monopoly, and was em-empowered to spend up to £50 of Society funds in so doing.

In the event the 1944 Transport Act did no worse than establish a new public transport organisation called Coras Iompair Eireann, which incorporated the GSR and the Dublin United Tramway Company. But this exercise in name changing did not change reality. The deterioration of the railways continued while road transport continued to boom. By 1950 another 3,000 miles of paved roadways had been built, bringing the national total to around 14,000 miles, and the number of private cars on them continued to soar dramatically. In 1947 we had 52,200 cars, ten years later it was 135,000, in 1967 the figure was 314,400, and in 1981 the total was a staggering 774,594.

2

Before World War II a number of people in the motor trade had been able to make enough money to give them a very comfortable living. It was not until after the war, however, that really big money could be made, and by all accounts the largest of those motor fortunes was that accumulated by the late Stephen O'Flaherty. If we are to accept Isaiah Berlin's definition of a great man as one who for better or for worse changes the course of events, then O'Flaherty was a great man, for it was he who broke the hegemony of English and American cars in Ireland by introducing the Volkswagen 'beetle' and, later, the Mercedes and the Toyota. He was indeed the first to assemble Volkswagens outside Germany.

Stephen O'Flaherty did not stand alone as a motor millionaire. The Booth Brothers, Vincent Brittain, Tommy McCairns and R. W. Archer could none of them be described as penniless. A. F. Buckley prospered mightily from handling the Hillman Minx, one of the most popular 10 h.p. models of its class, and his gains multiplied when Aer Lingus decided to equip itself with Viscount planes from Vickers, whose Irish agent Buckley was. In accordance with trade etiquette, business had to be done through the agent, so a shower of gold descended upon Alec Buckley. It would have descended upon Tommy McCairns if Aer Lingus had chosen an American plane fitted with GM engines, as it was considering doing. Nonetheless, as Mr McCairns philosophically remarked, he managed to survive, if not on the same scale as his former general manager Stephen O'Flaherty.

Stephen O'Flaherty was born in 1902 in Passage East, Co. Waterford, the youngest of five children. His father had come from the Aran Islands where, in 1896, Stephen's first cousin, the novelist

184

Liam O'Flaherty, was born. Stephen claimed descent from the princely O'Flahertys who had been driven from Ballinahinch Castle in Co. Galway on the orders of the first Queen Elizabeth,* being thereby deprived of over a quarter of a million acres of land. The chief beneficiaries of the confiscation were the Martins, the family which in a later generation produced the celebrated Humanity Dick Martin, although this did little to lessen the resentment of the O'Flahertys against their expropriators. During the second part of his life Stephen O'Flaherty, from any of his several homes in South County Dublin, could have had a fine view of Howth, scene of a famous visit to the local lord by Grace O'Malley ('Granuaile'), lady wife of an ancestor, Donal O'Flaherty of the Combats.

If Stephen O'Flaherty's claim to so colourful an ancestry is correct, then he and his novelist cousin can fairly be said to be not unworthy descendants of Granuaile, and her no less combative spouse.

Like his cousin, Stephen first tried his luck in England. He worked in Dunlops, then moved to a Dutch firm, Hans Reynolds. While working in Manchester he met a Shropshire girl, Dorothy Wilcox, who had been born in the same year as himself, and at the age of twenty-four married her. For both of them it was to prove a singularly fortunate partnership and, for many years, a happy one. Both were energetic and enterprising, and Dorothy O'Flaherty had decided tendencies towards a business career. Part of Stephen's surplus energy was devoted to developing sidelines. He worked the normal business hours in Hans Reynolds, but he was also devoting his time to a small manufacturing firm, in partnership with his wife. Its chief product was an instrument, closely resembling a pliers, which Australian and New Zealand sheep farmers found handy for removing hay and other seeds from the eyes of their flocks. Mrs O'Flaherty's lively sense of humour obliges her to emphasise that the instrument was not fantasy but sober fact. In about 1928 or '29 Stephen returned to Ireland to work in Fords' accounts department in Cork, then moved to Dublin to look after the accounts in McCairns Motors. The moving about from firm to firm was not so much in search of advancement as a consequence of his restless temperament. It was his nature to keep moving: he could not even settle in one house, for, like Dr Colohan, in the course of his life he had many addresses.

Tommy McCairns found O'Flaherty so hardworking and efficient that he appointed him, first, secretary of the firm, then general manager. As usual Stephen O'Flaherty kept a lookout for a sideline, but oddly enough at first he paid little attention to the sideline which was to evolve into the structure from which came his fortune. The sideline was a run-down engineering firm in Townsend Street

*Cromwell was more likely to have been the villain of this particular piece.

which Dorothy O'Flaherty had acquired, chiefly as an outlet for her own energy — 'to give me something to do' as she says herself. The firm was called Howard McGarvey & Sons.

The original Howard McGarvey was a civil engineer who worked in a large firm of engineers, plumbers, iron and brass founders, bell hangers and gas fitters in Middle Abbey Street in the 1870s. Later he branched out on his own in Lombard Street, and in due course became Howard McGarvey & Sons of the Lombard Works, 62 & 63 Townsend Street. He did well enough to live in a large house, Brooklands, standing in its own grounds on the Merrion Road.* When Howard McGarvey died, his two daughters continued to live in Brooklands, and when their brothers died these ladies carried on the business with the assistance of one capable engineer. Unfortunately this engineer did not drive, and since the work involved a considerable amount of travelling this was a handicap. Mrs O'Flaherty cannot now recall, at a distance of more than forty years, just how she and the Misses McGarvey met. It may have been at White Rock on Killiney beach where, in those days, the local fishermen brought in their catches of lobsters and offered them for sale at a shilling (5p) apiece.

At any rate the three women became friends, the sisters eventually telling Mrs O'Flaherty about their little business and how they were no longer able to carry on with it. Mrs O'Flaherty offered to buy it from them, believing that she would be able to run it with the help of the engineer, whom she also proposed to drive to his various jobs. The 1939 war broke out shortly after Mrs O'Flaherty had taken over, but somehow Howard McGarvey & Sons (for she continued to use the old name) managed to struggle on and even to show signs of reviving. At this point Stephen O'Flaherty became interested in the possibilities of Howard McGarvey & Sons and he and his wife went down to the Townsend Street premises, sometimes as early as six in the morning, he to put in a couple of hours with the paperwork before appearing on the dot of nine at his general manager's desk at McCairns Motors.

Naturally Stephen had not mentioned at McCairns Motors his connection with the other firm. He took the view that what he did outside office hours was his own concern. Tommy McCairns found out, however, although there was little he could do about the situation. He could find no fault with Stephen's work, for Stephen continued to put in a satisfactory day's labour and continued to take care of McCairns Motors' pence as carefully as if they were his own.† But when Tommy McCairns became convinced that Stephen

*Brooklands was demolished some years ago. It was situated at the junction of Merrion Road and Nutley Lane.
†Stephen O'Flaherty's docking of an 8s. 6d. (42½p.) luncheon claim from the expense account of Matt McQuaid, then a rep. for the firm, after he had landed a handsome order

was using contacts he had made in the course of his work at McCairns Motors to benefit Howard McGarvey & Sons, he brought matters to a head with a ruthlessly direct question: 'Are you working for McCairns Motors or are you working for Stephen O'Flaherty?'

After some hesitation came the momentous reply, 'I am working for Stephen O'Flaherty.' So they parted. Although Stephen O'Flaherty made the break with an appearance of reckless defiance worthy of a descendant of Granuaile, it was as a rather shaken man that he came home to his wife that evening. Financially he was not yet ready to give up his job, especially as the O'Flahertys now had two sons at the stage when education can be a dauntingly expensive matter. But the break had been made, and as the motor trade was still in its wartime crisis Stephen had no prospect of a general managership in any other firm. 'We realised we simply *had* to make a go of Howard McGarveys', is how Mrs O'Flaherty now recalls their decision.

3

During the remaining years of the war the O'Flahertys kept McGarveys afloat and McGarveys returned the compliment. After the ending of hostilities in Europe, the firm, now transformed into Motor Distributors Ltd, did business with a small number of Willys Overland jeeps and station wagons, Nash cars and trucks, Singers, Lagonda and Aston Martin, and Mulvihill dumpers. But the first real money Stephen O'Flaherty made came from Adlers. During the war years twelve unassembled Adlers had lain in their packing cases in the Dublin docks. Since no one claimed them the port authorities invited tenders for them. Stephen O'Flaherty's tender was successful. It had been a shot in the dark because no guarantee was offered as to the condition of the cars. Stephen might have got his fingers badly burned, a thing he was fully aware of. But he was always a gambler, and on this vital occasion his gamble paid off. The Adlers had been so expertly packed that the parts suffered little or no damage during their long sojourn on the quays. Stephen was able to assemble eleven perfect Adlers from the twelve cases and, a new car being at the time a precious commodity, got a good price for them.

In 1949 he secured the franchise for the Volkswagen for Ireland, thereby putting himself on the high road to fortune. Yet another gamble had paid off.

In retrospect it seems curious that the franchise should have fallen to Stephen O'Flaherty, since there were several other Irish traders much better placed to acquire it. For instance, his old boss Tommy McCairns almost certainly knew of its availability long

in Co. Donegal, caused Matt to complain to the boss. When Tommy McCairns supported his general manager, Matt McQuaid resigned and set up a partnership with McCarton.

before O'Flaherty did. McCairns claimed it could have been his for the asking because the American representative on the Allied body handling Volkswagen affairs in Germany was a General Motors man who told him about it. Much had been heard before the war of the 'miracle' car Hitler had promised the German people. Of revolutionary design, its low price and low running costs would place it within everyone's reach. But the revolutionary design was a discouraging factor. Would the public, long used to the rectangular car with the engine in front, accept a segment of a circle with the engine at the back? Most experienced traders would have answered 'no'. Besides, there was the much publicised link between the people's car and the vanquished Hitler, the full extent of whose iniquities was only then becoming widely known. Finally, there were the unattractive connotations of a 'people's car'. In 1949 a car was still an important status symbol and few people were prepared to settle for a people's car if they had any choice. So although the Volkswagen franchise was up for grabs no hands appeared to be reaching out eagerly. With English dealers this would have been understandable enough. Not so with Irish dealers, most of whom were quite used to dealing with foreign models. Cahills of the Iona Engineering Works experinced a certain stirring of interest in the VW, but while they were mulling things over Stephen O'Flaherty stepped in and secured the franchise. It was left to Cahills to accept his commission to set up the necessary jigs in his new works in Shelbourne Road, Ballsbridge. Yet Stephen O'Flaherty's intervention had not been at all as unhesitant as it later seemed to have been.

He had gone over to Wolfsburg to see the VW 'beetle' for himself and was appalled by what he saw. Apart from the strange shape and an engine uncooled by water and placed where Irishmen believed God intended luggage to be, the austere, strictly utilitarian trim suggested more a truck driver's cab than the interior of a conveyance for gentlemen. O'Flaherty came home, still suffering from shock, without having been able to nerve himself to make a decision. There had to be a second journey to Wolfsburg, but this time he was accompanied by his wife and the four-legged decision was to go for the franchise. Two more journeys were necessary before the agreement was completed.

The first VWs to take to the Irish roads were, needless to say, great curiosities. Their shape caused much amusement to drivers of British or American models, and this in turn engendered a feeling of special comradeship amongst VW drivers. When passing each other these otherwise total strangers were moved to toot their horns and wave cheerily. The VW soon ceased to be a bit of a joke. The economy and reliability of the air-cooled engine, and its thrilling acceleration, appealed to the non-snobbish. Sales figures rose. It was perhaps not just pure coincidence that the allegation crept into circulation that the VW was a dangerous car to be in in a crash, for there was no weight in front to take the brunt of the impact, leaving driver and front passenger to receive the full force. Presently it was counter-claimed that the VW was particularly safe because by folding up in front like a concertina when in collision it cushioned the occupants against the impact. Whether or not the counter-claim proved more convincing, VW sales continued to soar, Stephen O'Flaherty's fortune likewise. His rivals declared that he could be economical to a fault. For instance, it is said that the tyres on his demonstration car were let go bald, being fitted with a new set only when an important VW official from Germany arrived on an inspection tour. When the official departed, the bald tyres were restored. Even if true this would not make Stephen O'Flaherty unique as a businessman whose left hand pennypinched while his right hand lavished money on champagne parties. In any event it seems highly unlikely that the man heading an increasingly busy assembly plant would have the time to bother himself about the tyres of a demonstration car.

The VW assembly business quickly outgrew the capacity of the Shelbourne Road premises. It so happened that an almost completely built factory building on the Naas Road became available about this time. It had been commissioned by Montague Burton the tailoring magnate, who left instructions that should the factory not be completed at the time of his death, it was to be sold. Stephen O'Flaherty was the beneficiary of this instruction, for Burton died before the place was finished and so in 1955 it became the handsome headquarters of Motor Distributors Ltd.

O'Flaherty's success with the VW in Ireland secured him the franchise for the UK. He also acquired the lucrative Mercedes-Benz franchise for both countries and in 1958 the Renault franchise for Ireland. He eventually sold his UK franchises to Thomas Tillings, and his expired Renault franchise was awarded to Con Smith. His last coup was the introduction of the Toyota to Ireland. As he neared his mid-60s he handed over more and more of his responsibilities to his sons although, as is usual with men such as he, retaining a lively interest in the motor business which had occupied so much of his life. Heart trouble, followed by a stroke, naturally curtailed his activities; but although his speech was affected his mental faculties seem to have suffered little more than the normal wear and tear of seven decades.

So far as the outsider can judge he had few interests that did not involve money, its getting and spending. When he acquired the means he bought racehorses and works of art. If he bought and sold many stately homes, however, this was probably more the effect of his physical restlessness and desire for display than pursuit of profit, for unprofitable they certainly were to a man not interested in farming the land that went with them. Not ungenerous with family and friends he could freely bestow a gift while at the same time leaving the recipient with an uncomfortable feeling that he still regarded as his own what he had just given away. Apart from his domestic partners there was no one who could rightly claim to have got close to him.

According to Dorothy O'Flaherty he had read only one book in his life, *The White Seahorse*. Music made no appeal to him, and no sport or pastime held his interest unless he could stake money on the outcome. He was a keen poker player and often took a hand with that other man of millions Joe McGrath. He had no sentimental feelings about Ireland or the dignity of national independence, and since he laid no claim to have such feelings he cannot properly be charged with hypocrisy. He was quite willing to have Shannon Airport made a headquarters for NATO because this would provide revenue for the state. It goes without saying that he favoured the Napoleonic style in government on the grounds that one-man administrations are the best way to get things done. In an interview with the *Irish Times* when he was sixty-five he gave a clue as to the person he favoured for such an administration. 'I'd like to be dictator in Ireland for about three years,' he remarked. 'My first decision would be to halve the present Dail and double the salaries of the members. Big governments, like big boards of directors, invariably prove the least efficient.'

In middle life, like many another man with his financial muscle, he freely indulged his susceptibility to the attractions of young women; and a person who knew him well has said that when he went off the rails in this activity he did so very thoroughly. His wife seems to have accepted his adventures philosophically, and may even have done so with a certain amusement, for accomplished and independent-minded women can in maturity often rise above jealousy. But Stephen eventually dissolved his partnership of forty-five years with Dorothy and remarried. After a period of adjustment he began to pay regular visits to Dorothy at Sherlockstown House, Co. Kildare, an historic fifteenth-century building only a stone's throw from Bodenstown's famous churchyard, visits which continued up to a short time before his death. When it became clear that his life was drawing to an end, the second Mrs O'Flaherty asked the first to join her in taking leave of the remarkable man whose life they shared, and Dorothy did so. Stephen O'Flaherty died at the last of his scores of residences, the one in Monkstown, Co. Dublin, in the early hours of 16 April 1982. He was eighty.

Some months before he died his home was entered by a group of men claiming to be gardai. They tied him up and took away his wife's jewellery. They also took away a gold bar, the possession of which revealed that Stephen O'Flaherty, shrewd man, did not feel entirely secure with modern paper money.

Archbishop Walsh of Tuam blessing the fleet of Western Petroleum at Headfort, Co. Galway in 1954. Lord Killanin of Irish Shell is on the right.

13

Cabbages and Kings

1

Time changes the junk of one century into the antiques of another, although commerce has now reduced the time span to a mere twenty years or less. Thus the scrap car of the day before yesterday is today's 'vintage' car (the term used to be 'veteran'). What began as an indulgence of the antiquarian or sentimental strain in some people has developed into a profitable business. Vintage cars are no longer proofs of amiable eccentricity: they are assets like old silver or Sheraton sideboards. As the market grows, so does the definition of vintage car expand. It has long passed the stage of being an early model of significant intrinsic interest and/or no little beauty of design, which by a rare combination of circumstances has survived to a well preserved old age. A vintage car can now be made up from a score of old wrecks retrieved from farm sheds or scrapyards: a wheel from this, a mudguard from that, an engine from somewhere else, with a metal worker supplying the rest. The resulting miscellany of ancient and modern is then painted and polished to showroom perfection, entering on a new existence as a relic from 1905 or whatever.

But there are enthusiasts who, declaring themselves free from financial interest, maintain that the true 'vintage' content of many a vintage vehicle may be hardly more than an axle. These sceptics will also hint darkly that they have seen certain registration numbers appearing on different cars, presumably with a view to enhancing the historic interest. What is undeniable is that the vintage market now covers the most trifling accessories. I myself have been shown the brass cap of an old petrol can with a reverence one would have thought excessive with the Book of Kells. As for old cars, there are of course models still surviving which have genuine historical or artistic interest, but in many cases the interest appears to be a got-up thing, deliberately aimed at creating commercial value.

2

Traditionally, the Royal Irish Automobile Club has exercised general supervision over motor car competitions held in the twenty-

192

six home-ruled counties. In general, relations between the Club and the trade were harmonious. In connection with the first International Grand Prix held at the Phoenix Park in July 1929, the Club wrote to record

> its great appreciation of the work done by the members of the Society of Irish Motor Traders, Ltd, in connection with the promotion of, and the arrangements for, the first International Grand Prix held in the Phoenix Park last month, without which the event could not have been the success which it proved to be.
>
> The Committee desires to convey its warmest thanks to all the members of the Society who took part in the arrangements, and in particular to Mr S. T. Robinson to whose energy and ability so much is due.

The golden age in Ireland for such events was between the wars, but the hiatus caused by World War II seems to have blunted the public interest in car racing. A quarter of a century ago the RIAC could list seventeen Irish motor clubs associated with it, including groups like the Irish Volkswagen Club and the Austin Owners' Club (with an address c/o Lincoln & Nolan, the Austin people, in Lower Baggot Street), the very titles of the clubs hinting at the nature of their *raison d'être*. The RIAC could also list half a dozen notable motoring events in every month of the year. Today a blasé public seems neither to know nor care how many such events have survived into the television age. But the motor show retains its attractiveness. These shows aroused such widespread interest from the beginning that they quickly developed a commercial importance in their own right, so quickly that, as we have seen, in the early days the SMMT warned interloping entrepreneurs off the course in order to establish its own monopoly. In January 1907 the Irish Automobile Club organised a show at the RDS, the write-ups claiming that this had given an immense fillip to business:

> there is every prospect of it proving a vastly more important fixture in future, and that having once proved a success, motorists who have decided to purchase new cars will place their orders in Ireland, either at or after the Show, instead of travelling especially to Olympia, and there giving their order to English firms.*

But some prominent traders do not appear to have shared that view. When the Irish Automobile Club announced that it would organise another show at Ballsbridge in 1908, and on a larger scale, there were rumblings of discontent.

Many of the exhibitors complained that the profits from business actually done at the Show did not cover the heavy expenses. The

Motor News, 25 May 1907.

organisers replied that the advantage of displaying one's goods to an interested public must be regarded as a set-off to any paper loss. A hint was dropped that a 50 per cent reduction in charges for space would be given to Irish traders at the 1908 Show. The only response was a declaration signed by twelve traders (virtually the entire Dublin trade) that

> a Motor Show in Ireland is injurious to the interests of the established traders of the city and country generally, and the undersigned have, therefore, pledged themselves not to take space or support in any way the proposal to hold another show at Balls Bridge in 1908.

The Irish Automobile Club, through its secretary H. S. Chaytor, returned to the attack, alleging that the opposition to the 1908 Show had been organised by only one or two traders and that the prospects remained bright. If so they did not remain bright for long. The SMMT interposed with a reminder that the last word remained with itself, all members having signed the bond precluding them from exhibiting anywhere in the UK (which then included Ireland) without SMMT sanction. That put paid to motor shows in Ireland for many years.

In the 1920s the RDS quietly introduced the exhibition of commercial vehicles at their Spring Shows and Horse Shows, using the agricultural machinery umbrella. This was largely the doing of the RDS's agricultural director, the enterprising Edward Bohane CBE, who shared dictatorship of affairs at Ballsbridge with Judge Wylie, a smoother if not smarter operator. Bohane came to the RDS from the Lancashire Agricultural Show and perhaps through use of English connections secured permission to get private cars exhibited at the 1935 Spring Show. This naturally alarmed the Society, which protested to London and extracted the admission that the RDS had obtained permission through a 'misunderstanding'. In the autumn of 1935 the Society approached Edward Bohane with the proposal that he hire them part of the RDS premises for the purpose of holding their own motor show. Bohane swelled up like a turkeycock. From on high he told a deputation from the Society that 'it would not be possible for [the RDS] to consider the letting of [its] premises to any outside organisation owing to the very comprehensive programme which [it] has to get through each year.' Declaring that it was because of representations by traders that the Society proposed to go to the expense of erecting a new hall for the display of motor vehicles, Mr Bohane expressed the hope that the SIMT 'would co-operate with the RDS in its endeavour to encourage the display of Irish assembled vehicles by granting approval for the exhibition of private motor vehicles at the Spring Show'. He would expect the usual approval for the display of commercial vehicles 'and would not permit any interference with that phase of his Society's activities'.

The SIMT response was to remove the Bohanean flea from its ear by refusing approval for the display of private cars at either Spring Show or Horse Show for 1936. Mr Bohane now went public in all the Dublin papers. The SIMT replied, through the same medium, that it claimed the right to manage its affairs in its own way. Bohane now completely lost his head, publicly questioning the SIMT's ability to manage its affairs. Since this fatuity delivered Bohane into the motor traders' hands, they lost no time in despatching him.

> ... the position is simple. For reasons of vital importance to the motor trade itself the public display of private motor vehicles, unless at a time and under conditions suitable to the motor trade, cannot be entertained by our Society, which exists to safeguard the best interests of motor traders generally.

It might be that Bohane was not in the best of health during these exchanges. The following year (1936) he resigned as director, and in 1939 he died. Forty years after the Bohane-SIMT clash, when disagreements between the two societies were so much water under the bridge, the motor industry held its own first show in 1976 at the RDS premises. A resounding success, the SIMI Motor Show is now firmly established as a two-yearly event at Ballsbridge.

3

The work of the Society of the Irish Motor Industry, as it has been called since 1 January 1968, has inevitably grown more complex than that of its ancestors. Since 1967 it has had not only a secretary but a chief executive. It will be remembered that Seamus Moore, since becoming a TD in 1927, had combined his legislative function of doing nothing in particular with the task of doing nothing in particular as secretary of the two motor traders' associations. Since he was also acquiring other responsibilities (as a member of the Dail Commission of Inquiry into Resources and Industries of Ireland, as a director of Arklow Pottery Works, of Irish National Refineries, of Sabin Clothing, etc.) he took his departure in November 1934* and was succeeded by his assistant W. J. Lemass.

'Willie' Lemass was related to *the* Lemass. As he was wont to point out, all the Dublin Lemasses were related, they being descended, he believed, from one Le Masse, a Huguenot immigrant. After serving an apprenticeship to his solicitor cousin Peter Lemass, and putting in a spell as a professional singer (baritone) with the

*He died, still a Fianna Fail TD for Wicklow, on 14 June 1940, leaving £1,893. 11s. 11d.

McNally Opera Singers, he joined the IMTA in 1928 at the age of thirty-eight as organiser and assistant secretary. When he took over as secretary the change soon became apparent. The secretary's contribution was no longer merely that of a wet fish. Council decisions were followed through and implemented. Necessary initiatives were taken and we find the minutes of council meetings no longer recording that the same old ground is being gone over again and again, the same old problems coming up month after month and nothing being done about them. The brisk, efficient way the Bohane affair was handled during the Lemass regime and the speed with which the RDS dictator got his come-uppance, speak volumes for Moore's successor. It is pleasing to record that the council were not unappreciative, for shortly afterwards they raised Lemass's salary from £325 a year to £425, although this was still £75 less than Moore had got. They also brought Lemass's devoted lieutenant Miss Norah O'Brien from £2 a week to £2. 10s. (£2.50).

It should also be mentioned that Lemass, unlike Moore, was not niggardly in praising the work of those who assisted him.

One of Willie Lemass's shrewdest achievements was to steer the Society towards the purchase of its present headquarters, No. 5 Upper Pembroke Street. In 1939 the Society had moved from 31 Upper Merrion Street to 82 Merrion Square.* In November 1953 the landlady, Miss E. G. Butler, asked the Society to move from the 'return' section of the house to the basement, adding that the rent paid by the Society was much below the going rate and that she had asked Messrs Allen & Townsend to make a valuation which would suggest a more realistic figure. Willie Lemass seems to have gone househunting right away, and soon entered into negotiations on the Society's behalf to acquire the Upper Pembroke Street house, then a private residence. A preliminary offer of £3,500 having been turned down, the deal was closed at £4,000. The Society certainly did not lose on the transaction.

The bustling activity of his early years as secretary inevitably made Willie Lemass a very prominent figure, as his nickname, Mister Motor Trade, testifies. Being by nature extremely sociable he liked to do business by making personal visits rather than by phoning or writing, his hobbies providing additional scope for this attribute. During his secretaryship he was also hon. sec. of the Irish Motor and Cycle Trades Golfing Association; he was one of the oldest members of the Bohemians Musical Society and was by no means the least active member of the Dublin Grand Opera Society. Willie Lemass was to continue in office until the age of seventy-five, an age at which he could hardly be expected to cope with the increasingly heavy workload of secretary. The council was not unaware of the situation and ordained, a few years before the event, that Willie should at seventy-five be relieved of the secretaryship and allocated a post with less arduous duties and that Joe Quinn, the assistant secretary, if he succeeded Willie, should retire at seventy. So Willie laid down the reins at seventy-five and was appointed a director of Fiat (Ireland) Ltd, a position he retained until his death in May 1973.

He was succeeded by Joe Quinn, whose tenure of office was brief. It is generally acknowledged that Joe Quinn worked far too hard, so that although there was much regret at his sudden death in February 1966 after less than a year in the job, there was little surprise.

4

As has already been recorded, it had long been clear that much of the work of SIMT and IMTA had tended to overlap. The common-

*In the 1920s the home of William Butler Yeats.

197

sense amalgamation was planned during 1967 and the Society of the Irish Motor Industry officially came into existence on 1 January 1968. Billy Wilkinson was president at the time of the merger, and the members of the sub-committee who were responsible for making the recommendation for change were himself, M. J. McQuaid, J. T. Barton, Hugh de L. Crawford, J. D. Wyer, J. C. Dixon, and J. N. Sheridan. Leo Keogh, the Dubliner who had been heading RGDATA (the organisation representing the grocery trade in Ireland) was appointed chief executive of the new body and the sempiternally youthful looking Robert D. E. Prole, a son of Dundalk, became secretary.

As motoring in Ireland nears its first century of existence, it can be noted that a certain decorum, appropriate to the centenarian, has descended upon those connected with it. The decrease in the number of eccentrics or colourful characters is very marked, but then such personages are getting rarer in all walks of life. Eccentrics are a threatened species. Many of yesterday's amusing oddities of character are today's psychiatric disorders, the eccentric now becoming a patient who is either whisked off for hospital treatment or else has his symptoms suppressed with tablets. Who can conceive of any person today being allowed to manage a large and important motor business on the basis of weekend teetotalism followed by a Monday-to-Friday binge behind locked office doors on a case of Hennessy's brandy? This story, as related by Matt J. McQuaid, 1966 President of SIMT, is guaranteed by him to be fact not fantasy. Is there now in Ireland any car sales manager driving around the country in a Rolls-Royce, halting drivers of a certain model with a banknote? On the other hand there are no longer owner-managers of large assembly plants in a position to stand Napoleonically on their showroom staircases and bellow out a week's notice to a quaking senior salesman. For better for for worse they, together with pistol packing motorists like Dr Colohan, have gone the way of all flesh. But who shall declare that we'll never see their like again?

The modern age. Ireland's first motorway, the M1 between Belfast and Lisburn, which was opened in July 1962.

Motor People

Oswald Barton was born on 31 March 1895, in Chorley, Lancashire, served in World War I and when discharged decided to settle in Ireland. (He had a married sister living in Dublin and had spent his period of convalescence with her on being invalided home after the first gas attack in the Ypres sector. During this visit he married an Irish girl.)

In youth he had studied at the agricultural college in Preston and put his knowledge to use by setting up a farm machinery business in Rathdrum, Co. Wicklow, with a Mr Sutton. He bought one of the first tractors to become available in Ireland and, with Mr Sutton, designed ploughs and mowing machines suitable for use with a tractor. As the post-war economic depression affected agriculture, the farmers were in no mood to venture into hiring the new-fangled machinery, so Oswald Barton returned to Dublin. For a time he was an assessor for Lloyds, dealing with insurance claims in respect of cars damaged during the troubles. His reputation for fair dealing regardless of political affiliations gained him acceptance by all sides, so that the former British army officer found himself dealing quite comfortably not only with those who discussed differences on an intellectual plane but with those who might be shooting at one another within hours of lodging claims with Oswald Barton.

After an introduction to R. W. Archer, he entered the motor trade as a salesman in Lincoln & Nolan. This firm secured the Austin agency for Ireland in the mid-1920s and Oswald Barton believes he was the first man in Ireland to drive an Austin 7.

The Ever Ready Garage had been opened in Donnybrook in 1927 in part of what had been a potato field, and in earlier times part of the site of Donnybrook Fair. At first the venture did not prosper. The shareholders sold out to Freddie Smith who in 1929 offered Oswald Barton a partnership on a 50-50 basis. Barton accepted the offer and presently was appointed an Austin agent. Later he bought Smith's half of the business.

Oswald Barton believes the Ever Ready Garage was the first in the country to have its petrol pump area under cover. He got the idea while driving in England with his sister during a rainstorm. They needed petrol but she said she would keep on driving until they came to a covered-in station. Perceiving the sales advantage of such a cover, Oswald Barton had one erected at the Ever Ready on his return to Ireland and found it led to an enormous increase in sales. The Ever Ready was also amongst the first garages in Ireland to instal electric pumps.

The Second World War obliged the Ever Ready Garage to cut its mechanical staff to two, their work consisting mainly of occasionally starting up customers' cars laid up for the war period. But the garage's principal source of income was from offering parking space for bicycles at a shilling (5p.) a day. Virtually all their staff rejoined them after the war (one mechanic, Dan Kennedy, was with them for half a century).

Oswald Barton retired from active participation in the business in 1962, handing over to his sons James and Oswald.

Hugh Cahill was the founder of one of the oldest and most important firms on the north side of the city, the Iona Garage. He established it in 1923 and managed it until his death, after which it was run by his son Pearse. Hugh Cahill was very energetic and enterprising but, according to Pearse, 'didn't know the front of a car from the back'. His first venture was the Central Decorating & Window Cleaning Co., which had its offices above the Dublin Coal Co. premises at 5 D'Olier Street. Presently Hugh branched into the taxi business as the Irish Taximeter Hire Company, building up a large fleet of Maxwells, Hupmobiles and Buicks. There was a Rolls-Royce for those who required grandeur. In 1932 Hugh Cahill had an enormous fleet on the road as there was no tax that year, the government wanting to have as many cars as possible available for the Eucharistic Congress. He also became interested in the aviation business, founding Iona National Airways Ltd in 1930, first sited at Baldonnel but, from the following year, at Kildonan, Finglas, where he built Ireland's first civil aerodrome. Iona Airways boomed during the Eucharistic Congress, having a dozen planes in service to carry British newspapermen between the two islands. But the arrival of Aer Lingus put paid to Hugh Cahill's aviation business and he baled out after five years of spending a lot without making a penny.

Hugh felt he was entitled to be appointed an Aer Lingus director but, Pearse says, 'he voted for the wrong government'. Incidentally, Aer Lingus's early staff were drawn from Iona Airways, including their first pilot, engineer, and storeman. Hugh Cahill frowned on Pearse's determination to re-enter the aviation business after the war. (Pearse Cahill had learned to fly in the 1930s.) But in Pearse's view the car business had by then become too cut-throat and seemed to be utterly out of control.

However, the core of the Cahill business was the Iona Garage, which Hugh had built behind the famous pub, Brian Boru House, on Prospect Road. He took on the Dodge agency from John O'Neill Ltd of Pleasants Street, the importers of this model, using Dodges for the taxi business. The Iona Garage also did a lot of engineering work, fitting Gardiner engines to buses for the Wicklow Hills Company, converting fourteen of these to 5-cylinder Gardiner diesel engines. (As Gardiner also made marine engines, the Iona were able to fit these to fishing boats.) In the 1930s the Iona had the contract to service the tanker lorries of the Irish-American Oil Company (now Esso) and Shell. But towards the end of the 1950s the oil companies introduced their solo-site policy. Against Pearse's advice Hugh Cahill went solo, clinching a deal with Caltex, 'for a few shillings', says Pearse, 'whereupon Shell and Esso withdrew their fleets from us'. Since there were few filling stations in the area (for many years Iona's nearest competitors were at Phibsboro and Binns Bridge), Hugh Cahill built another garage at the top of Whitworth Road, which soon had the highest petrol sales in the city after the LSE Garage. This encouraged Hugh to open another garage on the other side of the street to catch traffic from the opposite direction. But he hadn't reckoned on the traffic congestion and when traffic lights were put up and cars couldn't easily get in or out of the garages, petrol sales suddenly dropped away to nothing.

Hugh Cahill and Pearse had gone to the Paris Motor Show in 1948 to look for an agency. Pearse was anxious to see the Volkswagens, but the French government would not allow German cars to be exhibited in Paris at that time. At almost every stand Pearse Cahill found that on saying he was from Ireland, the response invariably was, 'Do you know Mr Stephen O'Flaherty? He is one step ahead of you.'

Pearse Cahill is now (1983) still running his air-taxi and charter firm, Iona National Airways Ltd, from Dublin Airport. For many years he has been the agent for the Cessna plane.

His father died in March 1966 at the age of 86 and, being buried in Glasnevin Cemetery, is only a little distance from where he had lived and worked most of his long life.

Denis Dennehy, Snr, chairman of Dennehy's Cross Garage in Cork, who died in 1982, was a leading figure in the trade for many years. His father's farmyard was on the site of the present garage. They had a milk run and each of the five boys and two girls in the family had to deliver the milk in turn before going to school. 'We had two donkeys – one for the morning and one for the afternoon deliveries. But on Sundays we had a horse and van – and we all wanted to drive the van: it was like a Rolls-Royce to me'.

There was a little workshop in the farmyard in which Denis and his brothers used to do the occasional repair job on cars, but his first regular job was in a shell factory in Oliver Plunket Street. That was in 1916, he had just left school, and the wages were ten shillings (50p.) a week. He stayed until the war ended, by which time he had gained promotion and was earning £2 10s. 0d. (£2.50) a week. After some brief spells in an engineering works and a garage (Johnson & Perrott's in MacCurtain Street) he emigrated to the United States, returning four years later in 1932, the richer by experience of work in a firearms company, an oil company and a truck company. A brother and he bought an ex-War Department solid-tyre 5-ton truck for £37, stripped it down, painted it, and contracted with the County Council to draw gravel from Barryscourt, Carrigtwohill, to the Kinsale Road, which was then being concreted. There was no tipping gear on trucks at the time: it was a case of shovel in, shovel out. The prospering career of the ex-War Department truck was cut short after about a year when a bus crashed into it. Out of his £130 compensation Denis Dennehy bought a Leyland and a Ford truck, both solid-tyred, for £90. He immediately fitted them with pneumatics, presently added an old Dennis 4-ton to his little fleet, and, in due course, a 6-ton Dodge. He and his driving staff, a man named Crowe, traded as the Leeside Carrying Company. Before long they had expanded into parcel deliveries.

An Englishman named Smith open a haulage depot near Merricks and organised a delivery service to all towns on the main road between Cork and Dublin. He offered Denis Dennehy £25 for a full load each way, 'a lot of money at that time', as Denis remarked. During a railway strike business boomed. The nationalisation of public transport in 1936 brought an end to the Leeside Carrying Company, which was taken over by the Irish Omnibus Company at what Denis Dennehy described as 'very poor compensation'.

It was now that Denis entered the garage business. His brother was running a shop and some petrol pumps at the Cross, employing two girls but being hard put to it to make enough to pay their wages. Denis put money into developing the business. Another storey was added to the shop and an adjoining vegetable store was turned into a garage which was added to as business increased. Denis Dennehy's first dealership was for International trucks; he then went to Chevrolet cars and from these to Austin trucks and vans.

Denis Dennehy regarded the commercial vehicle side of the business as 'the dirty end of the stick' compared with the private car end. When Austins refused him a car dealership he went over to the Morris truck ('at a ½% more'), and began selling the Morris against the Austin 'although they were only the same trucks with different badges'.

The result was that an emissary from the Austin main dealers in Dublin, Lincoln & Nolan, arrived at Dennehy's Garage and carried Denis and his wife off to dine at the Metropole Hotel and discuss a return to the Austin fold. He refused unless he was given their cars to sell as well as their trucks, and this was denied him. But the emissary came down to Cork again and eventually the point was conceded by Lincoln & Nolan. They were, Denis Dennehy recalled, a very decent firm to deal with, and not people to dun you for cheques the very moment the money was due. But such gentlemanly restraint went by the board, he alleged, when Lincoln & Nolan were taken over by Brittains.

In January 1976 Dennehy's was appointed Ford main dealers.

Andrew Joseph Doyle (Andy Doyle to everyone in the trade), the first Roman Catholic to open a garage in Dublin and get a footing in the motor business, came from Baltinglass, Co. Wicklow, where various members of the family were publicans, grocers, butchers, carpenters and blacksmiths. In the mid 1920s Andy Doyle took Dublin by storm, opening in South King Street beside the Gaiety Theatre; around the corner in St Stephen's Green in what is now the Green Cinema; in South William Street, Dominick Street and Marks Lane, where he had his service depot. His eventual headquarters was in Bachelors Walk. In 1931 Andy Doyle engaged as service and production manager the now legendary Pat Flanagan, then newly returned from a five-year stint in America with Packard and other manufacturers.

One day a large crate arrived from America at Doyle Motors. It contained a knocked down Federal truck, for which Doyle had just secured the agency. Pat Flanagan is reputed to have assembled this truck with a 7-lb hammer, cold rivets and an anvil. He also assembled Graham cars, although whether by the same method has not been recorded by his friends.

Andy Doyle was not only building up his General Motors agency but was also into accessories and the electrical side of the business (Traders Magneto and Dynamo Co.). He also undertook to deliver the *Irish Independent* newspaper throughout the country, and to this end assigned a crack driver named Jimmy Fortune to the inaugural Cork run. Using a Bedford-Chevrolet van on what was to be called the Dawn Patrol, Jimmy, accompanied by an observer from the *Independent*, got to Cork in three hours and twenty-three minutes, collecting, according to Owen Hayes, twenty-seven summonses for dangerous driving. Jimmy Fortune seems to have been well named, for the twenty-seven offences were all expiated by a small fine. But that was the end of Andy Doyle's Dawn Patrol.

In 1933 or thereabouts, Arthur Cherrick, who had a garage on Upper Rathmines Road, started putting into action his plan to build a filling station on a site beside what was then the Harcourt

Street rail terminus. The deal fell through so Andy Doyle moved in, setting up a station called Auto Services. Andy seems to have been badly undercapitalised. In order to equip Auto Services he had to transfer pumps from his other premises and accept A. P. Reynolds as a partner. Unfortunately Andy Doyle fell foul of the Revenue Commissioners and as a result of what became known as the Weights Case,* went out of business, leaving Reynolds to take over. When Reynolds became general manager of the Dublin United Tramways Co., John P. McEnroe (see biography of Owen Hayes) took charge of the former Andy Doyle empire.

Pat Flanagan, who for more than forty years was a pillar of McCairns Motors at Santry, claims, 'There was a time when I could recognise every motor car in Dublin by its sound.' He drew up a list of all the models he could remember in the city streets from the time he began to take notice ('I was always mad about motoring') and it was certainly a nice trick to be able to identify each by sound alone. The list includes:

Cesan Nadin, SPA, Brasier, Clement Talbot, Napier, Swift, Daimler, Gregoire, Delage, Standard, Peugeot, Bayard, Chenard Walker, Hudson, Essex, Hupmobile, Nash, De Dion, Mass Paige, Bedford Buick, Belsize, ZL, Zebra, Mosley, Hotchkiss, Stellite Wolsley, Calthorpe, Thomond, Argyle, Scat, Schnider, Morgan (a three wheeler), AC (another three wheeler), GWK, Styer, Arrol Johnston, Rover, Dellany Benville (it had two pistons per cylinder), BSA, Pierce Arrow, Locomobile, Fiat, Bugatti, Renault, Cadillac, Stanley, Steamer, Adler, Stevens Dores, Overland, Franklin, Winston, Statts, Mercedes, Opel, Oldsmobile, Chevrolet, Ford.

The models Pat Flanagan most vividly remembers include the Charron Laycock, Ajax, Dixie Flyer, Case, King, Cleveland, Horseman, Marlboro, Aldayse and Onions, Studebaker, Chambers (the Belfast-made model, rather expensive), Bean (sold in Dublin, says Pat Flanagan, by a man named Byrne who was supposed to have drawn up the Irish Free State Constitution), Scripps Booth, Cubit, Citroën, Saldo, Stanley (a three-cylinder with the steering wheel in the middle, made by Armstrong Siddeley), Siddeley Deasie, Westbury, Tamplan Vision, Vinot, Beardmore, Triumph, Bristol, Marquette, Lee Francis, Cord, Saxton, Star, Marmon, Lincoln, Pontiac, and Graham.

*Road-Tax on commercial vehicles was calculated according to their gross weight. Vehicles were accordingly presented at their minimum weight, which was quite legal. But the Revenue Commissioners took action when they discovered that vehicles were being stripped of essential parts before weighing in, even the radiator and fuel tank being left empty.

Pat Flanagan explains the huge number of different models in Ireland as caused by the way in which cars were bought. In those early days the motoring enthusiast would visit the Paris or London show and select the model that appealed to him. It was then shipped to Dublin. As a result, when the car was due for overhaul it would be brought to a garage where the mechanics might never have come across a similar model before. There were few tools in such garages and the non-availability of spare parts had to be compensated for by ingenuity and craftsmanship. Overhauling a large car could take several weeks. The body was lifted off and taken away for repainting, polishing and refurbishing. The engine was assigned to one man, the back axle and gearbox to another. 'We could take down the entire engine. Worn parts would be replaced by copies made by a blacksmith or ourselves. Everything would be thoroughly cleaned before it was put back. We learned to do everything from straightening a chassis to putting glass in the windows.'

Many of the mechanics in those early days had come here from England or from France. 'They had high rates and were allowed expenses because of living away from home. They kept their craft to themselves and were slow to pass on information to the young Irish lads. As a matter of fact the trade didn't loosen up until Ford started to issue workshop manuals and other information!'

Nevertheless some Irish mechanics successfully held out for the 'foreign' rates, which worked out at 1s. 9d. an hour (about 8¾p), or £4.25 a week. The fitters were paid £3 a week. These rates remained standard until 1945.

Pat Flanagan was born in Dalkey, Co. Dublin (in a pub) in 1903. Shortly afterwards the Flanagans moved into the city where Pat grew up in the Dawson Street area, then a thoroughfare dedicated to the trade he was presently to join. The first cars he remembers were small Peugeots and De Dions driven by men with goggles, whose lady passengers were heavily veiled to protect their faces from the dust. 'As the roads weren't tarred, any vehicle moving at a reasonable speed in dry weather would throw up a cloud of dust which could be seen for miles around.' At sixteen he was apprenticed to the Central Service Motor Co., 54 Upper Baggot Street, which was run by William F. Kelly, a motoring enthusiast and something of an inventor who had himself worked with Waytes Bros of Harry Street. He served a seven-year apprenticeship at Central Service, starting by mending tyres on prams ('You can't start any lower than that!') and working his way up through bicycles and motor-bikes to cars. No spares for any car except Fords were available, and there was only one firm in Dublin, Robinsons of South King Street, which could grind out a cylinder.

Carrying out repairs in those days in small garages was not free from hazard. Pat Flanagan recalls trying to lift the engine from a car by means of a pulley and rope slung from a roof girder. The engine didn't lift: the roof fell down.

After completing his apprenticeship with the Central Service Motor Co., Pat Flanagan went to America to gain experience. 'There wasn't the same enthusiasm there as in Ireland. I soon found out the Irish mechanic was way ahead of his American counterpart.' He spent five years in America, returning to Ireland in 1931 when, aged twenty-eight, he joined Doyle Motors as service manager and production manager, remaining for seven years before moving to McCairns Motors to begin his forty-year stint with them. There he became general works manager, assembling Chevrolets, Buicks, Vauxhalls and trucks, holding this post until the 1960s when he was appointed to run the factory servicing operation.

He had bought his first car, a Maxwell, in America. Before that in Ireland he had owned eight motor-bikes, and was never short of a car to drive. He got his first driving licence in 1919 when he was sixteen: it was merely a matter of sending a five-shilling fee (25p) to an office in Dublin Castle.

During the troubles he had to get a special driving permit as well as a licence. Under the Defence of the Realm Act three people constituted a crowd, so a driver with two passengers needed a permit with his photograph affixed. Pat Flanagan was, somewhat to his surprise, readily granted a permit.

Owen Hayes was studying medicine when the death of his father, who held a post in the army's medical services, obliged him to earn his living sooner than intended. In 1930 he joined Tom Rogers of South King Street, agent for an Italian car called the Ansaldo and an Austrian, the Styer. His wage was 5s. (25p.) a week. Two months later he moved to A. J. (Andy) Doyle, a neighbouring dealer in South King Street, at double that wage. Andy Doyle had several premises at that time including a showroom at Bachelors Walk. Owen Hayes took over part of the territory for the Bedford-Chevrolet trucks. The demonstration models had no body, a garden seat being placed across the front of the chassis for the driver. Owen Hayes was obliged to wear cap, goggles and a leather coat lined with newspaper in order to keep warm. The sight of nude trucks rattling through Dublin on demonstration trips seems to have suggested there was an opening here for local coachbuilders. Kellegher & Barrington of 89–92 The Coombe were quick to seize the opportunity, as was an immigrant Englishman called Roberts, who did particularly well. Hayes remembers having to deliver a Vauxhall Cadet to a Fr McHugh in Galway. The following day he went to Sunday Mass celebrated by Fr McHugh. The church was crowded, but he and the priest were the only members of the congregation wearing shoes.

Meanwhile Doyle Motors had acquired a new manager and re-organiser in the person of John P. McEnroe, a Cavan man. Mr McEnroe, who liked to be recorded as possessing a B.A. and H.Dip.Ed. (N.U.I.), appointed Owen Hayes sales manager at the Auto Services Garage in Harcourt Street. Hayes, needing a salesman, enlisted Matt McQuaid, who had just left Brittain's. Owen Hayes believes the two of them 'made a very good go of it,' but he wasn't able to see eye to eye with McEnroe and left abruptly. However he was not out of a job for long. Johnny O'Hagan of Ferguson's of 134/5 Lower Baggot Street offered him a sales managership at £400 a year. They sold a lot of Austins until the war broke out 'and on the Monday morning I lost my job'.

It was a nasty blow to a married man with an infant son, but luckily he got a job as an inspector with the Pigs and Bacon Commission, until the opportunity came to join the army as a second lieutenant.

Several traders had been enlisted for a course to organise motorised transport, the army up to then having relied quite heavily on the horse. On concluding the course Lieut Hayes was posted to the Phoenix Park as transport officer although, as he recalls, 'we had no transport'. He left the army on 1 January 1946, rejoining Fergusons as sales manager the same day.

No new cars were available, of course, but Fergusons bought used cars and gradually built up the business with them. But at this time Harry Ferguson was actively developing his tractors and ploughs and since Owen Hayes 'did not want to get involved in agriculture' he accepted an offer to join the LSE Motor Co. as manager. Subsequently, he became a director.

The once famous LSE Motor Company — famous because from its foundation at 35 North Frederick Street in 1918 its petrol pumps remained open twenty-four hours a day — was founded by Edward Lemass and his brother Peter, dispensary doctor in Rathmines, Kevin Smith and Albert Eager, their surname initials making up the name of the company. They also ran a taxi-service, using Daimlers, and were limited Ford main dealers. Soon after taking up his position Owen Hayes persuaded his LSE colleagues to leave Ford and become Austin, Rootes and Morris dealers. Later they concentrated exclusively on Rootes (which ultimately became Chrysler), moving to the former Kennedy's Bakery in Dorset Street.

Owen Hayes describes as 'some of the great characters in the business', Bob and Arthur McMahon 'who built an empire in Donegal', Dermot O'Donovan and Dan Ryan of Limerick, and Fergus Cross of Cork.

Arthur H. Huet started in a flax mills, the Bessbrook Spinning Company, a couple of miles from Newry along the road to

Armagh. Dunlops used a lot of linen in manufacturing tyres, which circumstance, together with the Huguenot connection, brought Arthur Huet and Harvey du Cros into contact with each other. They got on well together and Arthur joined Dunlops. After a spell as manager in the Dublin branch he was transferred to Birmingham where he became 'commercial manager'. During the reorganisation of the firm under Geddes and Beharrel in the early 1920s he returned to Ireland as managing director of the Dublin branch, which was moved to imposing new headquarters, Dunlop House, in Lower Abbey Street. Arthur's active service with the company ended in the early 1930s.

But he was not the kind of man to retire and twiddle his thumbs. He had played a major part in setting up a garage and showrooms, Clanwilliam Motors, at Nos 1 and 2 Clanwilliam Place, Mount Street Bridge, originally a pair of private houses which had been badly damaged in the 1916 fighting. His junior partner was a local builder whose contribution included the erection of the new building, and who also managed the new enterprise. The 1929 depression knocked Clanwilliam Motors on the head, but after a couple of years Arthur restarted it as Huet Motors Ltd, with his sons Percy and Dermot as managers and himself as very active chairman.

It was Arthur Huet who brought Tommy McCairns into the motor trade in Ireland. This was really in the nature of a compliment returned because Tommy, in his capacity as Champion Plugs representative in Ireland, had divided the franchise between Huet Bros (Arthur's cousins and already well established as cycle agents) and Brown Bros. Huet Bros had the advantage in Tommy's eyes of possessing a depot in Belfast as well.

Huet Motors prospered mightily between its rebirth and the outbreak of the Second World War, chiefly because of Arthur's tightly controlling hand and his co-operative business connections. Huets had a lucrative arrangement with Bewleys and Findlaters (the grocery chain, extinct now) whereby they serviced their large fleets of vans and representatives' cars, supplying new vehicles as required. But at the end of 1938 Huets was obliged to share the prize with W. B. Crawfords, this causing a noticeable dip in their profits, which the outbreak of war deepened into disaster, as it did with most other firms.

After the war Tommy McCairns again put some valuable business in the the Huets' way. He had been pressed by Rolls-Royce to take on their Irish agency but was unwilling to do so, recommending Huet Motors in his stead. Rolls-Royce agreed, and a gratified Percy and Dermot Huet promised Tommy that if ever he wished to buy an R-R it would be at an agreeable price. Tommy had no intention of acquiring one, but later, in deference to his wife's wishes, he went to Huet Motors, cheque book at the ready. He was, he said, a little put out to find that the new management did not feel obliged to honour Percy's and Dermot's undertaking. This, however, didn't prevent Tommy making a purchase.

Arthur Huet took a fairly active part in the running of the Irish Motor Traders' Association in the early days, chairing many meetings in what appears from the minutes to have been a businesslike manner. For some years he lived in South-hill, Mount Merrion Avenue, Blackrock, Co. Dublin, which forty years earlier had been occupied by Harvey du Cros. The house had a long connection with the motor trade. In the 1920s it was occupied by Charles Jacob, the wholesale cycle and motor accessory factor of Pearse Street. Even now (1981) when South-hill is a Dominican convent, one of the community is Sister Dominic Joseph, a daughter of John O'Neill, the Dodge importer. Arthur Huet died on 19 May 1951, leaving £35,237.

Thomas McCairns — Tom or Tommy to all who knew him — was brought into the motor business by Gordon Selfridge, owner of the Oxford Street store. Selfridge had branched into car sales and presently found himself with a miscellaneous collection of vehicles in an offshoot of his store. The vehicles appeared to be making it their permanent residence. He invited Tommy McCairns to move them for him, which he quickly did. Selfridge then gave him an introduction to General Motors, thus putting him on the high road to success.

Tommy McCairns was born 29 October 1896 in Grimsby, Yorkshire, by his own account the son of a professional cricketer and footballer. Discharged from the British army in 1918, a victim of shell shock, he became Irish representative for the Champion Spark Plug Co. spending the next four years travelling, he said, 'almost every navigable road in Ireland'. He adds that a journey of any great length in those days was 'an adventure', neither cars nor roads being dependable. After four years of this he had firmly established Champion plugs in Ireland. There followed the Selfridge interlude and the introduction to General Motors and his appointment as their Irish representative. Since he was paid at GM's American rate of £3,000 a year, he was by Irish standards a plutocrat, an image Tommy strengthened by staying in a suite at the Royal Hibernian Hotel when in Dublin.

The then importer of GM cars was Andrew Doyle Ltd, who had a showrooms at 128 St Stephen's Green and other premises nearby. Tommy McCairns's job was to develop the sales of GM cars and trucks all over Ireland, which in effect were Buick cars and Chevrolet trucks. It was an uphill job. Sales in those days were few and knowledge of servicing limited. GM's first exports manager was an Irishman, J. D. Mooney, and it was he who negotiated the acquisition of Vauxhall and Opel. Thus the Vauxhall was introduced to Ireland and their Bedford trucks gradually replaced the Chevrolet.

Before being taken over by GM, Vauxhall Motors were producing semi-coach-built and somewhat expensive cars. (Bernard Shaw had one, of which he was very fond. He toured Kerry in it.) With the imposition of American methods and policy, the Vauxhall developed a more popular appeal at a more popular price.

When the native assembly industry was established, GM and Vauxhall arranged with McCairns to form an assembly company. Thus came into being McCairns Motors Ltd, with an assembly works at Alexandra Road, East Wall, a parts depot in Nassau Street, a sales showrooms in Dawson Street and a service station off Waterloo Road. The assembly works in the heart of dockland was of course ideally situated. It was secured by Tommy through the good offices of T. F. Laurie, managing director of the Irish-American Oil Co. (now Esso), which also had premises in Alexandra Road. (Mr Laurie was a shipping member of the Dublin Port and Docks Board.) In 1935, their first full year, McCairns Motors assembled 328 cars. The figures during the war years tell their own story: 1940 (206), 1941 (18), 1942 (2), 1943–4 (nil), 1945 (5).

During the war McCairns were asked by the British government to send a team to Northern Ireland to assemble four-wheel-drive trucks for use in the desert campaign. The factory was in Carrickfergus, and the McCairns team were able to train such unlikely people as farm labourers and milkmen to build the trucks. Tommy McCairns used claim that his company received a citation from the British Ministry of Supply in recognition of their contribution to the war effort. How all this squares with Irish neutrality must be left to readers to work out for themselves.

After the war Tommy McCairns got the opportunity to acquire a useful site with excellent prospects at Santry. It comprised twenty-two acres and was bought at the knock-down price of £620 an acre. The problem of getting steel to construct the works — steel being then in extremely short supply — was overcome by Tommy by the purchase of British government surplus girders for Bailey bridges. Tommy admitted that neither he nor any of his staff had the faintest notion of how these girders were to be assembled. But a way was found and the imposing new premises was ready for occupation in 1951.

Incidentally, a number of the surplus girders were used by CIE to repair the Loop Line railway bridge over the Liffey.

Not the least interesting document in Tommy McCairns's archives is an application to him for a job as accounts clerk. The candidate got the job, did well, was appointed secretary to the company and ended up as its general manager. His name was Stephen O'Flaherty.

In 1973, which was their last complete year in the assembly side of the business, McCairns assembled some 5,500 vehicles. But they were now obliged to move away from assembly because General Motors decided to set up their own distribution organisation here. An arrangement was come to with the government whereby GM would open a plant in Tallaght, Co. Dublin, and would be licensed to import a sufficiency of fully built-up vehicles. By the end of 1974 McCairns Motors were completely out of assembly and in 1976 the firm was sold to the PMPA, Tommy remaining as chairman until his death in November 1982 at the age of eighty-six.

Tommy McCairns was extrovert to a notable degree and very much in love with life. Life returned his affection, indulgently allowing him to reach patriarchal age although he was much over-weight and much addicted to smoking. His great interest was horse-racing and here again life was kind, for he won the Irish St Leger with Vimadee and the Queen Anne Stakes at Ascot with Upadee.

Needless to say he loved entertaining, not merely as host but as performer. At the Vauxhall Ball (of which memories still linger in the trade) and at personal parties he was seldom found unwilling to respond to calls for his comic rendering of 'Tiptoe through the Tulips.'

Matt McQuaid was born on 16 April 1907 in Cootehill, Co. Cavan, where his father was the dispensary doctor. The doctor got through three horses before acquiring his first car, a two-seater Renault, which was followed by a stately Humber which, according to his son, required two men and a suit of clothes to start. His mother was a Dublin girl, a pianist who had played in the Irish village at the World Fair in Chicago in 1893 and had had breakfast with Buffalo Bill. (Lest the wrong inference be drawn from this, Matt McQuaid emphasises that in those days it was as much the accepted thing to invite people to breakfast as to dinner.)

Matt McQuaid was training to be a marine wireless officer when a chance introduction to one of the directors of MacLysaght & Douglas secured him, about 1925, an apprenticeship at their premises in Dawson Street. The firm, which was chiefly an agency for Ajax tyres, also handled the Peugeot, Hupmobile and Beam. Matt McQuaid recalls that the Hupmobile arrived crated, the crates being 'marvellous'. His first job with McLysaght & Douglas was to fit tyres to the Peugeots which were unloaded tyreless at South Dock (where the big gasometer now stands). Between ten and twenty cars arrived in each consignment and young Matt became so expert in trye fitting that he believes he set up some records for the period.

Matt McQuaid has vivid memories of a Peugeot model called the Quad. The Quad had a solid back axle and no differential and the wheels used 'squeal like hell'. Nevertheless the Quad sold quite well but the Peugeot six-cylinder model which followed it did not. Matt McQuaid offers a good and sufficient reason: 'You couldn't start the bloody thing!'

Matt McQuaid ventured briefly into the motor-cycle and cycle business at the beginning of the 1930s with his friend Tyrrell Smith the racing cyclist. The venture didn't prosper, so after stints as salesman with Brittains and McCairns he tried another partnership: McQuaid and McCarton in Haddington Road. It was a good pitch: right opposite a church and a pub. The war finished the partnership. Matt McQuaid joined the Transport Corps in the army where, he says, George Briggs, Billy Wilkinson, Harold Ray, Alex Powderley, Matt Kavanagh and Cyril McCormack formed a happy band.

In September 1945 Matt McQuaid left the army and joined McEntaggarts of Percy Place, agents for Standard cars, as sales manager. After two weeks as sales manager he was told someone had bungled his discharge papers and he was asked to go back to the barracks two days a week just to walk around and be seen until, after a couple of months, the complicated task of getting Matt McQuaid's discharge papers right could be achieved by the military.

He remained with McEntaggarts and eventually joined the board. This firm was also the agent for the famous American model the Packard, which Matt McQuaid remembers as 'a wonderful car'. Not the least of the wonders connected with it was that no shortages were ever discovered when it came to assembly. McEntaggart's also built Hudsons for Ernest Bell of Assemblers Ltd.

Matt McQuaid was president of SIMT and IMTA for 1966–7, 'which was enough for them', he says.

Michael John O'Neill — generally known as John O'Neill — was a Co. Carlow man who worked in Dunlops, a firm, he told his children, that was very strict on its employees. In his thirties he set up in 13/14 South King Street as a maker of bicycles (the Lucania), taking larger premises the following year in Pleasants Street where he diversified into tinware and became an agent for gramophones.

In the 1920s he started as a motor agent in St Stephen's Green, with his four sons helping in the business, Tom being the chief salesman. The business, however, owed a lot of its success to O'Neill's excellent manager and right-hand man, James Moore, who had been with him from the beginning.

When assembly became the order of the day, O'Neills took on Dodge cars and trucks, which proved highly popular. The state cars of the 1930s were Dodges, and the model was much favoured by those businessmen who did not opt for one of the Summerfield Chryslers. John O'Neill, who had married an Elliott girl, one of the famous poplin manufacturers of Weaver Square in the Dublin Liberties, was a senator, served as president for 1927 of the IMTA, and as chairman of the White Cross. Pat Flanagan describes him as the perfect gentleman. 'I remember going to him to ask advice on assembly as it was new to me. He opened his factory door and invited me to see everything and ask any questions I wished.'

John O'Neill died, aged sixty-four, in December 1941. After his death the business was carried on by his four sons, ending up with Jack and Paddy. Jack was elected president of both trade organisations in 1948–9 and 1958–9.

Charles E. Warren, founder of the firm of chartered engineers in St Stephen's Green, by birth a Cornishman, came to Ireland in 1914 to take up a post as instructor in the Technical College at Waterford. During World War I he managed a shell factory there, later working with Thompsons of Carlow in general engineering. In 1932 he set up on his own as an agent for components and equipment. His firm introduced the first electric pump in Ireland, later bringing in from America the first computerised pump and supplying Wayne pumps to the petrol companies. Warrens also introduced Evinrude outboard motors here. During World War II they sold six torpedo boats to the government. But Charles Warren is best remembered for his work on the motor mechanic apprenticeship scheme started in 1945.

The Society, on the council of which Charles Warren served for forty years and of which he was president in 1943 and again in 1959, had long been aware that many dealers were abusing apprenticeships. These dealers took on youths to do odd jobs in the garage, collecting premiums from them but not giving any real training in return. Some dealers are alleged to have set up businesses merely to collect premiums.

There was another difficulty. Dealers were often pressed by the local priest or bank manager or a particularly good customer to take on a lad who had neither qualifications nor training. The Society therefore set up an apprenticeship scheme in conjunction with the Department of Education, the chief objective being to ensure that only youths with proper qualifications were taken on by garages. A form of day release was instituted for those already in employment, the release later applying to longer periods of training. The scheme, not then being backed by law, was voluntary, but according to Charles Warren, while there were dealers who could not be got to toe the line, most of the better type warmly supported it.

At the beginning of the Society scheme the trade unions were invited to nominate a member of the organising committee. The invitation was not taken up. Warren's explanation of this was that

214

since every city had a different union, agreement on a nominee could not be reached.

It is generally accepted that the Apprenticeship Act of 1960 followed the lines of the Society's scheme. In April of that year Charles Warren was appointed to An Cheard Chomhairle, and in May 1967 to An Chomhairle Oiliuna (AnCO). Every year the Society offers gold, silver and bronze medals for competition between AnCO registered apprentices who sit for the Senior and Junior Group Trades' Certificate Examinations in Motor Car Engineering of the Department of Education. Appropriately qualified apprentices are entitled to the Society's mechanic's or technician's diploma.

Holders of the technician's diploma may apply for a Charles Warren Bursary, which consists of the interest on a capital sum of £1,000. This is awarded annually to the student selected by a panel consisting of the president and chief executive of the Society and the principal of the Bolton Street College of Technology, Dublin. The bursary is to help students to pursue full-time professional courses at Bolton Street or attend short intensive courses at other institutions of international reputation. Charles Warren, having himself served a six-year apprenticeship with the British Admiralty at Devonport, took a special interest in the Society's scheme, and travelled around the country to present the medals.

Appendixes

Appendix 1

DR COLOHAN'S WILL

Clause 5: Subject to the provisions contained in Clause 2 hereof I make the following pecuniary bequests *videlicet:* (i) To Miss Flossie Rice daughter of the late Dr Dominick Rice One hundred pounds (ii) and her sister Mrs Frances Carlin Two hundred pounds (iii) To Miss Kathleen McDonnell (a child of a close relative of my wife's) or should she predecease me then to any child or children she may leave and who shall be living at my death and if more than one in equal shares Five hundred pounds (iv) To my Valet Richard McAllister of Dean Cottage Cookham Dean Four hundred pounds to be paid to him as soon as conveniently may be after my death (v) To Miss Maggie McAllister sister of the said Richard McAllister One thousand five hundred pounds (vi) To Miss Mary Mullen of Burton Street Sligo Ireland (at present Manageress of The Grand Hotel Brighton) Five hundred pounds (vii) To the said Richard Alfred O'Brien in recognition of the services he has rendered me for fifteen years, etc.

Appendix 2

Correspondence between Seán Lemass's Department of Industry and Commerce concerning the importation of the first cars to be part-assembled in the Saorstát.

SAORSTÁT ÉIREANN

ROINN TIONSCAIL AGUS TRÁCHTÁLA
(Department of Industry and Commerce)
5th April, 1933

F. M. Summerfield, Esq.,
Regent Palace Hotel,
LONDON.

A chara,
    I am directed by the Minister for Industry and Commerce to inform you that, after full consideration of your application to him, he is prepared to amend, in the coming Finance Act, the defintion of body shell for the purpose of importation at the lower rate of 26⅔% so as to include metal body shells containing a certain amount of wood. It should be understood, however, that the Minister is not prepared to guarantee that this concession will be continued for more than one year.
                    Mise le meas
                    R. C. Flynn

                    REGENT PALACE HOTEL,
                    LONDON
                    6th April 1933

The Minister for Industry and Commerce,
Government Building,
Dublin, Ireland.

A chara,
    I hasten to thank you for the letter I received from Mr Leydon this morning, conveying your decision to permit motor body shells of a composite type at the lower rate of 26⅔% import duty.
    This will enable me to make an experiment in body finishing immediately and to that end I have in the light of your letter placed a firm order with Messrs Renault Limited of Paris for 10 cars with

unfinished bodies to be shipped to Dublin as quickly as possible, and we shall do all of the trimming, upholstery and paintwork in Dublin, and we shall also fit in Dublin wire wheels and certain other fitments.

I certainly trust that this experimental job will come out alright and permit me to develop that permanent business that we all so much desire.

Meanwhile, I would like again to thank you not only for the concession that you have made now, but also for so kindly seeing me at so short a notice on Tuesday to enable me to place the case before you.

Mise le meas,
F. M. Summerfield

SAORSTÁT ÉIREANN

ROINN TIONNSCAIL AGUS TRÁCHTÁLA
(Department of Industry and Commerce)
12th October, 1933

Messrs F. M. Summerfield Ltd.,
138 Lower Baggot Street,
DUBLIN

A dhaoine uaisle,

I am directed by the Minister for Industry and Commerce to refer to your letter of the 20th ultimo, relative to the importation of Motor Body Shells.

I am to state that arrangements have been made with the Revenue Commissioners whereby Motor Body Shells may be imported at the special rate of duty of $26\frac{2}{3}\%$ ad valorem with:

(a) the roof covering attached, and

(b) the door locks including handles and window winding mechanism fitted.

Mise, le meas,
[Signature indecipherable]

Index

labour disputes, 150-51
Larkin, James, 81
Laurie, T.F., 211
Le Waters, William, 34
Lemass, Seán, 146, 149, 155, 173, 181-3, 217-18
Lemass, William J., 127, 140-41, 143, 182, 195-7
Leopold II, King of the Belgians, 72
Lincoln & Nolan Ltd, 145-6, 158-60, 163, 200, 204
Lloyd George, David, 51, 88
Loughlin, T. J., 139
Louth, 14th Baron (R. P. R. Plunkett), 11, 46-7
LSE Motor Co., 208
Lucas, Harry, 177-9
Lucas, Joseph, 175-8
Lucas, Joseph & Son, 176-80
Lucey, Denis, 37-8

McAdam, John L., 24-5
McAllister, Margaret, 17, 19
McAllister, Richard, 17-19
McCairns Motors Ltd, 176, 185-7, 207, 211-12, 213
McCairns, Thomas ('Tommy'), 184, 185, 186-7, 188, 209, 210-12
McCandless motor car, 44
McCormack, Cyril, 213
McEnroe, John P., 205
McGarvey, Howard & Sons, 186-7
McGrath, Joseph, 118, 122
McGrath, Patrick W., 165
McKee, J. A., 39
McMahon, Bob, 208
McMahon, Simon, 208
McMullen Bros, see Maxol
McQuaid, Matt, 1, 149n., 182, 198, 199, 208, 212-13
McSwiney, Terence, 90
McTaggart, William R., 23

Mahony, M. P., 152
Massey-Ferguson Ltd, 104
Maxol, 169
Maybach, Wilhelm, 106
Mecredy, R. J., 2, 46, 48, 58, 68, 83, 110
Michelin Tyre Co., 125, 128-30, 133-4, 137-8
Mooney, Frank, 180

Mooney, J. D., 210
Moore, James (Seamus Moore TD), 116, 126, 127-8, 130, 133, 134, 136, 139, 141, 151-2, 195, 196, 197
Moore, John, 3
Moro, Aldo, 196
Motor Distributors Ltd, 161, 187-90
Motor News, The, 11, 14, 46, 47
motor shows, 107, 109-10, 193; Dublin (1907), 83, 85, 110, 113, 193; Dublin (1908), 111, 194; and Royal Dublin Society, 194-5; and SIMI, 195
motor taxation, 20, 22
Motor Tour, The (1901), 18, 48-51
Motor Traders' Association, 106, 113, 115-16, 117, 119, 120
motoring, early developments in, 28-35
Mulcahy, Richard, 122
Murphy, Billy, 50
Murphy, C. W., 141

National Union of Vehicle Builders, 151
Nixon, St John C., 12
Nolan, Andrew F., 145
Northern Ireland, 119-20

O'Brien, Miss Norah, 196
O'Brien, Lord Chief Justice Peter (Pether the Packer), 34
O'Callaghan, R. G., 15
O'Donovan, Dermot, 208
O'Flaherty, Dorothy (née Wilcox), 184, 185-7, 189-91
O'Flaherty, Stephen, 161, 183-91, 202, 211
O'Neill, John, 149
O'Neill, (Michael) John, 139, 154, 202, 210, 213-14
O'Reilly, A. J. ('Tony'), 165
Organisation of Petroleum Exporting Countries (OPEC), 169
Ormsby, Lambert H., 56
Owner-Driver, the, 39-40

Penrose, R. W., 180
Perry, Percival, 85-6, 89-91
Petrol Distributors' Committee, 151-2, 171-2
petrol prices, 169
petrol pumps, 133
petrol rationing, 154, 173-6
Phelan, Edward, 82
Pigott, Richard, 63
Plunkett, Rev. and Hon. Benjamin, 48
Plunkett, Sir Horace, 7, 47
Pneumatic Tyre & Booths' Cycle Agency Ltd, 68-70. See also Dunlop Rubber Co.
Poole, W. J. ('Billy'), 158, 163
Poole, W. J. and Co. Ltd, 158, 163
Powderly, Alex, 213
private warning systems, 45
Prole, Robert, 1, 4, 5, 196, 199

Quinlan, Miss M., 117
Quinlan, P. F., 119, 128, 135, 136-7, 138
Quinn, Joe, 182, 197

railways, effects of road transport on, 181-3
Ray, Harold, 213
Reliability Trials (1907), 35, 85
Reynolds, A.P., 205
road accidents, 132-3. See also traffic
roads, condition of, 22, 23-4, 26-7; for the Motor Tour (1901), 49
Robinson, S. T. & Co., 145
Robinson, Sir Henry, 23, 33
Royal Automobile Club (RAC), 7, 46, 107, 110
Royal Dublin Society, 110-11, 193-5, 196. See also Bohane, Edward
Royal Irish Automobile Club (RIAC), 12, 46-7, 53, 110-13, 192-3
Royal Irish Constabulary (RIC), 23
Russian Oil Products (ROP), 169-70
Ryan, Dan, 208

221